TRIATHLON REVOLUTION
Training, Technique, and Inspiration

MOUNTAINEERS
OUTDOOR EXPERT
series

TRIATHLON REVOLUTION
Training, Technique, and Inspiration

Terri Schneider

Foreword by Scott Tinley

THE MOUNTAINEERS BOOKS

THE MOUNTAINEERS BOOKS
is the nonprofit publishing arm of The Mountaineers Club,
an organization founded in 1906 and dedicated to the exploration,
preservation, and enjoyment of outdoor and wilderness areas.

1001 SW Klickitat Way, Suite 201, Seattle, WA 98134

Manufactured in Canada

Copy Editor: Joeth Zucco
Book Design: The Mountaineers Books
Layout and Illustration: Jennifer Shontz, Red Shoe Design
Cover photograph: *Triathletes ready for start of race.* © Robert Michael/Corbis
Back cover photograph: *Virginia Tech graduate Phil Gregory crossing 2007 East Cooper Coastal Triathlon finish line in South Carolina.* © Sarah Benson/Mount Pleasant Recreation Department
Photographs on pages 2, 41, 55, 74, 83, 116, 175, 203, 212, 213, 218, 234, 257 © Shmuel Thaler; photograph on page 8 © Kathy Wynn, Dreamstime.com; photograph on page 13 © Serge Simo, Fotolio .com; photograph on page 21 © Tarzoun, Fotolio.com; photograph on page 63 © Ielecorti, Fotolio,com; photograph on page 72 © Anke Van Wyk/Dreamstime.com: photograph on page 77 © Thomas Devard; photograph on page 99 © Alan Phillips/Dreamstime; photograph on page 105 © Rob Bouwman, Fotolio .com; photograph on page 106 © RJ Grant/Dreamstime.com; photographs on pages 133, 143, 145, and 159 © pouvrem, Fotolio.com; photograph on page 171 © fotofimmel, Fotolio.com; photograph on page 239 © Lori Langona; photograph on page 242 © Norman Field.

Library of Congress Cataloging-in-Publication Data

Schneider, Terri.
    Triathlon revolution: training, technique, and inspiration/Terri Schneider; foreword by Scott Tinley. —1st ed.
      p.   cm.
    Includes bibliographical references and index.
    ISBN-13: 978-1-59485-096-7
    ISBN-10: 1-59485-096-8
1. Triathlon—Training. 2. Triathlon—Psychological aspects. I. Title.
    GV1060.73.S38 2008
    796.42′57—dc22

    2008018942

Contents

Foreword

It seems funny now to think that when I started competing in triathlons in the mid-1970s, the best way to learn how to do it was to make it up, but there's a bit of pathos in that realization as well. When you're talking about dragging your body through months and years of physical abuse, guesswork is never a good idea.

"Who knew?" is no longer an acceptable excuse. Common sense should have been a better coach, and a bit of self-discovery taken to heart and set down in some degree of rationality might have lengthened a few careers instead of shortening the soft tissue of youth. Everyone seems to know exactly how to train for a triathlon these days. There are hundreds of professional coaches, dozens of training camps, countless videos and books. But I sometimes think the myriad texts lining the "Sports: How To" section appear as leftovers from a weekend feast, filling hungry minds but mostly falling flat in their homogenized rehash of material that appeared as creative significance in a former iteration.

Once in awhile, though, a new title cannot be ignored for the power of its writing, or in this case, the history of its author. Terri Schneider's athletic resume may not include the requisites of a best-seller (there are no World Championships or Ironman wins included in her pedigree), but what you find layered in her book is that intangible insight gleaned from twenty-five years of just doing it. And that "it," you will find, is highly inclusive. When Schneider dips into the wanderings of the mental processes experienced during an Ironman or a seven-day adventure race, she is offering the reader the rare combination of the experiential, the scholarly, and the insightful. Rare are the great endurance athletes who have taken on the great adventures, studied them at the graduate level, and combined the two perspectives in a cogent and clear narrative.

When this writer-athlete riffs on the notion of triathlon-as-athletic-revolution, you can trust her—she was there in the late 1970s and early 1980s, making the same brilliant mistakes that every triathlete did in their quests for a new kind of somatic experience. When Schneider muses on both the technical and psychological elements required to take your skills to another level, know that there is a synchronicity of having done it well and having coached many others to do it better than they otherwise would have.

Maybe I'm too hard on sportswriters. Any book, if it tells an honest story, is worth at least a cursory look. But when a new title breaks through the choking weeds of so many surface texts, it requires our deeper attention. *Triathlon Revolution* is just such a book. Beneath the good advice, you'll find a lot of nuggets that only a great athlete with the intuitive insight earned in both the heat of battle and the halls of higher education might possess.

Scott Tinley

Acknowledgments

Triathlon is indeed a community-oriented sport and this book is a testament to that truth. I'm not very good at asking for help, but once I was able to put my feelers out, the support came on in droves!

A number of people not only read all or part of the manuscript-in-progress and enthusiastically offered invaluable comments, suggestions, and recommendations, they also listened patiently to my email banter while I completed the first draft. Thanks to Jane O'Connor, Greg Brock, Michelle Cantor, and Julia Van der Wyk for their encouraging words, critical feedback, and intelligent comments. Huge appreciation to Tony Lillios, Sherri Goodman, and Lori Cartwright for their consistent and specific suggestions, many of which were incorporated into the manuscript. My niece Sarah Gales, a visually impaired non-triathlete, read the entire manuscript start to finish and offered invaluable perspective. Thanks for your love and encouragement—you continually amaze me!

Thanks to Karen Burgess for not only reading and editing the entire manuscript but contributing a piece and offering consistent warm support. Kudos to Penni Bengtson for not only contributing, but offering an enormous amount of time creating the Resources section.

Numerous people enriched my triathlon life in various ways "back in the day"—many of these people also contributed to this book. Special thanks and big respect go out to Mark Allen, Bob Babbit, Mickey Wender, Sally Edwards, Mike Reilly, Dave Scott, Pete Kain, Heather Fuhr, Dave Liotta, and Jerry Lynch. It was wonderful connecting with all of them once again through their stories and our correspondence. I was thrilled to receive contributions from Terry Storm, Gaylia Osterlund, Kim Mueller, and Ned Overend—I enjoyed getting to know all of them a bit deeper through our interactions. Thanks to Robert Kunz at First Endurance for offering top notch products to the endurance world, and to the folks at Montrail for their continued support. Additional thanks to Jack Johnstone, Norman Field, Lori Langona, and Steve Goodman for their photos.

Kate Rogers, Mary Metz, and all at The Mountaineers Books could not have offered a more user-friendly environment in which to create this book—thanks for the opportunity and guidance.

Heartfelt thanks to: Kim Delaney for her intelligent support; Scott Tinley for his poignant foreword and our introspective interactions over the years; Flo and Charlie Stover for their steady support and for always lending an ear or a glass of wine; Steve Schneider, my bro and one of my favorite people, for kicking me in the ass as needed; and my mom, Mary Alsip, for making soup, doing laundry, and just being there. I am fortunate to have a large and loving family who offer consistent support; Mom, Dad, Steph, Mary, Steve, Julie, et. al.—"love you lots."

Triathlon is ultimately about the athletes and I have had the opportunity to work with hundreds of true warriors within the sport. Thanks to all of you who have shared your triumphs and challenges with me. You are my heroes and my daily inspiration.

Thanks to the Triathlon Revolution and its many revolutionaries—you've offered the masses a depth of endurance unprecedented—rock on.

The Triathlon Revolution

"These were not triathletes. There was no such thing at the time. None were into cross-training, a term not yet coined. Most didn't own racing bikes and some were marginal swimmers at best. Yet they had the adventuresome spirit to come out after a hard day's work and with only two weeks' notice to participate in a new athletic event."

Jack Johnstone, on the first modern-day triathlon in 1974

If modern-day endurance sports have ever experienced a revolution, triathlon is it! Were the first triathletes runners looking for a bit of pizzazz in their time on the roads? Had years of staring at the black line in a pool brewed swimmers' conversion to multisport? Did cyclists come along for the ride, or were the first triathlon cyclists made from the unrest in the running and swimming ranks? In any case, the modern triathlon was born via those initial restless participants on a warm summer evening in Southern California in the mid-1970s. None would have bet that a jog on the beach followed by a spin on one's cruiser bike could lead to an explosion unprecedented in contemporary endurance sport. Triathlon was born.

Multisport folks have consistently rocked the endurance genre for more than thirty years. Since the sport's inception, triathlon has been on the rise with a steady growth in participants and events through the 1980s to 1990s, leading into full-impact mode at the turn of the century. Progressive growth combined with the initiation of online registration for races has resulted in sell-out crowds in most prominent events today. Experienced athletes know to pull out the credit cards and get online prior to January in order to get into their desired events for the following year.

As the number of events increased, the sport took center stage in already-established fitness and outdoor industries, while new manufacturers emerged selling triathlon-specific products. Stand-alone swimming, biking, and running companies began to shift their design and marketing efforts when they realized triathlon wasn't going anywhere. Before long, companies outside the industry were putting energy into the sport in the form of prize money, and the professional triathlete emerged.

A CRAZY IDEA GONE MAD

According to triathlete Scott Tinley, triathlon dates back to France in the 1920s–1930s with "Les Trois Sports." This event, consisting of a 3K run, 12K bike, and a channel crossing, was held intermittently throughout the early to mid-1930s.

Triathlon as we know it today, however, was started in 1974 by a group of guys in San Diego.

This first race drew forty-six competitors and plans for future events immediately followed. Jack Johnstone reflects on the inaugural event, "It seems strange to me now that we thought it necessary to include the sentence about bringing bikes. I think someone must have asked me if they'd be provided. I haven't been able to find any record of the entry fee, but I think it was one dollar."

Over the next few years, this and other events became more popular, and athletes training in other sports started to consider triathlon their specialty. Among these were some of the original legends of the sport: Tom Warren, who would go on to win the second Ironman triathlon; Wally and Wayne Buckingham, persistent regulars in the top ranks; and triathlon champion Scott Tinley.

UPPING THE ANTE

Joining that early crowd at triathlon events were U.S. Navy commander John Collins and his wife, Judy. The oft-told story is that

---

RUN, CYCLE, SWIM: TRIATHLON SET FOR 25TH

The First Annual? Mission Bay Triathlon, a race consisting of segments of running, bicycle riding, and swimming, will start at the causeway to Fiesta Island at 5:45 P.M. September 25 [Wednesday].

The event will consist of 6 miles of running (longest continuous stretch, 2.8 miles), 5 miles of bicycle riding (all at once), and 500 yards of swimming (longest continuous stretch, 250 yards). Approximately 2 miles of running will be barefoot on grass and sand.

Each participant must bring his own bicycle.
Awards will be presented to the first five finishers.

BOB'S FIRST TRIATHLON BY BOB BABBITT

Okay, I admit it. I had absolutely no idea we were supposed to finish the whole damn thing in one day. I remember thinking when I found out that these people were absolutely, positively out of their skulls.

The year was 1980, there were only 108 of us in Oahu for the start of the third annual Ironman triathlon, and who would have figured that *everyone* would try to swim 2.4 miles, ride 112, and run 26.2, one right after the other? My plan was to hopefully dogpaddle my way through the swim, ride to the other side of Oahu, maybe 60 miles or so, then camp out. I'd get up in the morning, ride the rest of the way back to Aloha Tower and then run the marathon. Now, doesn't that sound more sensible? It sure did to me.

Before I left San Diego, I had racks put on my sixty-dollar police auction Centurion with the charred rear triangle, so I could hang my newly acquired panniers on them. Inside would be my sleeping bag and provisions. I was totally set up for the road. A red Radio Shack radio mounted on the handlebars and held in place with a bungee cord, solid rubber tires to prevent those annoying flats, and a little black electrical tape to cover up the charred stuff. I was ready to roll!

But when I got to the starting line that morning and met my support crew (everyone had to have one), they suggested that they carry the sleeping bag and the rest of my goodies in their Fiat convertible. Since they were going to be close by, I thought why not?

The day before the race, my roommate, Ned Overend, who went on to become one of the greatest mountain bikers in history, and I were standing on the balcony of a hotel overlooking the stormy Pacific in downtown Waikiki. The race organizers had called us together for a pre-race briefing. As Ned and I watched wave after wave hammer by, we both suddenly realized that the chances of us getting through the surf of the Waikiki Roughwater Swim course in storm conditions were somewhere between slim and none.

So when the race director announced that the Ironman swim was being moved to Ala Moana Channel, Ned and I were ecstatic. The deal was this: ABC was over in the Islands to film cliff diving on Sunday. If this Ironman thing went off on schedule on Saturday, ABC could film it. If the weather forced a delay to Sunday, there was no way. So they moved the swim to Ala Moana Channel, which was protected from the surf.

While Ned and I were excited to be given a chance to get out of the water alive, the hard-core swimmers weren't happy at all. "What a wussy event," they grumbled. Obviously, those dudes hadn't done all their swim training in a 120-length-to-the-mile condo pool like Ned and I had.

When I finally came out of the water on Ironman day, I was just slightly ahead of Olympic cyclist John Howard, who spent half an hour washed up on the coral. I ran to the shower

Bob, Hawaii Ironman, 1980

and, after waiting my turn behind a father and his son, put on a wool cycling jersey, my tennis shoes, jammed enough Hawaiian sweet bread into the pocket of my shirt to feed Guatemala, mounted up, and took off.

I was actually starting to get into this long-distance cycling routine when a member of my support crew set up on the side of the road for a food hand-off. I'd seen this sort of thing in the Tour de France. I readied myself, reached out with my right hand and, before I knew what hit me, became the proud owner of a white bag with golden arches on it. How did I know that a Big Mac, fries, and a coke weren't on the Ironman diet? It sure tasted good to me. At mile 80 my crew followed up with a root beer snow cone.

By this point, I'd given up the notion of making this a two-day adventure. My crew was so into it, I couldn't imagine pulling over and setting up camp just yet. And anyhow, I was enjoying the heck out of myself.

When I pulled into the transition area at Aloha Tower, my crew had a major surprise waiting for me: a full-on massage, complete with soothing music and massage oils. They laid me down on a bamboo cot and proceeded to give me the best massage I've ever had. Forty minutes later, I started out on the run.

I trotted through Waikiki and out onto the Honolulu marathon course. I ate Hawaiian sweet bread, drank water, and simply ran and walked my way through the first 20 miles. All of a sudden, though, just past 20, I felt this urgency to pick up the pace. I ran through the Hawaiian darkness silhouetted in the lights of my support crew's car. Those last 6 miles just seemed to fly by. I started to visualize the excitement that was waiting at the finish line. What would it be? Marching bands, cheerleaders, or maybe huge crowds of screaming Ironman fans. Suddenly, I came upon a white chalk line drawn on the street. I slowed and looked to my right. In the park, underneath a light bulb strung from a telephone pole, sat an official-looking guy with a pad of paper in his hand.

"Hey, are you in the race?" he yelled. "Yeah!" I replied. "Well...you're done. Good job," he said.

I walked toward the voice and sat on the grass for a minute to catch my breath. There were four other finishers lying there chatting with their support crews. No one was moving or saying much except one guy who, for some unknown reason, was doing handstand push-ups. After the official wrote my name down, my crew poured me into the back of the Fiat and took me back to the hotel.

I trudged up the stairs to my room. I vividly remember the moon coming through the window and illuminating the red-as-a-lobster scorched outline of Ned's back. I asked him how his race had gone.

"Well, Pam (his girlfriend, now wife, and support person) had a hard time getting through the traffic in Waikiki. She didn't catch me for awhile," Ned said.

"When did she catch up to you?" I asked. "Mile 80," he laughed. "I had run out of water and was drinking from a sprinkler, and then she lost me again in the marathon!"

I can't believe it's been twenty-seven years. It seems like only yesterday.

Bob Babbitt is owner and editor of Competitor *Magazine and* City Sports *Magazine. He has been a triathlete since the beginning.*

the Hawaiian Ironman triathlon was conceived during the awards ceremony for the 1977 Oahu Perimeter Relay—a five-person running relay. Members of both the Mid-Pacific Road Runners and the Waikiki Swim Club competed in the event, and a debate ensued as to who was more fit—runners or swimmers.

Collins pointed out that Belgian cycling legend Eddy Merckx was known to have the highest recorded maximum oxygen uptake, so perhaps cyclists topped the runners and swimmers in the fittest category. He suggested the debate be settled by combining three notable events on the island: the Waikiki Roughwater Swim (2.4 miles), the Around-Oahu Bike Race (115 miles; at the time those present didn't realize this was actually a two-day event), and the Honolulu Marathon (26.2 miles). Collins figured that by shortening the ride to 112 miles and riding counterclockwise around the island, the bike leg could start at the finish of the Waikiki Roughwater and end at the traditional start of the Honolulu Marathon.

Prior to the first Ironman in 1978, the fifteen competitors received a couple of pages of instruction, including the now famous tagline: "Swim 2.4 miles! Bike 112 miles! Run 26.2 miles! Brag for the rest of your life!"

The Ironman was born—and the Triathlon Revolution was launched.

CONTROVERSY ENSUES

The Ironman moved to the Big Island in the early 1980s to accommodate more participants; the advent of triathlon in print media and TV launched the Ironman as well as the sport of triathlon. As interest peaked, the sport became organized and defined, and the international distance (also known as Olympic) of 1.5K/40K/10K was developed for the masses. Jim Curl and Carl Thomas produced the U.S. Triathlon Series (USTS) with enormous success between 1982 and 1997. In the meantime, national governing bodies started popping up around the globe.

The International Triathlon Union (ITU) was founded in 1989 as the governing body of the sport with the chief initiative of putting triathlon on the Olympic program. In 2000, triathlon produced its first Olympic medalists with an Olympic-distance race with a draft-legal format.

But as with any revolution worth mentioning, triathlon didn't mature to this point without its share of controversy. When the draft-legal format materialized,

most American professionals, myself included, were opposed to draft-legal races. It's not that we didn't want the Olympics, we just wanted the backbone of the event to stand strong as a solo effort. If triathlon was our version of the race of truth, then wasn't a draft-legal race a completely different event? At the time it depended on who you spoke with—the majority of original triathletes or the ITU and their initial petite following.

ITU currently does not recognize nor sanction Ironman-distance events. It does not acknowledge the Hawaii Ironman as a world championship event despite its unparalleled popularity in the sport. So ITU tends to the Olympics, while World Triathlon Corporation (WTC)—owners of the Ironman brand—continues to grow the Ironman trademark. To this day they are strong opposing revolutionaries residing in the same house.

CHALLENGE AND CAMARADERIE

At every distance, triathlon offered endurance athletes like myself the opportunity to revolutionize themselves. Similar to others who got the triathlon bug, I focused my life on the sport. I continued to expand my strength and endurance as a person through triathlon as I graduated from college, tried a few different jobs, married, found my passion for travel, quit my day jobs to race full time, and divorced.

I learned immediately as a pro triathlete that I felt most comfortable within the discomfort of the Ironman distance. Since

CONVERSATIONS WITH DAVE SCOTT: TRIATHLON

Terri: What experiences marked you prior to triathlon and how did these experiences mold who you became as a triathlete?

Dave: I can look back even before high school, and I'm not sure what the trigger mechanism was, but I always had this uncanny ability to do a little bit extra. Even in swimming I was always doing a little bit extra, thinking that that would be helpful. Even in high school when the workout was over, I'd do extra. In college, I'd come in before water polo practice and throw a ball against the wall for an hour before everyone else got there.

I always had a high work ethic and I think it came from my folks. My mom was very poor and never was able to go to college. Her father died when she was fourteen, and she didn't even have a toilet in her house growing up. She'd tell these stories when I was a kid, and I used to slough them off. But I think it did make a difference in me. I realized that life is not always rosy and you have to work toward what you want. I think a lot of it has been attributed to my parents.

Terri: What motivated you to start racing triathlon?

Dave: I spent a lot of extra time trying to be a better swimmer in college. I was just a mediocre swimmer, but I recognized that I was really good at really long races and workouts. And if we combined things in training like running and swimming or weights and swimming, I found out that I could run reasonably well, despite my form, and it didn't affect my swimming. In fact I was noticeably stronger than everyone else on the team in the combined workouts. My teammates would be decimated and that seemed to give me more strength. So that psychological component worked well for me.

In college I felt really incomplete as an athlete. I thought, "I don't know what is out there for me, but I can hold a workload for a long period of time and maybe there is a sport that does that."

I started doing ocean swims first and realized I was a much better open-water swimmer than in the pool. Guys that beat me in the pool I would kill in open water. I then started gravitating toward some weird combined sport events. We did a run-swim event in the mid-1970s down in Foster City, and Scott Molina, who was fifteen at the time, won the event and I got second at twenty-two years old. Scott trounced everyone. I did a few more events like this pre-triathlon, then tried my first triathlon.

> *Dave Scott (www.davescottinc.com) is a six-time Hawaii Ironman Triathlon World Champion and the first inductee into the Ironman Hall of Fame.*

Opposite: Dave training near his home in Colorado

strategy, strength, and mental tenacity were my fortes, the longer the race, the better. Ironman became my companion over many years of racing. Some say you find your true self in an Ironman. I say that in an Ironman you find many layers of the person that you didn't even know existed within yourself.

In the early '90s, WTC decided to offer the Ironman World Series in which points were awarded at each Ironman race; Hawaii was a double-points race. There was prize money at each event as well as a series purse. Though this was quite enticing for the pros who excelled at longer events, it required a minimum of four Ironman events in a season for the possibility of ranking well in October.

This type of racing, in addition to the other events strategically placed on my race schedule, required a significant amount of overseas travel. There were only about eight Ironman events to choose from, and only one—Hawaii—was in the United States. I also had to squeeze in additional important ultra events such as Nice Triathlon in France, Zofingen (Powerman) Duathlon in Switzerland, and the Strongman in Japan.

Training for a predominantly ultra-distance race schedule requires finesse similar to walking a slackline—for the entire season. The athletes who participated knew this. They'd build their training bases back home, and come spring they'd hit the circuit, running into each other regularly in Europe, Australia, Japan, or

Terri on her way to winning Escape from Alcatraz 1990

New Zealand. Most athletes would show up to the big races a few days in advance to acclimate to the time zone, train together, have dinner, check out the sights, and then race against each other full out, but not before pranks were pulled and a lot of laughter ensued.

As professional athletes who lived, ate, and slept our sport, we rarely, if ever, talked about training when we hung out pre-race. So we discussed music and philosophy, swapped books, gave each other hard times, reviewed the latest happenings in the world—all the while quietly respecting that the people sitting next to you at dinner trained their butt off for their best performances—just like you. We gave each other that—but we didn't need to talk about it—it just was.

But come race day, it was no holds barred. A comrade might feel for me if I was having a bad day, but she'd pass me just the same and move on. Racing long for a living is a thorny endeavor. We all knew it and respected and supported each other in it because we mutually empathized.

In many ways hanging out with my competitors before races made me feel more at home than being at home. There's something about being surrounded by people of like-mind that helps you settle in and feel accepted. My family and close friends didn't fully understand the magnitude of what I lived as a triathlete each day; these people I vaguely knew did. Being around them was like coming back to home base at each race venue.

Adding any level of triathlon training into a full life is a juggling act. It's highly doable and vastly rewarding, but if someone tells you it's easy, they probably don't have a job or children. The main piece that helps a triathlete hold it all together is the community in which they share that significant challenge. You can toe the starting line of any race knowing that the people surrounding you have faced the same challenges. There's solace in that knowing. Triathlon is about challenge and within that challenge triathletes support each other verbally or quietly through their extensive community. And post-race we celebrate.

TRIATHLON IS FOR EVERYBODY

Most humans gravitate toward challenge in their lives. It is this inherent quality that entices individuals to take on triathlon. How an athlete tests himself within the context of the sport is specific to each individual. One person may decide to focus on learning to run in order to finish his first sprint-distance triathlon, while another athlete trains for her fifth Ironman. You want to try off-road?—triathlon offers that. Have your eye on doing a relay with your family?—just sign up. Interested in racing every weekend for eight months?— the sport can accommodate you as well. If challenge is what you crave, triathlon is for you in whichever size and shape you desire. Triathlon truly is for everyone.

Most sports inadvertently generate a

social persona over time based on the nuances of their sport. Triathlon is an inherently friendly, community-oriented sport with a significant competitive edge. Triathletes train just as hard as other athletes, but the nature of their training and racing allows them to enjoy each other more fully—while they're training, in races, and post-race. Triathlon is social and supportive, and within that cocoon is the opportunity to compete at whatever depth you choose.

TRIATHLETES AS HEROES

I have been asked many times who my heroes are in sport. In our society we often associate "hero" with being someone who has accomplished some monumental feat or has unusual talent or vigor beyond the norm for what they take on in life. Yet regular folks and middle-of-the-pack athletes have just as much emotionally riding on their accomplishments as do the more talented. Their road to success can often be even more vigorous than those for whom it comes a bit easier.

The significance of getting a personal record in your 5K or completing your first triathlon is as much of a champion move in your world as it is for Tiger Woods to bring in another million. We all find value and satisfaction in our accomplishments. How and why we get there may just look a bit different.

As a young girl I was intrigued by professional athletes, just like any kid, but I realized that true heroic feats were happening all around me—daily, by people struggling to live life while going after their dreams. My father worked two jobs to support a family of seven while going to school to get his degree so he could advance in his career. He taught me that no matter what we choose in life, we go after it with dignity and hard work and then we can respect ourselves. We can be our own hero.

The world is a tough place, and if you throw voluntary physical duress into your daily repertoire in order to offer your kids a

SKIN DANSKIN DANSKIN DANSKIN DANS
FINIS
SKIN DANSKIN DANSKIN DANSKIN DAN
DANSKIN
DANSKIN

stronger vision of humanity, I'd say that is a heroic decision. As I matured as an athlete, this picture of the everyman-hero became clearer.

In 1993, I coached a group of fifteen women who were interested in competing in the Danskin Women's Triathlon in San Jose, California. These women became my first sports heroes. Some of them didn't know how to swim. Others borrowed bikes for the occasion. A few had never run. All were moms with jobs and full lives.

After eight weeks, all fifteen crossed the finish line via life-altering experiences. For some, it was the first time they had given themselves a gift worth coveting— self-confidence. I admired them for stepping into the unknown to examine themselves. What they found was more woman than they imagined.

This concept that had eluded them seemed to come to me naturally—if you want something, go after it. In many ways it felt easy, and I drew strength from making these choices regularly. But I saw the magnitude of their initial fear and struggle and their choice to follow through with their goal. That was heroic. If that vision of "hero" rings true in your world, then you'll see that the sport of triathlon is full of heroes. If you don't believe me, look in the mirror.

GOING AFTER YOUR HERO

In the stress of work, family, and training, you can generate an athletic life that is rewarding and fulfilling, while creating a rich lifestyle that exceeds anything you have known prior. Why live vicariously through someone else you consider a hero when you can see in your own mirror a fabulous life?

Triathlon has taught me that the heroes in life are everyday folks who fall on their faces time and again, pick themselves up, dust themselves off, learn from their falls, revel at the opportunities of the difficult lessons and heed them. Your hero should be yourself.

Admire the decisions you make in your own reality. Your success touches your life and the lives of your family and friends directly. That's important stuff. Cross that finish line. Dream large.

CREATING YOUR TRIATHLON LIFE

You have a huge advantage over people who started in triathlon back in the early years. People like me had to get a couple of degrees, make a lot of mistakes, and watch the clients that I coached make mistakes in order to figure out how to train and race effectively. There is now an immense amount of information to help you effi-ciently create and develop your triathlon life, starting with this text.

This book will address the keys to a progressive training process and how to pull them all together. You'll learn about swim-ming, biking, and running for triathlon, as well as nutrition, strength training, and flexibility training for triathlon. No triathlon book is complete without covering the most significant aspect of your athletic life—and my favorite—the mental game. There are tips for taking your racing off-road and the virtues and means of going longer in your training and racing, as well as the gear that will make your time on the road more efficient and fun: designer foods, designer clothing, high-tech bikes, heart rate monitors, and more. If you get tired of listening to me or my stories, enjoy the many wise words generously shared by other experienced triathletes and a few of the sport's legends.

When I start coaching a triathlete, I let my client know that we are a team working together to get her to the start of her first race prepared and with a solid race plan. This book is a similar process that I'm starting with you. I'm pleased you're on board. If the information doesn't enlighten you, my stories or anecdotes don't inspire you, then let me know because that means I have significantly missed the mark as your teammate.

CHAPTER 1

Foundation for Training Success

"Excellence is an art won by training and habituation. We do not act rightly because we have virtue or excellence, but we rather have those because we have acted rightly. We are what we repeatedly do. Excellence, then, is not an act but a habit."

Aristotle

Whether you are starting a fresh fitness program with the sport of triathlon, transitioning into triathlon from another sport, or upping the ante on your current triathlon plan, it is critical to incorporate several basic concepts into your training agenda, while respecting your current lifestyle.

In this chapter you'll discover the key to finding balance in your life while incorporating important foundational issues into your training: consistency, variety, rest and recovery, and the means to avoid overtraining, burnout, and injury. You'll learn the importance of periodizing, or cycling, your program as well as look at what heart rate training is all about.

Addressing these issues will not only aid you in creating a successful and effective triathlon training program, it will keep your training healthy and fun. If you can keep "healthy and fun" in the front of your daily program, you're definitely on the road to personal success within your own triathlon revolution!

BALANCING TRAINING AND LIFE

When putting together your training program, there are several facets of life to consider. Look at your weekly and monthly life agenda and then decide how much additional time you wish to devote to your training program. Your life agenda may include work, family time, hobbies, classes and study time, socializing, and relaxing.

Avoid creating a training program based on what you feel you are supposed to be doing or on what other people are putting out. In order to generate a healthy sense of balance and eliminate the frustration or guilt that can emerge when unsuccessfully executing your training program, it's important to create a program only after you have evaluated your real life schedule.

EVALUATING YOUR LIFE SCHEDULE

Look at your calendar for a month and record how you spend your time. Make sure you are including time devoted to travel, commute, study, and work. Schedule in time with your spouse and children as well as important solo time needed to relax and recharge your personal batteries. Then honestly look at each week and decide how much additional time you might have for training. Base the training program you create on that time. Sometimes in the excitement of engaging in a new sport, you may wish to jump to a level of training that you think will give immediate tangible results. Rarely, if ever, can an athlete do this without getting injured, burnt-out, divorced, or fired.

Move into your training program in a realistic manner and not only will your body and mind productively adapt to the new stresses in your life, but you'll be able to maintain enjoyment in the process. Triathlon is a lifestyle sport and one you can do indefinitely and successfully if you are good to your body and keep your mind fresh by easing into your training time slowly.

Though the hours per week you are able to train may dictate the distance of triathlon you can shoot for, don't limit your aspirations to somebody else's predetermined guidelines. Athletes have successfully trained for sprint- or international-distance triathlons on several hours of training per week. These folks may need to alter their ultimate goals to be highly competitive in their age group or to complete a long-course event or Ironman race, but their goal to cross the finish line in the sport of triathlon is definitely in their grasp.

CREATING TIME AND MOTIVATION TO TRAIN

After you determine how much time you can devote to training, get creative in order to fit that training into your schedule. It might be easy for highly motivated people to simply place the training time into their calendar and execute it as planned, but for

most, syncing training and life becomes more of a balancing act. Triathletes just like you share their challenges and some solutions:

Striving for efficiency:

- "Since I have a family and a business, planning a month or more out is reasonable for me. I know what I need to get in, take into account organized group workouts, and then make a plan."
- "I like to put my training schedule into a calendar. Some computer options are Now Up-to-Date, or iCalendar. I'm a planner. I like to get my training into a program ASAP as most things in my life can be scheduled around my workouts. That said, I do need to rearrange things sometimes as surprises come up. I review my schedule throughout the day so I know what's coming up, not only today but tomorrow morning."
- "When I have to go out of town for business, I sometimes rearrange things so that I get in most of my key workouts before I leave or after I come back. Prior to my trip, I check to see if the hotel where I'll be staying has a gym, pool, or places to go to run outside. With satellite imagery available, I can often see the terrain and nearby trails that look interesting. I may find a nearby bike shop where I can rent a bike or connect with other triathlon club members at my destination who can recommend a place to rent bikes. Otherwise spin classes at a local gym work well. I can also do plyometrics

and use stretchy bands to get some strength training in."
- "Scheduling is the key for me when I travel. If I have a plan and get out the door, that's 90 percent of the effort right there."
- "I run errands on foot or on my bicycle sometimes to get in my workout."
- "Commuting on my bicycle to work keeps me in pretty good shape for my races, and it's a guaranteed exercise event. If you do it in all kinds of weather, people are impressed by you and may say, 'Wow, you're hardcore!'"

Maintaining motivation:

- "I use my motivational triathlon tape I had done by a hypnotist. It keeps me motivated and focused on my training schedule. If I listen to it daily for one week, it will keep me on track. If I find myself slacking, I will listen to it more frequently."
- "Having a new race challenge puts the 'fear of suffering' in my heart. Creating a new challenge keeps me motivated to show up to workouts as I'm not very keen on showing up to races underprepared."
- "Nothing keeps a training date like scheduling it with a buddy or a group. Volunteering to lead a training workout keeps me motivated to show up as required. Picking my weak link as my volunteer leader workout is the best way to keep me consistent in this area."
- "I make training plans with someone else and treat it like an important event that cannot be missed."

Enlisting support:

- "Having a good support system is really helpful. My husband races bikes so he knows the time I need to put in—that's really helpful."

- "I have to walk my dog in the evenings, so sometimes I combine my short run sessions with my dog. Or when I have a brick workout—bike/run—planned, I can bring my dog. He gets to dig while I'm biking and then gets to run with me and he loves it!"

- "Sometimes I get my husband to go with me for workouts. If it's a short workout or something he's interested in, he's happy to come along, but I have to make sure it's an easy workout for me. "

Cementing commitment:

- "When I'm traveling, I get my training in right when I get up before breakfast. This helps me get in that training especially if the day gets crazy later on."

- "I work on being committed to myself and my workouts, especially if a workout companion flakes out. That's important."

- "For me being creative and juggling is making compromises in all areas of my life. It is a give-and-take in all areas. Making these choices makes me feel grown up and that allows me to not feel overwhelmed or self-centered. It's a constant learning balance."

- "Our 6 AM masters swim is a really great way to get some exercise in before work, and it's a class, so you have to be there. Then if you have a crazy schedule for the rest of the day, you have already done some training."

- "I find that if I don't treat my training schedule as something I have committed to and have to do, then it's too easy to skip it."

Being adaptable:

- "Sometimes I realize I just have to be flexible. I know that 30 minutes in an evening rather than my prescribed workout needs to be enough sometimes—especially when I am pushing it too much in life in general."

■ "I often take walking breaks while working to get my blood moving. Sometimes I eat lunch quickly and use the rest of my lunch time for an energetic walk."

Gaining self-knowledge:

■ "I had to learn how to get up a little bit earlier on some days to get everything in. Over time it wasn't so bad."
■ "I tend to have strictly defined hours of the day where I know I will be productive in my work, and my workout times are usually before or after those times."
■ "Well, sometimes, I just go back to bed."

Balancing training and life is about being efficient with your time, committing to yourself and your fitness program, and having some self-knowledge in order to decipher what time of the day you train best and when it's best to take a rest day. Planning your training with others and gaining support from loved ones is motivating and will allow you to reap the rewards of your training adaptation.

KEYS TO YOUR FINEST TRAINING EFFECT

Training effect is the cardiovascular and structural adaptation that the body achieves through exercise and recovery—the effect your training has on you physiologically, structurally, and emotionally. In order to gain training effect you need both training stress and rest and recovery. In these next sections you'll see the nuances of both optimized via consistency, variety, and adaptation within your training.

CONSISTENCY

If you ask elite endurance athletes how they get results from their training, they'll put consistency at the top of the list. The unglamorous truth is that you need to get up day after day, week after week, month after month, even on days you're feeling unmotivated. The reward for this work ethic will pay dividends in performance.

When I raced triathlon, I knew I was not necessarily the most gifted athlete at

CONVERSATIONS WITH DAVE SCOTT: BALANCING TRAINING AND LIFE

Terri: If you were advising someone else who is struggling with finding time to train, what would you tell them specifically?

Dave: I have an unwritten rule that I follow every year, that if I have a minimum amount of time, if I can just do 20 minutes of something, I usually feel better than when I started. So even if time is squeezed, I just get in that 20 minutes and I know I'll feel better.

People should have a primary time that they exercise and make that the rule. But also have a secondary time that works. If you always run at 6:30 AM and you can't get it in, then have another time set up rather than just saying, forget it. Even if you can just get in a half hour at noon or in the evening, just do it.

Have short-term goals. My short-term goals are fourteen days of training. Short-term goals are very palatable and doable.

CONVERSATIONS WITH HEATHER FUHR: CONSISTENCY AND EXPECTATIONS

Terri: What general training advice would you give to a middle-to-back-of-the-pack age grouper?

Heather: Consistency is the key to any training program. There is no sense in trying to train at a level that you cannot maintain. This is not realistic. You will get faster and stronger by being consistent in your training over a period of time.

Heather Fuhr is a Hawaii Ironman Triathlon World Champion as well as a fourteen-time Ironman Champion, placing her second on the all-time Ironman Win List.

the start line. Much of my confidence was based on the knowledge that I trained intelligently and consistently, while listening to my body and optimizing my physical and mental strength. To use this confidence well required me to put my blinders on and play out my carefully designed training program, without getting sucked into what other athletes were doing on any given day or week.

Doing this consistently provided results I enjoyed and longevity in a sport that sees many pros fall through the cracks after a few years due to injury or burnout. Even though I was racing at a world-class level, I always kept in perspective the fact that I wanted to be doing this sport my whole life. I wanted to create a lifestyle through healthy and regular training that would feed my love of endurance sports. Whether you like it or not, you get only one body

this time around, and steady, consistent efforts help keep your body and mind healthy and fit for the duration.

Consistency means a sound workload each week within each component of training: swimming, biking, running, strength and flexibility, nutrition, as well as rest. These consistent weeks build on each other over time, while incorporating recovery weeks, event goals, and life challenges.

Let's say that you can do two bike workouts a week with a total time of 2.5 hours per week on the bike. One of these bike sessions may be an hour and include intervals, hill repeats, or tempo riding. The other session might be a longer ride of 1.5 hours at an easier pace.

Your body will respond well and generate a positive training effect if you ride two times each week, week after week, consistently. Even if you never increase the time on your bike, you will have better results if you stick to your plan, rather than shooting for more but accomplishing it only erratically.

Over the last twenty years of coaching triathletes, I have noticed a definite pattern in many athletes who come to me for assistance—their original program is not consistent. They may already be swimming, biking, and running, but they are not doing all three regularly. Without drastically changing the duration of their workouts, I have seen huge changes in athletes who can fine-tune their training by being regular in their efforts.

Our bodies want to adapt! They're great at it! They are built for work and they will change and become stronger if you give them a sound workload over time. Consistency comes from patience and dedication, which is not very glamorous or exciting but works well in the world of endurance sports.

VARIETY

To become fitter, bodies want consistency, but they also want change. Within this consistent world you've created, you also need change and variety in your levels of effort.

MULTITASKING: A MOM'S MIDDLE NAME BY TERRY STORM

Mom, athlete, wife or girlfriend, employee. Which is most important? How do you fit it all in? I divorced when my kids were one and four, went back to work three days a week, and started working out at the YMCA for stress relief. Back when my kids were young, I could not have done it all without the daycare offered at the Y. I could swim the masters workout or run on the treadmill while my kids enjoyed their daycare and friends.

Alternating weekends with my ex and helpful grandparents gave me time to bike and run outside. One day in 1993, a gym friend suggested we try a triathlon. We figured since we all swam and ran and biked, we may as well put it all together. It was a very short sprint distance (I think the run was 3 miles) and my bike at the time still had a kickstand! After that first race, I was hooked, and despite my super-busy life, I've never looked back.

There have been many compromises along the way. I've struggled with guilty feelings that maybe I was selfishly not being a good enough mom/girlfriend/wife/worker because of the time spent training or racing. Should I go for a bike ride or should I do all the laundry? I had doubts many times in the past fourteen years. Perhaps I had made the wrong choices? Was being a triathlete that important?

I also wondered if my kids missed out on something, or if they ever felt that they weren't a priority for me. But today, now that my kids are fifteen and nineteen, I know that I made exactly the right choice because I know for certain that that they have benefited greatly from my athletic example as they grew up. I heard my nineteen-year-old daughter complain recently about her friend's mother, who does not work outside the home. She noticed that

Variety is the second key component to your allotted weekly training hours. Variety of efforts and scenery keeps the spark in your physiology and in your perspective.

Most endurance athletes have a comfy pace that they fall into naturally when they train. It's the pace you will do if you are riding along without interruption for an extended period of time, or if you are running with a friend and catching up on the week's news. It may be approximately 80 percent of your maximum heart rate (MHR) while running. This pace feels natural and healthy but if it's the only way you run, you won't get faster. Consistency in the number of sessions per week in each sport is important, but within these designated sessions it's best to vary intensity levels to gain the best overall training adaptation.

Change Your Intensity

Many well-trained runners will run a 10K at around 85–90 percent of their maximum heart rate. But you can only hold these effort levels in a race if you have trained for that type of output and distance. If you want to run your 10K at a pace consistently faster than 80 percent of your max, you will need to train regularly at least one session per week at an effort level above your

this other mother "didn't do things like you would do, mom, if you had that time—you know, sports and stuff."

My fifteen-year-old son was recently running with his high school cross-country team at the same park where I was doing a run workout. He waved and yelled to me. I thought I might embarrass him because I am so slow, but instead he told me afterward he liked to see me run. "Most other kids' parents don't even run," he commented.

I recently went running with both my kids. I watched them take off together ahead of me and noticed the similarities of our bodies and running styles—the enjoyment they have of an activity I love and have loved throughout their entire lives.

And I notice almost every day in the media that America's children are getting fatter, less active. For my kids, it is a given to be active in their lives. Sure they like the TV and computer, but they also like to run, bike, hike, and spend time outdoors. This example of a healthy lifestyle has been one of the greatest gifts I could give them.

I often look back at how I juggled all that I did to fit triathlon into my life. How did I do it? I take a look at my kids and myself together outside on a run, and I ask myself, "If this time together is the result of all that effort, how could I not have done it?"

Terry Storm was not athletic as a child; she took up swimming, running, and biking as an adult. Working full-time as a research scientist and the mother of two, she fits in her triathlon life through creative multitasking. She's competed in many sprint- and international-distance triathlons over the last several years.

natural 80 percent pace. Doing intervals, hill repeats, or tempo runs at higher heart rate levels will force your body to adapt over time to a greater effort and allow you to bring your 10K time down in the process.

Yet running (or cycling) at these stronger levels is stressful on your body. One good dose of this effort each week on each of the bike and run is quality stress and will help you get stronger. Too much of this stress (more than one to two sessions per week per sport) can hinder your ability to recover and may leave you feeling flat, overtrained, or injured.

An example of an effective weekly training situation for a 10K is to do one session at a very easy aerobic pace (65–75 percent of max), one session of intervals at a higher intensity (87–92 percent of max for each interval), and one longer, hilly session with varying intensity levels within the run (70–87 percent of max). In doing this, you implement a variety of intensities into your training, which sets you up for optimal training effect and ultimately a faster 10K time than you would get running solely at 80 percent of max. It's also much more mentally interesting than the same standard pace day after day.

Change the Scenery

Along with their familiar pace, many athletes like to run the same course each run session or bike the same roads each time they ride. Humans are creatures of habit who derive comfort from sameness and structure. But if you want to excel in triathlon, you need to become an adaptable creature as well. Adapting not only helps in coping with the rigors of training, but also in muting the emotional challenges of a race, which will allow you to have some fun!

Within the consistency of your three sessions of running per week, vary the intensity of each session and change up the location and terrain. Make one an easy run on flatter dirt trails to strengthen your lower legs and change up your stride and foot plant while running on uneven surfaces. Run on the track for a speed workout on a smooth, quick surface, which will train your legs for higher speeds. Finally, go for a longer, moderately paced run on a paved road that undulates with a couple of climbs and descents on its course. This variety not only gets your body used to different types of terrain, it also allows your mind to feel comfortable with change.

CONVERSATIONS WITH DAVE SCOTT: ELIMINATING DISTRACTIONS

Terri: What would you say to someone who is having a hard time sticking to their goals and who easily gets distracted or is too busy or can't hit the mark?

Dave: I think a lot of people have too many gadgets. I advise people to use them at times and build them into the programs I give them. But you sort of take away the euphoria and the fun feeling you have from feeling good about yourself by exercising with all the tools. It doesn't have to be programmable, and you don't have to look at your power meter, your GPS, or heart rate monitor. Just go out and do it.

An athlete's perception of the difficulty of a race course can be based partially on her experiences in training prior to that race. If you never swim in the ocean in training, you may feel nervous about getting through surf or chop in a triathlon with an ocean swim. If you never train in wind on the bike, you may struggle mentally, as well as physically, when you are forced to deal with headwinds in an event. But if you train on hills, then a hilly course will not faze you, and you will know how to deal with climbing. Making unknown quantities known entities will help you to perform your best come race day.

After I ran my first marathon when I was seventeen, a 20-mile run didn't seem so tough. Following my first Ironman, I realized that racing for 10 hours was challenging but doable. Having completed a 100-mile trail race, 12 hours of trail running was just another tough day of training. After my first nine-day expedition-length adventure race, sleeping in mud puddles while sleep-deprived and starving didn't seem so bad. As I slowly upped the ante in my athletic life, my view of what was tough changed again and again. Perception can rule your ability to adapt. The more you face adversity, the less you view your adaptation as a struggle, and the more you observe it as an opportunity to get stronger. Facing adversity teaches you to face further adversity.

Varying the intensity of your workouts within each week of training can help you grow stronger and faster as a triathlete. Adapting through race and training course experiences can allow you to be ready for anything that may happen during your event and, most important, give you the confidence you need to truly enjoy your race experiences!

The chart below uses run-training as an example to show what a week of training may look like when you incorporate consistency and variety into your running. Once you've determined your allotted training time per week, how many sessions of each sport you'll do, and how you'll vary them, you can start building such workouts into your periodized training program.

PERIODIZING YOUR TRAINING

Periodization of training was initially tested and documented in the early twentieth century by the Russians. It generally means dividing your training into periods in order to accomplish specific goals. You can periodize a few weeks of training, a few months of training, a year of training, or other peaks and recovery phases within your season in order to best plan build phases.

The idea of planning a year of training is an excellent one and will allow you to hit your peak at precisely the correct time (in theory). But in twenty years of coaching, I have rarely found an athlete who executes a long-term training plan perfectly. It is common to alter and fine-tune the original plan as you go, due to missed workouts, illness, or time constraints. That doesn't mean that you shouldn't create a macro-periodization plan for an entire year; it means that if you do, you need to be adept at adapting it as problems arise.

A four-week cycle is a common and effective micro-cycle of training that allows you to best capitalize on your consistent weeks of building fitness. This four-week periodization process requires an athlete to build on one or all of the following: distance, intensity, or quantity of training sessions within each sport. This is done over a period of three weeks; the fourth week

SAMPLE WEEKLY RUN TRAINING	
Monday	Rest day
Tuesday	Run 20 min. off the bike at 70% of MHR flat terrain; do the middle 4 min. at 85% of MHR
Wednesday	Warm up 10 min.; 6 x 400 on track at 88% of MHR, 200 easy jog between each; cool down 10 min.
Thursday	Rest day
Friday	40 min. at 75% of MHR rolling hills
Saturday	Rest day
Sunday	1 hour continuous on trails. Incorporate 4 hills of 2 min. each into the run at 87% of MHR

of the cycle is for recovery. Continuing to build your training each week or stabilizing your training at a peak level for weeks on end will not allow your body the rest and recovery needed to adapt to the stresses of training. The body and mind want consistency, variety, and positive stress to become stronger, but they also need recovery to optimize this fitness-building process. See Appendix B for two four-week sample training schedules.

Adapt Within Your Adaptation Process

The amount that you build each week during the initial three weeks of your training cycle and the quantity that you reduce your training intensity and duration during your recovery week are dependent on several factors, one being the amount of time you have chosen to devote to training.

Athletes who have some years of base in triathlon or similar sports can build more

in distance and intensity and take less of a drop in these during their recovery week. But most need to spend some time ascertaining the cycle modifications that are best suited for their goals, time constraints, and bodily limitations. One of the reasons it can take endurance athletes many years to start seeing satisfactory results is that numerous cycles of training are needed to learn to dial in a program for which they are best suited.

But there is one constant: all dedicated, motivated athletes will stray from their prescribed program at some point or other. Whether it is work, travel, injury, social or family commitments, stress, or lack of motivation, most folks miss workouts now and then. If this happens, there is no point in fretting or guilting yourself into piling on extra workouts to make up what you missed. Evaluate where you left off and use the following guidelines to keep your program moving forward. If missing workouts happens frequently, you may need to start at the beginning and reevaluate your realistic time commitment to the sport.

If you miss a few workouts during an initial phase of a build cycle, keep moving forward and take your recovery week as planned. If you blow almost an entire week of build training, you may want to repeat that week the following week, and then continue with your periodization process as planned. Consistency is key, but sometimes life just gets in the way and you have to adapt.

It is essential to take your recovery week unless you have missed several key workouts in a week's time. If you are a new endurance athlete starting triathlon or have tendencies toward illness or injury, try a three-week periodization cycle (two-week build, one-week recovery) initially to allow your body to adapt to the stresses of training. This also allows you to adjust to the new demands that training makes on your life schedule, such as getting up early or squeezing in a lunchtime workout and eating at your desk.

Patience Yields Progress

There is no reason to hurry your build process. Just as your body adapts slowly to losing fat in a weight loss program, your body adapts best if you ease into your program and give it a chance to grow tough slowly. Methodical training, rather than force fitting a prescribed program that is too challenging for your current level of fitness, will help keep injuries, illness, and mental stress at bay.

In addition to making you physically and mentally stronger, learning to endure in your training can offer some intangible virtues that you can carry into all aspects of your life: patience, confidence, and adaptability to name a few. Ask any athlete who does an Ironman triathlon what the major driving force is during their event. They'll tell you that recalling the weeks and months of consistent smart training motivates them.

In Appendix B, you will find some sample training schedules with four-week periodization cycles in each sample. To get a better feel for how to periodize your training, refer to a sample schedule that might work for you.

TRIATHLONS—FOR ME? BY SALLY EDWARDS

Ganbatte Kudasai! fills the air on the streets around Lake Biwa during the Ironman-Japan, as throngs of spectators scream encouragement to the triathletes. Translated into English, the phrase means "Do Your Best!"

Each person doing their individual best is what triathlon is really all about. Triathlon is a way of living that everyone can accomplish by living an active, healthy (swim, bike, run) life.

At the extreme, though, the sport of triathlon has been identified with the concept of the Ironman—the 2.4-mile swim, 112-mile bike, and 26.2-mile run—a grueling ultimate test of one's mind and body. That need not be what triathlon is; it can be for everyone. Sure, it is for "iron" men, but even more it is for those of every age, for women and for men, for those with special needs, for every person.

During the past twenty-five years, I have completed sixteen Ironmans on five continents. I know that triathlon training works to enhance my fitness and quality of life, and I know that it will do the same for you. I'll tell you my secret. I follow what I call the principles of the four Fs. The four Fs are like sports ingredients that you can use every day, in different proportions, as you train.

Sally greets finishers at the Danskin Women's Triathlon.

FUN. If you aren't having fun, then you aren't getting it. During your workouts, you must invariably ask yourself the *why* question. For me, it's mind chatter that sounds something like, "*Why* am I doing this to myself?" Everyone has different answers to the *why* question, but, among the plethora of responses, one of them had better be "because of the fun."

(CONQUERING) FEAR. Triathletes themselves can be intimidating, as can the sport of triathlon. Risks and fears are involved: fear of water, risk of injury, fear of taking time away from family, fear of failing, and the list goes on. But no matter how strong the anxiety, remember that *everyone* experiences it, and that one of the thrills of cross-training is learning to conquer those fears.

FITNESS. Tri-training will make you fit, and fitness is the cornerstone of your most valuable possession, your health.

FAIDO. Another chant that the Japanese triathlon spectators shout repeatedly is *faido*, which means "to fight." In Japanese, *faido* means to fight against that part of yourself that keeps you from doing your best—*ganbatte kudasai!*

Start. And discover that one of the greatest transitions of all is to cross that finish line as a triathlete: The woman who starts the race is not the same as the woman who finishes.

Sally Edwards has been at the forefront of a revolution in fitness training fusing technology with science. She created the Heart Zones Training System, the first to use zone training. She is also the leader of The Sally Edwards Company and author of twenty-two books. Sally is a Triathlon Hall of Fame inductee and the national spokeswoman for the Danskin Triathlon Series.

RECOVERY

If you do not recover adequately, you may not make gains in your training. A healthy combination of active and passive recovery, sticking to your periodization schedule in training, and intelligently adjusting your overall program when life gets in the way will allow you to see positive results.

Recovery refers specifically to de-stressing your body—muscles, tendons, ligaments, and your physiology—as well as your mind after bouts of positive training stress. Using various means of active recovery in your training such as warm-up and cool down, positive hydration and nutrition, light movement on rest days, and hard/easy training methods in your periodization progress helps you make huge gains in your training adaptation. At the same time, you can learn to enjoy the more passive methods of recovery such as massage, cold and hot baths, and getting to know the sleeping patterns necessary for constructive health and fitness. Rest and recovery is not just part of your training process but extends into that daily balancing act called life.

Active Recovery

At the beginning of every workout, it is imperative that you spend some time warming up your body and preparing your muscles, cardiovascular system, and mind for the task ahead—sort of like lubing the engine before asking it to do work. Warm-up time is part of your prescribed workout; it's just done easily, prior to a potentially increased workload. Warm up for five, ten, fifteen minutes or more. It is important that you move easily and allow your HR to come up slowly during this time.

Many athletes notice that the longer they train in distance, the longer it takes them to warm up or feel as though they are in their natural pace. This can be true for their cool down as well. A fit endurance athlete needs to incorporate cool-down time into each workout, not only to ease into the next phase of their day, but to initiate the active recovery process for that specific workout. Cooling down after hard bouts of exercise slowly de-stresses the cardiovascular as well as the muscular system.

Immediately following cool down, it's time to actively restore your body with fluids and vital nutrients that will aid your recovery and allow you to feel better the rest of the day and into the next day's training. Along with plain water, a recovery drink will do wonders for your recovery process. There are many excellent products on the market specific to recovery.

Choose one that you enjoy that contains a carbohydrate to protein ratio of 3 to 1 or 4 to 1. Mix your drink prior to your workout and have it ready in the fridge or in your car to sip right when you are done with your training. Drink your mix within a 15-minute window of completing your workout. If you are doing multiple workouts per day, drink your recovery drink after the most difficult or the longest workout of the day.

Fill a garbage can with water and some ice (designate a can for this use) and stand in it for 15 minutes while drinking, reading, or returning phone calls. The neighbors may think you are a bit odd, but that's nothing new—you're a triathlete!

You do not need to drink the full prescribed amount of drink (as stated on the package) unless your workout is longer than about 1.5 to 2 hours. Scale back the amount you use for shorter workouts. These are guidelines to your nutritional recovery process. Play around with quantities and drinks to get a feel for what is best for you.

Active recovery does not have to take an enormous amount of time from your day; it can be easily incorporated into your life schedule.

With active recovery you'll be amazed at how you can come back off of some really tough days of training to throw it down again the next day or week.

It is vital to the recovery process to work with some form of a hard-easy schedule within each sport and within each build week of your training cycle. After an interval workout on the bike, follow up the next day or two days later with some easy spinning in your small chain ring to incorporate active recovery into your build training phase on the bike. These workouts are not just filler workouts, they are a fundamental part of your recovery, base building, and aerobic conditioning for each sport.

Some athletes combine a more challenging week of running with an easy week of cycling or a challenging week of cycling with an easy week of running. This is another way to incorporate recovery into each sport as well as safely build more distance into your cycling and running. The best solution for your recovery process is what works best for you. This may take some time

to decipher. Pay attention to what you feel is working for recovery and keep a training log for further information gathering.

Passive Recovery

Passive recovery methods have been found to accelerate recovery, which can be quite useful for athletes juggling three sports. Sleep immensely helps your recovery process, but many triathletes fail to incorporate it into their day! Just like a meeting at work or time with your family, you need to schedule in sleep time. Going to bed at the same time each night will allow you to get adequate sleep. Start to unwind well before bedtime or you will not hit the mark. If you are not tired when the time comes, do some easy stretching or read a book. Your sleep time is as critical as your active recovery time in helping you come back from difficult bouts of training and perform at your best.

The amount of sleep each person needs varies. To figure out how much you need, turn off your alarm clock for a few days and allow your body to wake naturally. Note the time before you fall asleep and when you naturally wake up. Take these sleeping samples on days that are typical, not after a day or week that has been particularly stressful.

You should start to notice a pattern of how much sleep your body needs. This amount will generally increase when you are in the build phase of your training and may remain higher during the first few days of a recovery week, and then taper off a bit as your batteries start to recharge. If you can allow yourself to sleep your natural amount, you will set yourself up to gain positive recovery in your training.

You may be saying, "I don't have time to sleep the 8 hours that my body is craving!" but you are capable of finding the time if it is a priority. As a result, you'll be more productive, less injured or sick, and more rested for your workouts.

If you are really serious about gaining critical recovery from your workouts, take naps. On the weekends after your post-workout ice bath/hot shower/recovery drink extravaganza, top off your recovery by hitting the couch for a 20- to 30-minute power nap. Getting the most out of your limited time may require some power-nap gear: ear plugs, eye covers, or just a soft pillow to shield your face from daylight. Instruct your kids, dog, spouse, or alarm clock to wake you (or not) as needed, and you'll be ready to take on the rest of your day recovered and refreshed.

Many people believe that massage is just a fluff-feel-good sort of endeavor. Massage does feel quite excellent, but for athletes it can be vital, particularly in the recovery process. Massage not only promotes nourishment and blood flow in the muscle tissue, but it helps you to get in touch with potential problem areas in your body. Massage can help prevent injuries by treating tight or compromised areas before they become a problem. As a neophyte professional triathlete, I could not afford regular massages, but I would spend some time each night listening to music, talking with friends, or watching TV while giving myself a leg massage. I followed the massage with some stretching, and voilà! I was ready for some good sleep time. Later in my career, and especially during the most important time of my season—training cycles leading up to the Hawaii Ironman Triathlon World Championships—I had weekly massages and continued the daily leg massage routine. I was amazed at the training workloads I could produce by engaging in this type of passive recovery.

AVOIDING OVERTRAINING, BURNOUT, AND INJURIES

It is common to have occasional days of moderate to heavy fatigue, but if it lasts for a week or more, you may need to re-evaluate your training process and your lifestyle choices to eliminate the possibilities of overtraining. If left unattended, overtraining can lead to burnout and injury—two predicaments that are much more serious than overtraining. Looking at the causes and symptoms of overtraining can help you to avoid this situation.

Areas in your training process that can cause overtraining:

- Inadequate (passive and active) recovery within weekly training
- Inadequate decrease in volume and intensity of training within periodized recovery week (third or fourth week) as well as inadequate passive and active recovery within this week
- Too much overall volume of training or too quick of an increase in volume

- Too much intensity of training or too quick an increase in intensity
- Too many race efforts
- Striving for unrealistic goals in training or racing
- Failure to adjust training process to lifestyle stresses
- Increase of training too quickly coming off some downtime (i.e., off-season or injury)
- A training program that lacks enjoyment and fun

Areas in your lifestyle that can cause stress and result in overtraining symptoms:

- Perpetually rushing around
- Lack of routine
- Lack of adequate sleep
- Not enough recovery or relaxation time
- Imbalance in diet including inappropriate carbohydrate, protein, and fat intake; inadequate water intake; inadequate vitamin and mineral intake; excessive alcohol, caffeine, or simple sugar intake
- Poor living or interpersonal conditions including unhealthy surroundings; regular conflict with family, coach, friends; unhappiness in relationships; not enough time alone
- Poor work conditions including regular conflict with co-workers, too much work, unhappy with job or career
- Excessive travel
- Exposure to sick children or co-workers
- Asthma, allergies, and all illnesses

Psychological symptoms of overtraining:

- Feeling indifferent about your training and life
- Mental lethargy
- Mood disturbances such as irritability
- Poor focus
- Frustration
- Inability to accept that you are overtrained
- Decreased self-esteem and self-confidence
- Change in interaction with others

Physical symptoms of overtraining:

- Altered sleeping patterns
- Excessive craving of water or sugar or significant change in appetite
- Consistent or excessive fatigue
- Consistent muscle soreness
- Increased or persistent illness, injury, infection, swollen lymph glands
- Morning heart rate changes
- Performance change including an inability to work at usual intensity levels during training or racing
- Amenorrhea
- Decreased libido
- Change in body weight

You may glance at these lists and say, "I have some of those symptoms right now!" It is common to experience some of these challenges, especially during build phases of training. You may feel tired one day, crave sugar the next, and lose a bit of sleep a couple days later. It is common for your morning heart rate to increase after strenuous training efforts. You do need to ride an edge of peak training weeks during the crux of your build in order to gain the maximum benefit, but the key to riding that edge is to do it infrequently and for short periods of time. That would mean that for one week or a few days out of a four-week cycle, you may feel considerably on edge.

The key to deciphering whether you are experiencing regular training stresses or overtraining is to note the duration and quantity of your symptoms. If you are experiencing several symptoms over a period of ten days or more, you are most likely overtrained. Back off immediately! Take one or two recovery or rest days before you get to this point and notice if you bounce back. If you ignore the signs and forge ahead with your training, you may put yourself into a deficit that will take many weeks to recover from.

One of the most significant challenges in your training process is knowing when to push and when to back off. Your training log can help you become more in tune with how you are feeling mentally and physically. Look for patterns. Be honest. Listen to your body. Write down your observations. Your body communicates with you in the form of fatigue, hunger, pain, and so on. If you listen, you can keep yourself on the positive side of that training edge and go to your events primed and healthy to race. If not, you may head into the vortex of burnout.

BURNOUT

You need stress in your training in order to make gains. Positive training stress allows for successful psychological and physiological adaptations to the training process.

Overtraining is a psychophysiological malfunction in training adaptation. Burnout is an exhaustive psychophysiological malfunction in response to repeated efforts to try to adapt to training. Burnout = game over.

Many people use the term "burnout" loosely when they feel tired or unmotivated, but in reality, burnout is a very severe reaction to overtraining. You can pop back from mild overtraining with two to three days of recovery. If you let yourself hit burnout, it may take weeks or months of mental and physical recovery in order to train and race at a peak level again.

Symptoms of burnout include a lack of commitment to training and a belief that the costs of time and energy put into training are too great for the rewards—the investment feels too high. The joy and love you have for fitness and sport are shrouded by excessive mental and physical fatigue.

Once an athlete hits burnout, there is no other option than to back away from training for sometimes an extended period of time. This is the time to create more balance in your life with activities outside of sport or triathlon. Find ways to make your minimal training fun again. Generate impromptu off-season activities to help you recharge your batteries and get the love of sport back into your life again.

You are your best friend in recognizing the signs of overtraining and burnout. Listen and learn to balance the edge of positive training stress and overtraining. You will make mistakes—heed them—learn from them. Listening to your body will help keep you in the game of endurance sports.

TAKING RESPONSIBILITY FOR YOUR INJURIES

There are two types of endurance athletes: those who have been injured and those who are going to get injured. And there are two types of injuries that athletes tend to suffer from: traumatic injuries and overuse injuries.

Traumatic injuries in triathlon can come in the form of bike crashes, stepping off a curb incorrectly while running, or getting smashed by a wave and hitting the sand. Trauma happens suddenly, and you know immediately that something has gone wrong.

Overuse injuries are the most common form of endurance sport injury. Just like your car, with regular tune-ups in the form of passive and active recovery as well as a smart training program, you may stay out of the shop. But if you head out of balance in any direction, you may fall victim to injury. Most people do not have perfectly aligned, perfectly bilateral moving parts. Due to inherent structure, strength, or flexibility imbalances, you can cause problems simply by moving your body parts in one plane of motion for extended periods of time.

Think of the number of times your foot hits the ground, your pedal turns over, or your hand enters the water during 1 mile of movement. That's a lot of repetitive motion over hours, weeks, and months. The body adapts amazingly to this level of repetition if you give it time to do so, but if you force your training volume or intensity before the system is ready, you may throw something out of balance and cause a malfunction.

Overuse injuries tend to come on gradually, though some may pop up quickly due to a long training session or a race effort. The latter are what I call "injuries-in-waiting"—compromised body parts just waiting to go sour. Injuries-in-waiting can be the most frustrating because on the surface you can't figure out where they came from—they just show up on race day. But if you look a bit deeper you may find the source of the problem waiting to happen.

It is important to note that injuries are often a symptom of a problem somewhere else in the body. The body is connected in total. For example, if your pelvis is out of alignment, it may cause undue stress on certain tendons and muscles in the hip. If the attachment of your iliotibial tendon on your hip is torqued, it may tug on its insertion point on the lateral knee area. The pain may show up in your knee (ITB syndrome), but the cause of the problem may be coming from your hip (or feet). A compromised area in your neck may cause a problem in your stride or foot plant. Work regularly in your recovery with a health care professional who understands this concept and understands that you need to address the symptom but that ultimately the issue is defining the source of the problem. Sound complicated? It is (see Attending to an Injury later in this chapter).

Your training log can hold the clues to overuse injuries. For example, I can look back in my training log and see a dramatic, inappropriate increase in training—I got greedy and increased the volume or intensity of my training too quickly. I may note the date on my running shoes and realize I am long overdue in replacing them (if you listen to the aches in your legs while running, they'll tell you when your shoes are "flat" or "dead"). Or I may have gotten a new piece of gear, or changed position on my bike or in my swim stroke.

I could have noticed signs of overtraining creeping in but ignored them. Or I could have gotten intermittent twinges of tightness, excessive fatigue, or weakness in a specific spot but failed to make adjustments to my recovery program.

If overtraining is unattended, it can lead to injury. Psychological, physiological, or structural, too much stress can cause the body to break down. Injury pain is a sign that you are doing something incorrectly. If you listen, you can fix the problem. If you don't, then you will be dealing with an injury.

THE MIND/BODY CONNECTION

About midway through my career as a pro triathlete, I went through a divorce. Prior to that time, I had had a few minor injuries but nothing that set me back or took me out of training for more than short periods of time. I found that the combination of my knowing my body very well, having solid health professionals on my side including an excellent massage therapist, having a healthy diet, sleeping well, and generally paying attention to recovery process, meant I was able to stay pretty solid despite the long hours of weekly training. Until the divorce.

This emotional stress seemed to manifest itself in my body in various negative ways. I was constantly fatigued, lethargic, couldn't sleep, didn't care about training, was constantly sore, and as a result had a slew of injuries. Normally the signs of overtraining, they are also signs of severe mental stress or depression—in my case situational depression—which can lead to injury or illness. Over time as I walked through the mental stress and settled into my changed life, my body became stronger and healthy again. But this process took several months to a year, and in the meantime my body paid a price.

But don't take my word for it. There is a school of sport psychology that explains the psychological predictors of athletic injury. In other words, there is an academic model that explains the interactive relationship between athletic injury and certain psychological factors. The way you deal, or not, with stressors in your life can create precursors to injury.

Injuries are not just caused by your physical life. Unhappiness can cause an injury in a convoluted, round-about manner. Too much stress, inability to deal with anxiety, and excessive anger can do the same. If injury comes knocking at your door, review your training and lifestyle while being honest with yourself about what is happening in your personal life, and you just might find the culprit to the problem.

Common training injuries:

Tendonitis. Pain or tenderness on a tendon near a joint. You may also experience numbness or tingling, stiffness that restricts movement, a mild swelling, or locking of the joint.

Help: If tendon pain is severe, stop doing the activity that causes the pain for a few days or up to two weeks. If pain is minor, reduce activity by 50 percent. Ice the area for 15 minutes, two times a day. If pain persists, seek medical attention.

Muscle strain. Weakness of the muscle causing an inability or decreased ability to use the muscle, or pain in the strained muscle or corresponding joint. Tends to come on slowly over time or you may notice the painful area once you stop training.

Help: Stop doing the activity that causes the pain for a few days or up to two weeks. If strain is minor, reduce activity by 50 percent. Ice the area for 15 minutes, two times a day. If pain persists, seek medical attention.

Muscle tear (or pull). Usually a sudden tearing of a muscle or piece of a muscle. Many people mistake a strain for a pull; if you pull something, you'll know it immediately. Muscles pulls cause exaggerated strain symptoms with prolonged pain and swelling. You probably won't be able to continue with the activity you are doing unless you modify movement significantly.

Help: Stop the activity that causes the pain until pain free. Ice the area for 15 minutes, two times a day. Seek medical attention.

Joint issues. Ache or discomfort in joint area. Swelling and reduced range of motion. There are many issues that can cause joint problems.

Help: Stop the activity that causes the pain until pain free. Ice the area for 15 minutes, two times a day. Seek medical attention.

Stress fracture. Pain on the affected area and on the bone in general during exercise. Tenderness and swelling at the point of the fracture. Sometimes swelling does not occur.

Help: Stop the activity that causes the pain until pain free. Seek medical attention. No matter how you slice it, bone breaks take some time to heal. Usually six to ten weeks. Period. Force your return from a stress fracture, and you'll end up on crutches or worse.

Attending to an Injury

The complex challenge of obtaining appropriate medical attention for a sports injury is one of my biggest pet peeves as an athlete and coach. I have walked enough athletes through the difficult process of getting an injury diagnosed and properly treated to realize that athletes must be proactive in researching and obtaining whatever means possible to help their injuries. Heed the following advice in attending to an injury.

#1: Take action toward healing your injury. Once you've established that you have an injury, it's important that you let yourself grieve over it (briefly), then look at your options for taking action and come up with a plan. An injury means that something you love—training for a period of time, or perhaps an important race—has been taken away. Acknowledging that you are really bummed that you are injured is part of the healing process. Then it's time to look at your options for seeking medical help, getting rehab, and continuing your training while addressing the mental stress that may come along with your injury. You should feel confident that you have everyone you need on your team to help your cause.

While this process is in motion, evaluate your training program to determine what you can and can't do during your healing process. Cross-training is the beauty of triathlon. So if your running is temporarily taken away, you can still bike, swim, lift weights, and deep water run. If you can't bike and run, you can still swim, strength train (perhaps with modification), and deep water run. That's a whole lot of positive activity with which to maintain your current fitness.

Your body will heal faster if you train through your injury. You'll feel better mentally, and you'll increase blood flow to the affected areas for progressive healing. Many doctors are shocked at how quickly athletes can come back from injuries. If you train through your injuries, you will maintain a base of strength that will help your body's overall healing process. Don't use your injury as a license to quit training. If you want to race well again, revamp your program with the guidance of your sports medicine doctor and keep getting out there.

#2: Go to a sports medicine specialist who is also an athlete to have your injury diagnosed. Get a referral from someone you respect who has been to this person. A sports medicine physician who is an athlete will understand that unless you have severe trauma that limits movement, you can continue to train with an altered program. He will recommend that you do activity that doesn't cause pain and will set your rehab program in motion, which should include additional modalities such as physical therapy, massage, or other forms of soft tissue therapy, as well as a proactive protocol for getting you well.

Be wary of a doc who wants to inject drugs, such as cortisone, into you regularly, or wishes to do surgery right off the bat (for non-traumatic injuries). Also be wary of a doctor who sends you home telling you to ice, take anti-inflammatories, and do nothing for two weeks (yes, some doctors amazingly still do this). There is a lot you can do to rehab an injury before resorting to these modalities.

Don't hesitate to get several opinions about your injury. The first person you see may not address your problem effectively. Shop around. The more information you gather, the more ammunition you'll have to deal with the problem.

#3: Don't be a cheapskate with your body. You may pride yourself on being a smart shopper when it comes to getting a deal on gear, but if it's your body you're talking about, don't scrimp. You may have to go through standard, sometimes convoluted, channels before getting proper attention for a sports injury, and still the person you finally see may not be the best at dealing with your injury. So if they aren't—pay out of pocket for someone who is. Yep, you heard me!

In endurance sports you abuse your body. Believe me, it's much healthier abuse than sitting on the couch eating bon-bons and watching TV, but it does cause wear and tear just the same. You train smart. You rest and recover. And still sometimes you get injured. In the latter case, seek the best medical professionals.

#4: Research your injury. Before your appointment, research your injury via books, magazines, or the internet. You will reduce the amount of frustration in your injury healing process if you arm yourself with knowledge about what might be happening with your body. At your appointment, ask questions. This will also make you an active teammate in your healing process, rather than someone on the sidelines.

#5: Try various forms of therapy for your injury, and stick with the ones you like for your ongoing passive recovery process. Standard western medicine is one way to deal with an injury. There are many modalities available to you—seek them out and be willing to experiment. Post-divorce I had an injury that was threatening to indefinitely put an end to my running. I tried doctors, podiatrists, chiropractors, acupuncture, massage therapy, and physical therapy (PT). I spent so much time at the PT office that I told them I was going to have to start renting space. But I still couldn't run—fast. When I tried to increase speed, my calf

would lock down and stop me. Another triathlete suggested I try myofascial release therapy, so I paid out of pocket to try a series of treatments.

I knew from the first session that I had found what I needed. The work was painful but it was the good pain that addresses the core of an issue. It took two expensive sessions a week to break up accumulated scar tissue in the problem area, and it worked. In several weeks I was running—better than ever and pain free for the first time in a year.

Since that time, I have gotten additional work with craniosacral therapy, scar tissue massage, rolfing, directional non-force chiropractic, and more. Each modality addressed my body in a different manner. Some I continue with—I have been going to the same massage therapist for fifteen years—while others don't speak to me as strongly. Don't wait to get an injury to do serious maintenance on your body. Get those regular tune-ups by trying different health practitioners. When you find those you enjoy, stick with them.

#6: Consider deep water running and other training options. Deep water running can be useful not only for injury rehab but also for recovery run days. If you are building your running back up after an injury, start with a short 10- to 20-minute run on roads, then immediately hop in the pool to finish your running time with an additional 20 to 45 minutes of deep water running. Deep water running is uneventful (use music), but it works. Learn how to get creative with your workout by getting a videotape or book on the topic. Vary your workouts just like you would running on a track. Very few injuries will not allow you to deep water run. It's a very effective fall-back for most injuries, and it feels great to unweight yourself and run freely in water.

Other options for training through an injury include the stairmaster, elliptical trainer, or similar equipment. As you start back into running again, try the treadmill or a turf field for a cushy means to ease up the stress. A few cycling alternatives include hiking uphill, stationary bike, and inline skating. To substitute for swimming, try a Vasa Trainer, different swim strokes, and weight training.

#7: Ease back into training. Once your injury starts to heal, do not jump right back into your pre-injury training volume and intensity. Decrease volume 60 percent from where you were prior to the injury, then make slight increases of 10 percent per week as you test the injury. Do not test for speed unless you are fully healed. Speed requires maximal use of your muscles and joints, and if they are not solid, you may set yourself up for a relapse.

Coping Mentally with Injuries

Training for triathlon not only gives you strength and endurance, it offers you a means to gain confidence in yourself as an athlete and as a person. You may start to see yourself—your identity—more fully within your athletic life as you gather success through your sport. This is all wonderful stuff, but when injury requires

undesired cessation of an activity, it can be a huge mental blow.

One of the best things to do to ease your mind during injury recovery is to come up with a plan of action. When you don't take action, you are setting yourself up for injury-induced depression or low self-esteem.

Here is a practice I have used successfully many times. It has helped me toe starting lines post-injury that I never thought I'd touch. This injury-specific mental-training

process will keep you positive and present during your injury healing process:

- Review each day of healing. Each morning when you wake, review the training you will be doing that day, as well as any appointments that you might have related to your injury. Make mental notes of how many times and when you will ice, stretch, or engage in any other forms of rehab.

- Review your healing affirmations. On 3 by 5 cards, write three positive affirmations: (1) reference yourself within the sport in which you got injured, (2) address the healing of your injury, and (3) reference yourself as an athlete.

    For example: (1) I am a strong and fluid runner, (2) my calf will come back stronger than before, and (3) I am a dedicated, committed athlete.

    Read these at the start and end of your day. The idea is to train your mind to engage positively in your healing process. You may think that you are lying to yourself by making statements that may not come true, but in actuality, you are stating the possibility of what can come true.

- Visualize your healing. In the morning as well as evening take a few deep breaths and breathe into your injury. Send breath and energy to that area. Close your eyes and imagine the cells healing, the swelling decreasing, the area getting stronger. Do this in a calm, positive manner.

- Visualize your entry back into sport. During training each day, visualize yourself doing the sport you currently cannot do. Picture yourself running easily, with no pain, in a place you enjoy—your favorite trail, the beach, or with friends. See the strength and ease with which you are running and let your body feel that motion as you are seeing it. Combine this visual with your affirmation: "I am a strong, fluid runner."

- Gain support for your healing process. Enlist a friend, training partner, your doctor, or a sports psychologist. Make a pact with that person that you can contact her whenever you need her support and she will commit to being there for you. Work with someone who will be realistic and affirmative about your progression, not someone who will treat you as a victim. For example, she should ask you questions like, "Did you read your affirmation cards today?" or, "What is your training plan for the day?" rather than, "Oh poor you, you're injured, I feel terrible for you."

- Do one constructive thing each day that replaces the time you would be spending training in the sport in which you are injured. Have you been wanting to catch up on some reading? Write more in your journal? Take that photography class you've been eyeing? Now's your chance. Take the time you would be spending running and use it to engage in another highly constructive activity. In doing this, your injury will actually be offering you an opportunity for positive activity in your life at an otherwise unproductive time.

- Practice patience. Part of becoming a

THE RULES OF THE ENDURANCE GAME

1. YOU WILL RECEIVE A BODY.

You may like it or hate it, but it will be yours for the entire period this time around.

2. YOU WILL LEARN LESSONS.

Each day as an athlete, you will have the opportunity to learn lessons about your body. You may like the lessons or think them irrelevant and stupid.

3. A LESSON IS REPEATED UNTIL LEARNED.

A lesson about your body will be presented to you in various forms until you have learned it. When you have learned it, you can go on to the next lesson.

4. LEARNING LESSONS DOES NOT END.

There is no part of endurance sports that does not contain its lessons. If you are training and racing, there are lessons to be learned about your body.

5. WHAT YOU MAKE OF YOUR LESSONS IS UP TO YOU.

You have all the tools and resources you need to make the most of your lessons. What you do with them is up to you. The choice is yours.

6. YOUR ANSWERS LIE INSIDE YOU.

All you need to do is look, listen, and trust.

---

mature athlete is acquiring patience. Ask any elite or professional athlete and they will tell you about the extended amounts of time needed to fine-tune their craft. Along with that time comes patience, acceptance, and love for this process. As you see yourself grow, mature, and cope with the stress of sport, you calmly ease into your sporting life each day. There is power in that calm. There is vast power in patience—especially with yourself.

Remember one very important fact: The body will heal when it is ready to heal, and you can't rush that process. You can offer it your best shot, embrace your newfound patience, and then sit back and accept what is given. Ultimately, it is your best option.

PRINCIPLES OF HEART RATE TRAINING

While most triathletes are interested in knowing a bit about the principles of effective heart rate (HR) training and enjoy cool new gear, like a HR monitor, many are not that keen on taking the time to become experts on the topic or learning the nuances of how to use a monitor's various features, let alone analyze the detailed information the monitor can regurgitate.

Because understanding this sometimes-baffling topic can offer efficiency in generating training results, it's worth learning the nuts and bolts of the topic of HR training. I will not present the intricate detail or the finer art of the craft. This overview of HR training will be more than enough to get you started on this exciting part of your training program.

HEART RATE

Each time your heart beats, a defined quantity of oxygen-filled blood is pushed out of this important vessel to be used in various parts of the body. The heart is a highly specialized type of muscle, and if you train the heart by requiring it to work harder, it will get stronger—analogous to a quad muscle getting stronger from the repetition of turning the pedals on a bicycle.

When you do cardiovascular training such as swimming, biking, and running, your HR increases. The rate increases partly because you need more oxygen in your muscles in order to do these activities. The faster you go in any sport, the faster your heart beats because oxygen demands become higher and the heart tries to accommodate by increasing blood volume output.

HEART RATE MONITORS

Heart rate monitors instantly record your heart rate, thereby giving you feedback on how hard your heart is working. Knowing your heart rate during training can help you make significant and precise gains in your fitness level by verifying that you are working at the correct level to make those gains.

If you train too fast too often, you can set yourself up for overtraining or injury. Your heart rate monitor can assure you that you are not overstressing your body by helping you follow your training plan. Your monitor can also alert you if you are not training hard enough given your MHR (maximum heart rate) and goal training pace.

Recovery is just as critical as speed work in helping you gain training effect. A heart rate monitor can let you know if you are working at the correct level for your training recovery workout.

HR monitors can be an excellent tool for races, especially while you are learning the nuances of pace, fueling, and how to race in heat, wind, and other outside factors. The monitor can give you valuable information about your effort level and how your body reacts to stresses of an event.

With a heart rate monitor, you can measure your various training and racing levels, while having a "companion" to train with. You can measure recovery, training intensity, and resting heart rate while taking the guesswork out of your training process.

RESTING HEART RATE

Resting heart rate (RHR) is the number of times your heart beats in one minute when you are at complete rest—for instance, prior to getting out of bed in the morning. The lower your RHR, the longer rest interval between heart beats. This means the heart has more time to fill with blood. The more blood that fills the heart, the stronger the contraction and the greater the amount of blood pushed out with each beat.

Even at rest, a stronger, fitter heart will be more efficient at pumping more blood with each beat. An average adult has a RHR in the 70s to 80s. Many fit athletes see this number drop into the 50s and some top-level endurance athletes have RHRs in the 40s or even the 30s when they are in peak form.

It is helpful to have a good understanding of what your RHR is on average during general levels of base-building training. Take your RHR over a week's time during base-building training and then compare this average number to your RHR during higher levels of training. This comparison can give you some valuable information.

If you try to increase your training load too quickly or for longer than prescribed periods of time, it may show as an elevated RHR. You can also develop an elevated RHR as a result of improper hydration or nutrition, lack of sleep, too much stress, or a combination of any of the above. If your RHR increase is sustained for several days or longer, it may be your body's way of telling you that you need to reflect on your training process to determine which variables may be causing this issue. (See more detailed information in "Avoiding Overtraining.")

Sometimes this increase is expected due to a planned, healthy increase in workload. But if the increase lingers for extended periods, take a look at your overall program and your general life stress levels to see if making some adjustments to decrease stress will help bring your rate down to your normal average or even lower.

RECOVERY HEART RATE

Your recovery HR is measured one minute after you stop exercising and is an excellent indication of your current fitness level. When you start your training program, take note of this drop after each workout. Over time you will notice a consistently quicker rate drop during this minute. This is an indication of increased fitness.

You can also use recovery HR to note increases in fitness in certain benchmark workouts. For instance, let's say that the first Wednesday of each month you do a running track workout of 6 intervals of 400 meters each (6 x 400). When you begin incorporating this workout into your routine, note your HR as you finish each interval and then again one minute later during your recovery for that same interval. Run these 400s at the same intensity for the first couple months of your training program, and after month two, you may notice a decrease in your recovery HR during your recovery interval. Log this information in your training journal and note changes over time.

MAXIMUM HEART RATE

Your maximum heart rate is the maximum number of times your heart beats in one minute's time. This number varies from person to person and is foundationally based on your genetics. You may be able to drive your MHR up higher as your fitness increases due to neuromuscular and physiological gains that allow you to push your body faster and therefore your HR higher. But your MHR itself is not an indicator of fitness. It is important because it is the number that allows you to measure all of your own personal training efforts accurately.

There are several formulas that try to predict a person's MHR, but research points to the need to test an individual's physiology in order to get an accurate measure.

A MAXIMUM HEART RATE TEST

It is best to execute a MHR test either in a lab setting or on a running track with a HR monitor. Here is a running MHR test you can do on your own at a track.

Caution: Attempt this test only if you are feeling quite fit in your running, you are injury free, and you are rested and healthy for the test.

This is a very challenging test—a maximal/race effort. It is helpful to get someone to time you and cheer you on—to help push you to that max effort.

Doing the pre-test warm-up is key. Do not attempt the test unless you are warm, sweaty, lubed, and ready to race.

WARM-UP:

- 2 miles of very easy jogging.
- Light stretching of all major muscle groups of the legs and hips.
- 6 x 100-meter strides—build speed on the straights of the track and do an easy jog on the curves of the track between each.
- 2 x 200-meter at mile race pace with a 200-meter brisk walk between each.

Do some additional stretching before the test as needed in order to feel very warmed up.

TEST:
1-mile time trial broken at the 800:

- First lap at 85 percent of max (estimate this); second lap at 90 percent of max.
- Stop after lap 2 and walk briskly for 35 seconds. Be ready to go right into the next 800 at the end of recovery.
- Third lap at 95 percent of max. Fourth lap all out!

Wear your HR monitor and note your HR 10 yards before you finish, when you finish, and 5 to 10 seconds after you finish.

Use the highest number you see on your monitor for your MHR.

Make sure that you cool down with at least a mile of easy jogging after this test.

Note: If you feel as though you didn't give it your best shot, or you didn't feel up to an all-out effort, wait a few weeks and try the test again. If you feel as though you have made significant fitness gains since your last test—test again.

The current formulas are not precise, and in my experience as an athlete and coach, they have proven to be incorrect more often than not. You can test your MHR in an established lab setting on a treadmill, or you can do your own max test on a track (see "A Maximum Heart Rate Test"). Check out your local hospitals or universities for labs that conduct MHR tests. There may be a small fee, but it is a solid investment if you are planning to use a HR monitor in training.

Studies have shown that the MHR you can attain while running is on average 5 to 6 beats higher than what you can attain on a bicycle. MHRs while swimming can be significantly lower than running—around 10 to 14 beats per minute. But as a multi-sport athlete, it is best to test your max while running and then adjust and extrapolate that number into your biking and swimming efforts.

Before you do your max test to determine your MHR, go ahead and wear your heart rate monitor for a few weeks in training and observe what your rate is during different levels of each workout. What is your HR when you are warming up? When you are running or biking at a moderate level? What does it shoot up to when you do a run interval or bike up a hill really fast? Note what your heart is doing during these times and you'll start to get a sense of how your cardio system works at different stress levels.

HEART RATE TRAINING LEVELS

Once you have established your MHR, you can use this number to determine training HRs for all of your workouts. If you want to do a set of 4 x 2 minute running intervals at 88 percent of max (or approximately 10K race pace), calculate MHR x 88% = interval heart rate, or, for example, 170 x 0.88 = 149 beats per minute for each interval. With this number, you can design your training heart rates for each of your workouts, including your very important easy workouts. Using MHR is an easy and accurate way to start using HR in your training.

Each of the five training levels in the box (see page 62) have been categorized, described, and then assigned a HR range or a "% of max" range. There is also a brief description of how you can use each specific level in your training. The percentages designate a HR range relative to your MHR. For example, 80 percent of your MHR is MHR x 0.80. You can choose whichever method of evaluating intensity level suits you (by description, perceived exertion, or % of MHR); however, in order to use the "% of max" numbers within each level, you must know your MHR (see the "Borg Scale of Perceived Exertion" in chapter 3).

TRAINING LEVELS

LEVEL 1: RECOVERY

Used for: Recovery, warm-up, cool down, baseline endurance
Perceived Exertion: 9–10, you can talk easily, effort is extremely easy
HR Range: 65–75% of max

LEVEL 2: AEROBIC

Used for: Improving aerobic capacity, warming-up, cooling down, longer races until fitness increases
Perceived Exertion: 11–13, conversations are comfortable, effort is easy
HR Range: 75–80% of max

LEVEL 3: HIGH-END AEROBIC TO LOW ANAEROBIC

Used for: Improving lactate system, intervals, hill repeats, tempo training, long to moderate distance races depending on fitness
Perceived Exertion: 14–15, short conversations are possible, effort is moderate to challenging
HR Range: 80–85% of max

LEVEL 4: LACTATE OR ANAEROBIC THRESHOLD

Used for: Improving ability to mobilize lactate for longer periods, intervals, hill repeats, moderate to short races depending on your fitness
Perceived Exertion: 16–18, difficult to speak; effort is challenging to difficult
HR Range: 85–90% of max

LEVEL 5: SUB-MAXIMUM TO MAXIMUM EFFORT

Used for: Training fast twitch to develop speed, intervals, hill repeats, sprint events
Perceived Exertion: 19–20, breathing is labored, effort is very difficult
HR Range: 90–100% of max

CHAPTER 2

Swimming in Triathlon

"My strokes felt powerful, and I felt strong, alive, as if I awakened for the first time. Nothing in the swimming pool gave me this pleasure. I was free, moving fast, feeling the waves lifting and embracing me, and I couldn't believe how happy I was."

Lynne Cox, Swimming to Antarctica: Tales of a Long-Distance Swimmer

In a triathlon, you'll swim a course in a lake, river, canal, or ocean as efficiently as possible, while surrounded by many other bodies trying to do the same. Because that is the crux of swimming in this sport, the main focus of this chapter will be all things open water. You'll learn about gear, swimming in open water in training and in a race, including negotiating associated fears, as well as some key areas of swim training for triathlon. Most important, you'll get psyched to develop that amazing relationship with open-water swimming!

ESSENTIAL GEAR FOR SWIMMING

Approximately half of triathletes spend $25 to $100 a year on swim gear for triathlon. Purchasing a wetsuit will drive those numbers up, as will frequent swimming in a pool, since their chemical systems dissolve swimsuits.

Swimsuit. You can purchase a swimsuit for training and for racing, or you can opt to purchase different clothing for your race. There are too many types and brands of suits to list here, but the main thing is to find a suit that is comfortable, streamlined in the water, and that you enjoy wearing. Some use their suits to make a fashion statement at every workout, while others wear an inexpensive suit even after it starts to sag in the butt due to dissolving elastic. I have seen many larger breasted women wear a sports bra underneath their race bathing suit for extra support. Try various suits, then stick to the brand that you intuitively pull from your drawer most often.

Goggles. Goggles not only protect your eyes in salt or chemical-infused water, but they help you see clearly both above and below the water while swimming. With goggles, you can see the guy's feet you're drafting off of, as well as the buoys that are guiding you. Goggles need to fit your face

and be comfortable to wear for long periods of time. If they are adjustable in the nose piece and head strap, you have a better chance of getting them to prevent leaking or fogging. Try them on in the store. If they hug your eye area with ease, make the purchase, but you may need to try a few pairs before you find the one brand that works on your face while swimming.

When testing the goggles in the water, adjust them to feel snug but comfortable. Prior to getting in the water, spit in the lenses and swish the spit around, or use a defog product (as directed on the package), then dip them in water before putting

them on. Try wearing the goggles for half or more of your swim workout without taking them off; they should feel comfortable after this length of time. If they start to bother your face or feel like they are sucking the eyeballs out of your head, adjust the strap to ease the pressure. If you can't relieve this discomfort or eliminate leaking or fogging, get another pair and start over.

If you have large eye sockets, you may need a larger goggle with adequate padding where the goggle sits on the rim of your eye area. For eyes that are very sensitive to sunlight, opt for a darker lens. You can wear a lighter lens for early morning or evening swims, but you'll want the darker lens for midday swimming or open-water swimming when there is a strong possibility that the sun will hit you in the face. Your goggles need to be comfortable enough to wear for distances of 1K up to 2.4 miles of focused swimming. Trying to swim in open water is challenging enough without being distracted by your goggle strap simulating a vise grip on your face. To find 2.4 miles of comfort, you may have to shop around, but it will be well worth the effort.

Swim cap. Your swim cap helps keep your head streamlined and insulated in the water, hair out of your face, and visible in open water. That's some pretty solid work done by a light, cheap piece of gear! When you do a triathlon, you will receive a race swim cap when you pick up your event packet. You can save it as a souvenir or use it for training to save a few bucks and advertise to your training partners that you did an event.

If you purchase a swim cap for training, choose one that doesn't rip the hair out of your head when you put it on, is visible in open water (bright color), and stays on your head when swimming long distances. A popular choice is silicone. They are more comfortable, longer lasting, and warmer than rubber race swim caps, but they do cost a bit more. Some opt for lycra swim caps for comfort, but take note that water can move through a lycra cap, making your head much less streamlined in the water than a sealed rubber cap. Because lycra is permeable, your hair will get a direct hit from the chemicals in a pool.

Earplugs. Some would consider earplugs to be optional, but for a few reasons, all swimmers should wear them. When your ear is regularly exposed to excess moisture, water can remain trapped in your ear canal. The skin inside can become waterlogged, diluting the acidity that normally prevents infection. The soggy skin will also more readily allow bacteria to penetrate your skin. Bacteria and fungi from contaminated water can grow and cause swimmer's ear which is an infection of your outer ear and ear canal. All of the above can be prevented by using earplugs in your swimming. In addition, many athletes who have a predisposition to seasickness sensations when swimming in open water have eliminated this problem solely by wearing earplugs.

Earplugs are available in two varieties: soft moldable silicone plugs and pre-molded rubber plugs. As with goggles, earplug brand and type is a personal preference. Use the type that is comfortable and keeps the water out of your ears. Because I can mold the silicone plugs to the inside of my ear, I use these for maximal comfort and seal.

OPTIONAL GEAR FOR OPEN-WATER SWIMMING

There are a lot of extra goodies you can buy to help your swim cause for both open-water and pool swimming. The following are the basics:

Wetsuit. A swimming-appropriate wetsuit will not only keep you warm, it will also make you more buoyant—offering the ability to move higher and faster in open water. Long sleeve, swimming-specific wetsuits tend to have thinner, more pliable rubber in the shoulder area, long zippers for quick removal, and a smooth, often fragile surface.

Energy output has been found to be lower using a wetsuit. This suggests that your effort level in open water can be lowered with a wetsuit, which bodes well for your subsequent cycling and running efforts.

Once you submerge yourself, water will start to seep in between the suit and your skin. The water will remain in this space and that thin layer of water along with the insulated neoprene will keep you warm.

If you are an apprehensive open-water swimmer, the wetsuit will be your security blanket in the water. With your suit on, you are a moving buoy. Even if you stop moving and lie still, lifeguards will find you floating on the surface of the water. Excellent news! But keep in mind that the USA Triathlon rules surrounding wetsuits state that they can only be used if the water temperature on race day is below 78 degrees F. Check with your race for specifics regarding water temperature and wetsuit use.

Do some homework on what you can afford and what type of suit interests you, and then spend a bit of time trying them on before buying. You may be able to get your local triathlon club or your training

A neoprene hood will help keep you warmer in cold water.

partners to let you try out their suits. The more wetsuits you can take for a test drive, the more confident you'll feel making your purchase.

In an ideal world, an avid triathlete would purchase both a sleeveless and a long-sleeved suit, but many triathletes are not interested in tying up that much money in neoprene. A long-sleeved suit may be faster because the added neoprene in the shoulder and arm area helps you ride higher in the water. However, even if you have a suit that fits you well and has minimal neoprene thickness around the

shoulder and arm area, the downside to a long-sleeved suit is that it may start to feel confining after swimming for a while.

Many athletes, especially those with apprehension in open water, hyperventilate or become severely anxious in their long-sleeved suits. Because the suit needs to fit tight on land in order to fit best once it gets wet, the chest area in particular can feel like it is restricting breathing. If you have issues with this, wear your suit often to get used to it. If the sensation remains, try using a sleeveless suit to ease pressure on the chest and lung area, and do some concerted work to address your open-water fear issues.

A sleeveless suit may not be as warm or as fast as the long-sleeved, but it will give you greater mobility—literally and emotionally. When deciding which type of suit to purchase, assess the water temperature for the majority of the races you'll attend. Do some additional research on the pricing for sleeveless versus long-sleeved, and then go try on what interests you.

Trying on wetsuits will be the biggest downer you'll encounter in your relationship with your new suit. It's a hot, confining, time-consuming process—bring snacks, water, and a friend for moral support. But once you find that perfect suit, your open-water swimming experiences will become significantly more pleasant.

Once you get your suit, try it out in the pool first to get used to it in a controlled setting before jumping into the ocean or lake. Others in the pool may think you're a bit odd, but it's worth the confidence boost.

Neoprene hood. If you live in a cold water area, race in cold water, or are prone to getting cold even if the water is balmy, try using a neoprene hood. Since you lose a significant amount of heat through your head, insulating that area will help you feel warmer in the water. Before swimming, put your brightly colored swim cap on over your hood.

To keep the hood on your head, it needs to have a strap that fastens under your chin. Look for a hood that has an adjustable Velcro strap so you have some options on how tight it fits. The downside to a hood is that it can chafe or constrict your lower chin and neck area. You may need to decide between warmth and comfort.

Lubricant. If you purchase a wetsuit, or if you swim with just a swimsuit in very salty ocean water, you'll want to have some kind of lubricant to prevent chafing. The most popular products apply like deodorant and come in similar-shaped containers. Some athletes use spray lubes similar to those used for cooking.

At minimum, apply the lube in your armpit area and around your neck. It's common to chafe on your chin from the chin brushing your shoulder while swimming. The lubricant can also be used around your wrists and ankles to make wetsuit removal easier.

I also put lube on the inside heel area of both my cycling and running shoes to help my heels slide easier into my shoes, especially if I am racing sockless. In longer events, I store a blob of lubricant under my bike seat so I can reach down while riding, grab some lube, and apply it between my thighs and my bike saddle to prevent chafing. You can never have too much lube for your crotch on the bike. Keep a bit handy under your saddle, and no matter how long the ride, you'll always be prepared.

OPTIONAL GEAR FOR POOL SWIMMING

Much of the gear listed below will be available for you to use at your local pool but some people have their own preferences or may not want to use gear others have been using. Whether you use shared equipment or buy your own, these are options to make your swim training creative and fun. Enjoy your gear without becoming dependent on any one piece. Pull with a pull buoy, swim with paddles, kick with a board or fins all in one workout, but steer clear of doing an entire workout with only one apparatus. Train to be an adaptable and versatile swimmer by diversifying your gear, strokes, and workouts.

Kickboard. Use a kickboard for kick sets in training, but also learn to do kick sets without one. When using a kickboard, wrap the fingers of both hands around the top of the board, and extend your arms out and over your head. Your forearms will naturally rest on top of the board.

Pull buoy. Using a pull buoy can simulate a wetsuit, as both draw the legs up behind you. Using a pull buoy will help you focus on how your upper body does—or does not—affect your stroke. Many new swimmers and triathletes with a less than adequate kick will gravitate toward using a pull buoy. Again, use this device to help refine your stroke and keep your workout interesting but do not become addicted to the pull buoy.

Paddles. Using swim paddles not only requires you to move your arms and hands effectively through the water, but will help you gain strength. However only use swim paddles if you don't have shoulder issues and feel that your stroke is fairly competent. If you are unsure, have a coach assess you for paddle use. If you move your arm through the water with a paddle in an improper manner, it can cause undue stress on the shoulder joint; do this often, and you're setting yourself up for injury.

Fins. Use fins to strengthen your legs and teach yourself proper body position in the water. But if you are repeatedly using fins to keep up with other swimmers in the pool or to compensate for poor leg position, use them sparingly. Just like paddles or the pull buoy, fins can be an excellent teaching aid but should not be the focus of your swim workouts. If you are looking to generate a more productive kick, put the focus on proper upper body technique or increase your heart rate a bit using the chopped-off style of fins, such as Zoomers.

EMBRACING OPEN-WATER SWIMMING

While learning to embrace open-water swimming, you'll learn about efficient sighting for straight swimming, drafting and maneuvering techniques, swim starts in triathlons, working with waves and swell, and specific techniques to work with fear and apprehension—all with the goal of developing a positive relationship with the water!

FINDING THE VIRTUAL BLACK LINE

In order to swim in a straight line in open water, you need to regularly sight off of objects in line with the direction you are moving. When you are in the water, your ability to see and your awareness of your surroundings is diminished, so it takes a concerted effort to gain vision. Many swimmers have an imbalance in their swim stroke, which may cause them to veer to one side when they don't have a black line to reference. Some triathletes swim in circles due to pulling stronger with one side of their body. If you notice this in your open-water experience, have a coach assess your swim stroke to work on balancing out your stroke. In addition, learn to sight consistently in open water to keep yourself on track.

Sighting requires you to know what object you are moving toward—a buoy, boat, or something on shore that is in line with your swim direction. Once you know what you are heading toward, you can count—ten or more strokes—and then pop your head up for a peek, or swim one or two head-up strokes to lock eyes on your desired destination. Once you see your objective, count another cycle of strokes before you peek again. Some need to sight after just a few strokes in order to keep their line. Practice in open water to determine what works best to keep you going straight.

Once you get your count-and-peek technique down, you'll execute it without disrupting the timing of your stroke. While swimming in swell or chop, you may need to take your quick peek a couple times in a row before you spot your objective. Sight in this manner with regularity, and you will always swim straight.

If you are swimming in a group or drafting another swimmer, do not assume that your swim companions are going in the correct direction. Continue to sight as you would if you were swimming solo. If the swimmer giving you a really great draft starts to head off in the wrong direction, abort your draft partner and move toward your objective.

DRAFTING AND MANEUVERING

In addition to swimming straight, it is to your advantage to learn how to draft off of other swimmers in open water. Drafting not only offers a speed advantage, it has been shown to give an energy advantage as well. If your draft offers more speed and ease than solo swimming, you will have more to offer your bike and run segments.

In order to draft, swim either a few inches behind a swimmer's toes or to one side or the other of the swimmer's legs. You will notice that while drafting, your effort feels a bit easier than solo swimming. To gain the highest speed advantage, draft someone whose pace is slightly faster than your maximal speed for the distance. In this drafting situation, you are actually swimming faster than you can solo, and with less effort.

It is common to bump or brush other swimmers while drafting, but etiquette in open water is to swim in close proximity while not touching. If someone is drafting you and continually touches or bumps you, use your body language to send a signal that you are not happy. Execute a few hard kicks to get someone off your feet, take a stroke to the side to move another swimmer off of your shoulder or hip.

It is worth the reward to work for a draft, but it does take some skill and a high comfort level in the water. Maneuver assertively yet respectfully in the water to let others know that you are standing your ground within your swim space. You've

paid a hefty entry fee to swim in your race. Own that piece of real estate in the water by letting others know it's yours. If you aren't interested, or don't feel comfortable with your skill level to mix it up with the masses, then choose a swim start position to the back or side of the other swimmers in your wave start.

CUSTOMIZING YOUR RACE START POSITION

You can wisely decide to choose a non-aggressive swim start position on race day such as the side or back of your wave. But if you do opt to start in the middle or front of your group, be aware that swimming in a triathlon is a contact sport. Through the myriad of mass start Ironman races on my resume, I've come out of events with broken teeth, scratches down my back, and bruises. It can be part of the business of swimming in triathlon. Remember that no one is trying to hurt you—in truth they don't care a bit about you or your swim position—they are working for their own fast swim time, as should you.

If your race start requires that you run into the water, check out the shoreline before the race. Is it flat, steep, rocky, or smooth? Doing a bit of research may help you choose the best place to run into the water. In a deep water start, swimmers tread water. When the gun goes off, many bodies quickly move from vertical to horizontal. This will cause an extremely crowded situation until the group has made some forward movement to break things up. Choose your starting place to either avoid or engage in this inevitable frenzy, then use your assertive maneuvering to establish your horizontal space in the water.

MOVING WITH THE ELEMENTS

If you train or race regularly in the ocean or a lake, there's a good chance you've had to swim through waves, swell, or chop. The swell in a lake can be from boats or wind, and if the wind is severe, the chop may turn to sharp rises of water or even whitecaps. Unless it is a calm day, or an enclosed area, you will most likely encounter waves in the ocean as well as swell or chop. Swell in the ocean is part of its natural rhythm and can vary from very mild to quite deep with peaks and troughs.

Whatever your view of the conditions from shore, they will be magnified in your mind once you enter the water.

In the troughs of rolling ocean swell, your visibility is low to zero, so it is helpful to sight when you are at the apex of a swell. If you have developed the skill of breathing on both sides while swimming freestyle, you have the option of breathing with your face away from wind chop. Oftentimes in chop or swell, if you tuck your face in toward your armpit, you can grab your breath quickly without getting water in your mouth. You will swim slower in choppy waters. Expect this and you won't be surprised when your swim split in big swells turns out to be subpar.

Swimmers often get munched by waves because when moving out through surf they either stand in place or try to jump up and over an oncoming wave—both situations produce an undesired result. When coming back in from swimming, swimmers usually collide with waves if they're not paying attention to what is happening behind.

Neither situation is pretty to watch, and both are avoidable. A wave is a very heavy, powerful mass of water, moving at a reasonably fast speed. You cannot move through a large breaking wave unless you are streamlined in the water. Your best bet is to take a deep breath, then dive through the wave or mass of white water, aiming your streamlined body at the base of the water mass. As you move through, you may get jostled around a bit before you pop up on the backside of the wave. Stay streamlined and relax. Tuck your chin to avoid goggle loss.

Once you pop up, keep swimming! Waves often come in pairs or groups, and it is common to have to dive through a few before you clear the surf line and have clean water in which to swim.

When returning to shore through the surf, take a peek over your shoulder, or a quick backstroke every 30 seconds or so and note the location of the waves. Once you are in the surf line, where the waves will start to break, you have a couple of options. First, try to bodysurf a wave to shore.

Practice this first, so you have some skill base, but even if you mess it up, there is a good chance the wave will pick you up and move you closer to shore—just not in a way that you might enjoy. Or tuck and submerge yourself while letting the wave crash over you, then pop back up and resume swimming. Whether you are in the ocean or a lake, you should keep swimming to shore until you brush the bottom with your fingers. Once you touch, stand up in thigh deep water and run or walk to shore.

A wave is much heavier and more power-ful than you, but you are streamlined and wetsuit buoyant. Don't fight wave movement; move through this power of nature unobtru-sively, and you'll fare quite well. New ocean swimmers should spend some time playing in waves. Practice diving through them; float around in small surf and notice the pull and push of the wave and white water—and relax. The more you grow accustomed to this force of nature, the more you'll realize that you are small compared to their power and therefore privileged to be able to move with and through them with ease.

The angle of the sand at shoreline can affect your ease of entry as well as the speed and height of a wave. If you are swimming in an unfamiliar area, ask locals or lifeguards the easiest spots to enter and exit the water, and if there are any notable currents or areas that are problematic.

SWITCHING FEAR TO FUNCTION

If you are new to swimming, new to swim-ming in open water, or new to both, you may have some fears about venturing into a lake or the ocean. In open water, you don't have lane lines or the pool edge to hang onto or to push off of. Waves, currents, and swells create a dynamic situation in open water that you don't contend with in a pool. In total, these elements make open water a change from what is familiar. A change can create apprehension prior to it becoming familiar.

The more you expose yourself to change, the more quickly it becomes a known entity. But during that process of making the unfamiliar familiar, there are some mental tools you can use to help this process along. Chapter 9 covers mental training in more depth, but here are a couple of areas you can incorporate into open-water swimming.

Do your first few swims with support from someone who has done open-water swimming. Stand on the shoreline and recognize your strengths in swimming. You know how to swim. With your wetsuit on, you are a buoyant swimmer. Keep these facts in the front of your mind when you step in the water.

Take your time getting in. Notice that water will start to seep into your wetsuit once it hits the bottom of your zipper. Submerge your body slowly, then your face. Move into the surf when you feel ready to take on the waves and dynamically move through the surf line. Once you get past the surf, stop and float in your wetsuit. Roll onto your back, let your arms and legs float, and com-pletely relax your body. Put your head back, soak up the sun, and take a deep breath. Enjoy this moment of complete relaxation. Remember that at any time in your swim, you can roll onto your back and float and take a break—this is your open-water equiva-lent to hanging onto the edge of the pool.

When you start swimming, practice sighting off of objects in the water or on land that are in line with your direction of travel. Count your strokes—10, 15, 20—then sight again. Take turns practicing drafting with your swim buddy, while you continue to refine your sighting techniques. You only need a few feet of water in which to swim,

AFRAID NO MORE BY GAYLIA OSTERLUND

As a young adult, I was diagnosed with panic attacks following a traumatic event in my life. And attacks they were . . . and sometimes still are. They can come on in the middle of a dinner party with colleagues, in the grocery store that I have been shopping at for many years, but most often in large crowds. As a result, over time I started limiting my activities for fear that "it" would happen again. I really began to doubt myself. I had no self-esteem. I became a prisoner to this uninvited guest. Routine and familiarity became critical. I have come to realize it is all about fear. Fear of failure, success, pain . . . basically fear of everything. Eventually, I really believed I could not function outside of my box and just stopped trying. Perhaps this mind-body connection goes to the heart of why we choose to test ourselves in sport.

When I decided to do my first triathlon, I was scared to death of water. I have no idea where the fear came from, but it was present and in full control. To learn how to swim, I did what the little kids do. My husband would stand in chest-deep water several feet from the wall and I would push off into his arms (dog paddling!). Gradually, the distances increased, I learned how to freestyle, and I made it halfway across the pool. The day I swam the full 25 yards was a real turning point. I realized that with a lot of encouragement I could do so much more.

Next to conquer was the "fear factor" of open-water swimming. Unfortunately, I have yet to find lane lines on the bottom of a lake or ocean! I started reading about the art of visualization and how I could apply it to my life. Initially skeptical, I now rely on it every single day. When you can see the experience in your mind, it seems familiar when you get there.

Triathlon has truly challenged me to step outside of my self-imposed boundaries and beliefs and begin to explore the possibility that I can choose to take risks yet continue to keep myself safe. Something as simple as a run in uncharted ground was a huge success. A solo 1-hour bike ride gave me so much personal glory. From these small steps, I am learning to trust myself, and my confidence grows with each new workout challenge. As a result, I am much more confident in new and formerly frightening situations. I have conquered my fear of swimming and successfully completed the swim from the infamous Alcatraz Island! I have even made it to the starting line of the Hawaii Ironman four times. It is such an empowering experience.

I consider myself one of the lucky folks! I am surrounded by supportive, encouraging people every day. My husband, my coach, Terri, and a community full of endurance athletes nudging me to the top of the mountain. They have kept me calm in my panic, faithful to myself even through my disbelief in what I was capable of trying. Most important, they have taught me that my spirit is much stronger than the limits my mind had imposed.

Gaylia Osterlund was a non-athletic child turned adult tennis player turned six-time Ironman competitor. She raises her kids and keeps working to live life to the fullest.

so your first time out swim along the shore past the surf line so you have the option of hopping out of the water to take a break.

At any point during your swim, you may notice distressing thoughts creeping in. Perhaps you are thinking about what might be below you in the water or maybe you are doubting your ability while you are swimming. These thoughts may cause some fear or apprehension. At the first notice of such thoughts, say to yourself, "STOP!" Then replace the distressing thought with something positive about yourself as a swimmer, such as, "I am a smooth, relaxed swimmer," or "I get the job done in the water." Say this phrase to yourself while watching your hands move through the water under your body. When the unfamiliarity of open water creates anxiety, then infuse a familiar entity. Focus on counting your strokes and watching your hands move through the water underneath your body. Think about your technique and body position. Once you count to 20, sight, then start counting again to 20. Do it again.

Each time you get in the water, allow yourself time to warm up and engage with the new surroundings. When you swim, practice counting and use your phrases as tools to dispel distressing thoughts. Over time you'll learn to change fear to function and in that process embrace this new medium of movement.

Embracing open-water swimming is partly about gaining knowledge. Review the above information as many times as needed to help you develop a healthy relationship with open-water swimming.

TRAINING FOR OPEN-WATER SWIMMING

Open-water swimming is a dynamic activity. You are required to adapt to and be in motion in various conditions, temperatures, and directions while other people in close proximity around you are trying to do the same. An effective open-water swimmer is versatile in his skills and incorporates various training techniques into his pool swimming.

To feel fresh for the other two events in a triathlon requires you to be a fit and efficient swimmer. The stronger and more fluid your swimming, the less effort you expend in this portion of a triathlon and the more energy you have for biking and running.

Join a masters program or swim fitness class overseen by a coach. An organized group workout is motivating and challenging. If you have a set of expert eyes on deck

guiding your technique, your time in the water will be highly productive. Introduce yourself to the coach, let her know your goals in triathlon and that you are interested in having her help you with your swim technique. Most masters coaches are quite helpful, but sometimes they need to be reminded to focus on you.

Freestyle is the most efficient stroke for triathletes and should be the predominant focus of your swim training. Each slight movement you make in the water can affect your speed. Take a seminar, have someone film you, watch videos on proper technique, take swim lessons from a qualified coach. Olympic swimmers and professional triathletes continually work to refine their swim stroke and so should you. If you are not seeing results, either focus on your stroke or change up your swim training in some way (usually both are in order). These take effort and time, and the amount you put in will be dependent on your motivation level and life schedule.

In addition to your coached swim training and continual work on your technique, there are several things you can do in your pool workouts that will help you become a better open-water swimmer. To be more versatile in the dynamics of open water, become competent at breaststroke and backstroke as well as freestyle. There are many situations in a lake or ocean when taking a quick backstroke to peek behind yourself or a couple of breaststrokes to catch your breath can come in handy.

Learn to breathe easily on both sides during freestyle sets. When you are swim-

ming fast in open water, you will most likely breathe on one side for your highest oxygen uptake. But in order to get the sun out of your face, sight off of buoys to your side, or change up the stresses on your neck area, it's best to have bilateral breathing as one of your open-water swim tools.

Practice a strong water polo, or head-up, stroke. Swimming a few strokes with your head high out of the water might be

THREE KEYS TO SWIMMING WELL IN TRIATHLON
1. SET GOALS

When I met Terri, we were both training for Ironman triathlons, and I was coaching the university and masters swim teams. She joined our training group of hard-core triathletes and instantly became one of my favorite people to coach for one simple reason: She had a sense of purpose and reason for doing what she did. This is the first and most critical step in any endeavor—set a goal. She had specific, pre-determined goals that were measurable and realistic. She was committed and willing to do whatever it took to achieve them.

Micky Wender, head coach, USMA–West Point

There is nothing more important in athletics than setting goals. You must have a reason, a mission, and a sense of purpose. The two most important questions to ask yourself are *what* do you want to accomplish and *why*? Take the time to really figure that out for yourself and the rest will take care of itself.

2. GET A COACH OR TAKE LESSONS

Swimming is a technique sport. It is much more like golf or tennis than it is like biking or running. Going harder does not equate to going faster. As I tell my athletes, practice does not make perfect, it makes permanent. You can practice the wrong thing all day. At the end of the day, it will still be wrong. Perfect practice makes perfect.

It is critical in the sport of swimming that you get instruction in the basics of body position, balance, rhythm, and timing. When I first started coaching Terri in the early '90s, she knew this better than I did. She would bring her personal video camera to the pool, have someone film her, and force me to watch it with her. That level of instant feedback is priceless.

She was also very tuned in to distance per stroke. As a swimmer you must be keenly aware of how many strokes you are taking as it relates to efficiency and energy expenditure.

The best triathletes get through the swim with minimal effort and stay in the pack. The race is won on the bike and the run. Therefore you must develop the efficiency and fitness to get through the swim without letting it negatively impact the rest of the race. The best way to do that is to get some coaching.

3. HAVE FUN

It is critical that you build the basics of your swimming in the pool. Then progress to open water. Make your progressions from pool to open-water swimming as fun as possible. Make your initial open-water swimming experiences short and sweet. Go to the lake with some friends and do a short out and back. Go to the ocean and do a little bodysurfing. Build your comfort level slowly and take the time to have fun. It's a lot easier to get in the water on a cold morning when you have a few friends to do it with you. Make a routine out of it. There is safety, fun, and power in numbers. Not to mention the social obligation that gets you out there.

> *Mickey Wender has led highly successful swim programs at the University of Washington and the University of California, Santa Cruz and is currently head swimming and diving coach at USMA-West Point. He has done two Ironman triathlons and Eco-Challenge Expedition competitions. Mickey has his masters degree in sport psychology and is the author of the swim DVDs for www.coacheschoice.com.*

necessary when you are sighting in choppy waters. Incorporate these stroke varieties into your swim workouts on a regular basis.

Many triathletes feel it is unnecessary to learn how to do flip turns in the pool, but in doing flip turns, you are adapting to being underwater in various positions, learning to exhale out of your nose, as well as becoming streamlined in the water. Being streamlined transfers to "all things speed," and the more you practice this position, the more intuitive it will become. Your times will become faster as a result of your flip turns, which will give you more confidence in your swimming performances—confidence you will bring to your open-water experiences. Take some time each week to practice your flip turns. Watch others who flip well, and ask them to help you refine your turn.

There will probably be a few other swimmers in your lane at your masters workout. Switch off leading and following until you feel comfortable in all positions within your group. Wait for 10 or more seconds before you take off behind the person in front of you, accelerate to catch him, and then use his draft. Practice sighting off of objects on the pool deck. Get a group of willing triathletes and practice swimming in close proximity to each other to simulate a race start. With no lane lines and in a confined area, your large group can simulate a triathlon swim start, complete with crawling all over each other and struggling to find your own piece of real estate in the water. After a while, these exercises will become familiar and matter of fact.

What should you do if your goggles are kicked off your eyes? Put them back on and keep swimming. Use some training time to adapt to the stresses of a race so their execution becomes second nature and you can focus on more important stuff—like your stroke technique and pacing yourself properly.

Once a week, perform a swim set in the pool that simulates a race start. This might be a set of 300s where you swim the first 100 at sprint pace, then swim the last 200 at race pace for your next triathlon. These types of sets will make you comfortable with the anaerobic nature of a triathlon swim start as well as get you thinking about the pace you'd like to swim your next race.

Refine your swim training to help yourself become a fast, well-rounded, efficient swimmer. Take the skills from the pool to become an effective open-water swimmer. Swim with an open-water buddy. Practice in open water, and you will continue to improve your open-water swimming prowess and overcome any apprehensions of the unknown.

CHAPTER 3

Cycling in Triathlon

"One's destination is never a place, but rather a new way of looking at things."

Henry Miller

By sandwiching the sport of cycling between swimming and running, you have triathlon. This three-in-one event sets you up for a unique bike racing experience. Though you are surrounded by many other cyclists in a triathlon, you are required to generate your own space in order to time trial—this is triathlon's exclusive genre of the "race of truth."

Determining how to ride in a triathlon can be more challenging than performing its counterparts, swimming and running. If you are fit, you can swim all out for the distance you are covering. Once you come off the bike, you can hang it all out on your run before you finish. But the learning curve on riding after swimming and before running can be long, steep, never-ending, and incredibly rewarding.

ESSENTIAL GEAR FOR CYCLING

The majority of triathletes spend under $500 on bike accessories, while about a quarter or more will spend over $1000. That doesn't include the bicycle. Cycling can be an expensive sport, and the one in which you will acquire the most gear for triathlon. There are various ways you can buy speed on your bike, in particular by reducing the weight of your gear or increasing its aerodynamics. But speed is not the only entity you are seeking on the bike. Suitable gear should also take function and comfort into account. In combining the three, let's look at gear needs and options for cycling in triathlon.

Bicycle. The bike that you use for triathlon should fit you perfectly and must pass basic USAT safety standards.

A poorly fitted bicycle will be uncomfortable to ride and potentially dangerous, and it can be the cause of both major and minor injuries. If your bike fit is in question or if you aren't sure if it is in question, ask around and get a referral to a reputable shop with a bike fit expert. Most quality shops should have at least one knowledgeable person on staff who can properly fit you to your bike.

THE BIKE ACQUISITION PUZZLE

When looking for your perfect bike, there are several pieces to the puzzle: how much to spend, what you'll use the bike for, frame

A FITTING MESSAGE

One of my greatest frustrations with my industry is the way we allow you—the buying, racing, riding public—to leave our stores with poor-fitting and poor-running bicycles and equipment. I am constantly amazed that cyclists accept such freaking discomfort and pain as "normal." I've talked at a woman's cycling forum over the years. I always ask the 200–300 women to raise their hands if they're comfortable and usually see 85 percent of the hands go up. I follow with specific questions like, "How many of you get sore in the neck and upper shoulders?" "How many of you have soft tissue contact on the front of your saddles?" "How many of you can't stay in aero position for long?" Numb fingers? sore knees? locked elbows? can't quite reach your brake levers? As you probably guessed, nearly 100 percent of the room finds something to raise their hands about.

When I do a fitting with someone, I request that they put their best princess-and-the-pea attitude on and expect me to NAIL it!! Not just get sort of better—I really expect to have someone leave shocked at how much better they feel. No, I don't nail it every time or with every issue, but a competent fitter can do wonders if you give them the opportunity.

After you have been fit by whomever you end up with, ask yourself, am I comfortable? Do I still have pain? A yes means you need to be refit by the same person or start looking for someone new. I ask people to only use me for a few fittings as there is so much to work out, and one session may not be enough to ferret out all of the issues.

How do you find a competent fitter? I would say the best method is to ask as many cyclists as you can and see which name comes up the most often. There are a few fitting schools and "universities" putting out a lot of "certified" fitters. You may go to their websites and find the local "graduate."

Wade Hall has worked in the bicycle industry for twenty-eight years and currently owns The Spokesman Bicycles in Santa Cruz, California. The Spokesman's motto? Feel the Love.

material and geometry, and where to purchase your bike. Gathering the pieces takes some time.

The shop you ultimately use may need some additional time to order the bike you want. Once you get the bike, there will be a period of time when you are learning the nuances of your new ride. Take these issues into account when you figure out your deadline for wanting your bike completely

dialed in. Depending on your ability to make decisions in a timely manner and the shop's ordering challenges, this can take anywhere from a couple of weeks to a couple of months, or more.

Once you have gathered the information needed, shop around, ask a lot of questions, test ride a lot of bikes and then choose the bike your gut tells you you'll love. One sign that you have purchased the perfect bike for you is that you won't think about your bike when you are out riding—the bike will be one with you and your experience on the road. You won't futz with your position in the saddle because it will be correct. You won't worry about shifting problems or whether you will be able to come out of your pedals at the next stoplight, because your gears and pedals will be perfectly adjusted for ease of use.

Aerodynamics is critical on the bike in triathlon, and it is essential to spend some time with your bike fit pro refining your position on the bike to be as aerodynamic as possible. But if your pricy aero bike and handlebars are uncomfortable, you won't look forward to riding in this position or riding at all. What's the point in buying speed if your body rebels? The better your bike fits, the more you'll want to ride and the fitter you'll be. Most important—the more enjoyable your racing experiences.

Let's dial into that perfect bike by addressing the following:

How much do you want to spend?

Approximately half of triathletes spend $1500–$4000 for their bicycle. Buying used is an excellent option because, just like your car, your bike depreciates significantly the second you ride it out of the shop. You can also capitalize on the not-so-smart-shopper who bought impulsively, then let their several-thousand-dollar bike collect spiderwebs in the garage. The challenge with buying used is that it's tougher to find the "perfect" used bike unless you have

some time to shop around. If you have to compromise in any area when buying used, particularly fit, don't make the purchase.

I know many people who start in triathlon with a very basic, heavy bike and evolve their equipment as they mature as an athlete. That is an excellent way to get your feet wet without spending a lot of money. Know you are going to dig the sport before you make a considerable investment.

If you do opt to buy, have your price range set and then look at the type of bike you are interested in using within that range.

What type of riding will you be doing?

Your riding style and goals dictate your frame geometry preference. Is your goal to be a pure triathlon time trialing machine, or are you interested in doing some century rides, bike touring, bike racing, or all of the above? If your answer is all of the above, then your puzzle just got a lot bigger, because a bike set up for triathlon and one dialed for bike racing are two different animals. But if your focus is mainly triathlon with some other organized rides thrown in for training, you can work with one bike to meet your needs.

Most triathlons, with the exception of the "most grueling" or "world's toughest" genre, are flat to rolling with some longer steady climbing thrown in. But what does the terrain look like where you live and train? Do you live in Florida or Kansas or do you ride long mountainous climbs or rough roads on a regular basis?

Bike frames that are designed for all-around road riding tend to have relaxed seat tube angles in the 75–76 degree range. Many European and some North American time trial designs also embrace this road style geometry. In general, this style of frame creates a relaxed climbing and descending experience as well as an overall comfortable ride. U.S.-born time trial frame geometry embodies a steeper seat angle of around 78 degrees. This frame geometry tends to shorten the top tube and broadens the angle between your leg and abdomen by pitching you into a more forward time trial position.

Which frame geometry is better?

The simple answer to the question "Which frame geometry is better?" is "the one that works best for your riding style." Look at the type of riding you will be doing (climbing versus flat or both) and the type of riding style that suits you (forward or laid back).

A question often raised is which type of geometry is predominant. For years, Dan Empfield and his crew at slowtwitch.com have gathered bike and bike gear data from the transition area of the Hawaii Ironman World Championships. In 2005, they did an analysis of the number of riders who rode each type of geometry and compared it to how they did in the race. Though this is only one (pretty important) race, they looked at about 1600 bikes and riders, and they found that close to 60 percent of the racers rode steeper seat angles. Those who rode steep not only ran, but swam, faster than those who rode a more relaxed angled

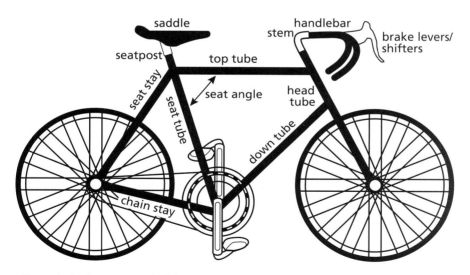

Figure 1   Basic anatomy of a bike

bike. As intriguing as these statistics are, Empfield notes, "This isn't to say that riding steep made them better, just that steeper seat angles and faster finishing times were associated with one another."

Whichever type of bike you purchase, train and race on the same bike or be sure that your training bike and racing bike are set up with exactly the same measurements and general gear. That includes frame geometry, wheel size, pedal type, bike shoes, seat height, handlebar height, and distance between seat and handlebars. When you train, you are training your body to transfer power in a very specific position to your drivetrain. If you change that position when you race, your power will not transfer optimally in your changed position. You want your race set-up to feel fast and light but not dissimilar to your training bike. Add race wheels, but don't change frame style or material.

What type of frame material do you want?

For each type of frame material, there are countless cyclists who will argue why each is best. Often the budget for your new bike will automatically eliminate certain frame materials. Once you determine which materials are in your price range, you can start to examine the properties of each material, the ride qualities they offer, and then compare those to your preferences.

Aluminum is light and stiff—one of the stiffest frame materials out there. Aluminum frames don't have much flex, allowing direct power transfer to the drivetrain. But all that stiffness can lead to body fatigue over the long haul or on bumpy roads. A heavier rider might do the best job subduing an aluminum bike's tendency to pop around on rough roads. If you are all about a quick ride on smooth roads while sprinting out of corners, seriously consider aluminum.

Carbon fiber is about as light and comfortable as it gets. Carbon absorbs road shock so you don't have to, and it is very popular for longer rides, varied terrain, or achy back problems. It is tough and stiff but not as stiff as aluminum. Because of its shock-absorbing flex, carbon has been thought to be a poor sprinting or climbing-out-of-the-saddle bike, but many of these properties depend on the design of the frame. The type of carbon, and the way it is put together (molded or lugged) can define power transfer properties (quality and feel varies with manufacturer). If you want a light, comfortable, high performance ride at a relatively reasonable price, carbon is for you.

Steel is the standard from which all bikes evolved, and some will ride a steel bike to the death. It is durable, shock absorbent, and comfortable, and, though not as quick as aluminum, it has an energetic feel. Steel is a pound or so heavier compared to titanium, carbon, and aluminum, but if you want a classic, all-around versatile feel on a tough frame, steel is for you.

Titanium has incredible qualities, for which you'll pay a pretty penny. It is extremely light, shock absorbent, stiff in all riding situations, and durable. Titanium is unique in that it has a consistent and quality ride for athletes of all weights. Downside? Your titanium acquisition could cost you the down payment on a house in some areas of the United States.

There is quite a bit of aero or wing-shaped tubing available in current bike frames that has tested positively in wind tunnels at speeds of more than 20 mph, meaning that there isn't necessarily an advantage to riding an aero frame at speeds below that. I'll ride the frame material and geometry I prefer and then work on my fitness, skill base, and position on the bike to gain speed before I let the frame shape determine my preference. I wouldn't be averse to trying a titanium bike for a while if an opportunity landed. But all said, I'll take carbon fiber over any other frame material any day. That is—me and thousands of other triathletes.

650c or 700c wheels?

We can argue wheel size as long or longer than we can argue frame materials or geometry, and we'll still come up inconclusive. Both wheel sizes are viable depending on the size of the rider and bike, and both handle and accelerate differently. Despite the market's increasing use of 700c wheels for triathlon, it is generally agreed that bikes 50cm and smaller should be built with 650c wheels, especially for steeper seat tubed bikes. Test ride both, especially if you are a smaller to mid-sized rider and then make your decision based on feel and the wheel size that corresponds to the bike frame of your preference.

What about all the components on the bike?

Unless you are planning on putting your new frame together as an off-season project with bits and pieces from different component manufacturers, you will probably buy a bike that is fully built, with the exception of pedals and aero bars (oftentimes those are included as well). If you know on the front end that you want to switch up any components, negotiate those changes into your original purchase. You'll save money on the ultimate bike price as well as mechanic fees on later changes.

Make sure you walk out the door with bottle cages and water bottles, a seat pack with a couple tubes, tire levers, patches, CO_2 cartridges with valve adapter, and a small pump to carry along on your rides.

Your mid- to high-end bike should have some solid training wheels to use that will be fine for racing as well. If you stick with the sport and decide you want to buy some speed, I recommend keeping the training wheels for training and purchasing a set of race wheels. Yes, race wheels will make a difference in your speed, and next to aero bars are the best way you can upgrade your existing or new bike. You know the amazing feeling when you take off your training shoes and put on those super light racing flats for your weekend 10K? Putting your race wheels on your bike for a triathlon feels even better!

It will probably take some trial and error to get a saddle that works for you. Women's saddles are made a bit wider in the sit-bone area and many women swear by them. But

I know a few women, myself included, who have had issues with a wider women's saddle putting too much pressure on the upper hamstring area. Many saddles have a center cutaway feature that minimizes compression to the pelvis and protects blood flow to the soft tissue of the crotch area, eliminating pain or numbness issues for both men and women.

Ask your shop if they will let you test ride various saddles. There are many styles and designs to choose from, so there is no need to suffer with an uncomfortable saddle. Find one that you don't think about when you ride.

If you are planning to do even a couple of triathlons, get aero bars for your bike. Aero bars seem to be that "I should have gotten those a long time ago!" piece of gear. Once you ride them and notice their comfort and speed advantage, you never want to go back. Even if you are planning some century rides or bike touring, aero bars come in handy to take pressure off your hands over long distances. If set up appropriately, you will notice significant

aerodynamic and comfort advantages immediately.

It's quite normal to feel apprehensive about using your first set of aero bars. There is a perception that you won't have as much control or safety edge as you do with standard drop bars. Just like using your first clipless pedals, there is a learning curve with aero bars, but as you gain confidence over time, the new bars (and pedals) will feel natural.

Your choice of tire width depends partly on your comfort level on the road. If you are new to road biking, start out with 23–25mm or wider. If you want a thinner, faster tire for racing, check out your comfort level on a 20mm tire. Your tires are your connection to the ground, and it is important that they are well taken care of. A couple of days before a race, I always put new or virtually new tires on my race wheels. During this process, I inspect my rims for damage or frayed edges and make sure my rim tape is intact. I check again for any cuts or problems the morning of the race.

What is available to buy in your area?

If you've done some research and test riding and know exactly which bike you want and which size you need, you can purchase your chosen bike anywhere it's available, including the internet. But this may or may not be your best option. Sometimes purchasing online can save you some money, but when making that internet purchase, take into account the cost of shipping, having the bike built at a bike shop, as well

as your initial tune-up. Most shops will include the build and the first tweak with the price of the bike.

The major advantage in using a local shop for your purchase is the relationship you will build through that process. Finding and keeping a good mechanic and bike shop relationship is priceless. It may help you get your bike in for a quick pre-race tune up or prompt repair. Many shops will give repair preference to regular customers, which can help you get back out on the road quickly.

Reputable shops, who sell mid- to high-end bikes, should employ knowledgeable, experienced staff. If your local shop doesn't, or you don't feel comfortable with the person you are dealing with, ask to talk to someone else in the shop or go somewhere else. Although it's extremely helpful, you don't need to know a lot about bikes in order to make a solid purchase. But you do need to have a positive feeling about the sales staff, so you can develop a trusting relationship. If they're smart and they care, they will recognize the value in that relationship as well.

ESSENTIAL BICYCLE ACCESSORIES

Helmet. Always wear a helmet while riding your bike. You may be the best cyclist on the road, but the other riders and drivers may not be as competent or aware. You only need to look at one broken helmet to realize that it can save your life, or even better, save you from the possibility of staying alive with brain damage. There are

so many light, comfortable, and attractive helmets on the market, there is no excuse not to wear one.

Most helmets purchased at a reputable bike shop in the United States will follow USAT legal helmet standards. If you are doing an Ironman event or racing in a foreign country, check to make sure that your helmet will pass the event's safety standards.

In order for your helmet to work for you, you'll need to wear it low on your forehead so that the sides of the helmet can protect the fragile part of your skull on impact. Your chin strap should be comfortably snug. If you crash and your helmet takes a reasonable impact, throw it away and get a new one. Most helmets are not designed to stand up to multiple crashes.

Floor pump. Topping off your tires with a high-pressure pump each time you ride should be part of your bike maintenance process. It is common for your tires to lose 10 pounds or so of pressure after a few days. You can also use this pre-ride pump to do a quick check for any significant cuts or bulges in your tires that could cause problems on the road.

The pressure rating on the sidewall of your tires is a number chosen for many reasons, most of which are not scientific. It can be chosen for legal or marketing reasons but does not necessarily represent the amount of pressure you must have in your tires. For the same tire, a heavier rider will want more pressure than a lighter rider. An underinflated tire can cause rim or tire damage and pinch flats. If you know you are riding on smoother roads and you want to gain speed, reduce friction or the chance of pinch flats, or create a quick feel to your bike's steering, pump up your tires 10–30 psi higher than what is stated on your tire. A smart rider will experiment with different tires and tire pressures and take note of what he enjoys and what feels comfortable. What feels best for you might not for your highly experienced bike racer friend who weighs 20 pounds more.

Pedals and shoes. Many people start out with a cycling shoe or running shoe combined with clips and straps on their pedals. But if you know that you want to continue cycling either in triathlon or for fitness, I recommend you opt for clipless pedals and work through the initial learning process right away. There are two types of riders: those who are going to fall over on their bike at a stop sign while trying to get out of their clipless pedals and those who already have. Once you get past the initial discomfort of clipping in and out, it will become second nature. Be patient with your progress and remember that the benefit you gain is worth the effort. Being connected to your pedals allows you to ride faster and more efficiently and truly become one with your bike.

If you have a pedal/shoe combination that makes it very difficult for you to come out of your pedals, get different pedals. Most of the higher end pedals have a smoother release mechanism that allows you to clip in and out without thinking about it.

Get a road pedal that allows you to clip in on both sides. Once you roll on your bike, you'll just place the cleated area of your shoe onto the pedal and press down. Easy. Getting a lower-profile pedal will also ease your mind if you decide to pedal through corners.

Road cycling shoes are designed with a stiff platform to best transfer the pressure from your foot to your pedal. Your road shoes should feel comfortable. If your shoe presses unduly on any particular part of your foot or repeatedly causes numb areas, try different shoes (or a different saddle). When you have your professional bike fit done with your new bike, have the technician look at your shoes and feet, how they are placed over the pedals, and how they track when you pedal. Inconsistency in any of these areas can cause foot issues on your bike.

OPTIONAL BICYCLE ACCESSORIES

Bike shorts and other clothing. If you are new to cycling or have sit bone or crotch issues on your bike, try new bike shorts or a new bike saddle. Shorts designed for racing triathlon have narrow, shallow padding in the crotch, which make then easier to run in. A cycling short for training should be comfortable and offer more padding and zero chafing. Do not wear underwear with your bike shorts. The extra pressure can chafe or create discomfort—cycling shorts are made to wear alone.

There are many other clothing accessories you can purchase to make your cycling experiences functional, comfortable, and fun. Evaluate the weather in which you ride and make your clothing choices accordingly. Consider wearing gloves when you train to protect your hands, but try racing without them—there is a strong chance you

USING A POWER METER BY DAVE LIOTTA

Have you ever wondered if you are really getting better after riding all those training miles? Power meters are the most objective way of measuring a cyclist's fitness and training progress. These devices are usually attached to the cranks or rear wheel of the bike and constantly measure the amount of work a cyclist is doing.

The primary issue that separates a great cyclist from the rest of us is that great cyclists can pedal at higher power outputs for longer periods of time without fatiguing. Assuming that two cyclists' stature, equipment, aerodynamics, and technique are equal, the rider with higher power output will win—every time.

Dave winning the Sandman Triathlon

In the most basic terms, a power meter calculates how much force a cyclist creates when pushing on the pedals. This wonderfully simple number (expressed in watts) can be used to measure changes in fitness and predict performance and is even used to make equipment adjustments resulting in better performance.

Power meters trump speedometers and heart rate monitors because they are not affected by variables such as weather, road surface, hydration, and so on. There is no gray area involved in deciphering power output information. However, you can use a heart rate monitor or speedometer with a power meter to measure efficiency on the bike (high efficiency is when a cyclist produces a lot of power with low physiological strain as reflected by heart rate).

Increasingly, many coaches and training plans encourage the use of power meters. Manufacturers have responded to this demand and are now producing devices that simultaneously measure speed, heart rate, and power output. The price, weight, and complicated nature of these devices are dropping quickly. For the more tech savvy and affluent, some power meters come with software that allow triathletes to download and graph training information.

The future promises that most performance bikes will have this device built in and at little additional cost. Until that day, aftermarket power meters must be added at an additional cost ranging from $800 to $2500.

Dave Liotta is a four-time Hawaii Ironman finisher, has his master's degree in exercise physiology and is a Level 2 USAT triathlon coach.

won't even know you are not wearing them in a race.

I live in an area that oftentimes has morning fog that can roll back in come afternoon. For longer rides, even in the summertime, I always carry a windbreaker that I can wad up as small as my fist, in case it gets a bit chilly. You can get bike jerseys with pockets, long-, short-, or no-sleeves, tights, leg or arm warmers (my favorites). Stay away from cotton; once cotton gets wet, it stays wet, and becomes cold against your skin.

Shop around, look for sales, and enjoy outfitting yourself for your new sport!

Bicycle computers. Depending on the bike computer you purchase, its functions may include GPS (global positioning system), odometer, trip distance, auto start/stop functions, stopwatch, clock, tire size memory, heart rate monitor functions, timer, alarm, cadence, altimeter, temperature, and current, maximum, and average speed.

If you are someone who gets really excited about specific data concerning each of your workouts, or you or your coach specifically plan your training output for each bike workout, you may want to consider getting a power meter as well.

At minimum, your computer should provide information on how far you went, how long it took, and what your average speed was. This is helpful data for you to learn more about your cycling prowess, as well as note improvements. Just like your heart rate monitor, a bike computer of any kind is not essential but can be a helpful tool in refining your skills as an endurance athlete.

When wondering how much gear to purchase, consider how involved you want your training to be. Are you interested in getting out and enjoying your activity or fine-tuning your skills as an athlete? The gear you purchase can help you refine those decisions.

There are many options for every part of your bike and your bike accessories, and I could write an entire book comparing each. Check out slowtwitch.com or similar websites for current discussions on what's hot in the bike medium and who is using what and why in triathlon.

DEVELOPING A RELATIONSHIP WITH YOUR BIKE

Just as learning more about open-water swimming will allow you to feel more comfortable with that aspect of your triathlon life, developing a relationship with your bicycle will increase your comfort and speed on the roads. This includes understanding bike maintenance skills and taking those skills out on the road while safely riding with cars, pedestrians, and other riders in close proximity.

Part of understanding your bike is being able to perform basic maintenance while out riding. Learning to recognize tire problems, fixing them on the fly, and changing a flat will increase your confidence in your cycling abilities.

Take a flat tire changing class from your local shop. Many of your riding buddies have their own versions of proper flat tire changing, some of which may be inefficient.

Get the beta on quick tire changing from a professional who does it regularly; then practice once a week until you can change your tire in a couple of minutes or less. You must practice. Bring spare tubes on each ride and replace the punctured tube with a new one. You can then take your time at home patching the tube to use again while training.

While you're at the shop for your tire changing class, sign up for a bike maintenance class, which should cover tire and rim inspection, chain cleaning and lubing, and how to check the following:

- handlebar stability
- saddle and seat post stability
- brakes and brake pad condition
- crank arm stability
- derailleur condition
- if your wheels are true (uniform when rotated) or wobbly

Once you learn these skills, do a weekly inspection of your bike. With the exception of chain cleaning and lubing, it will

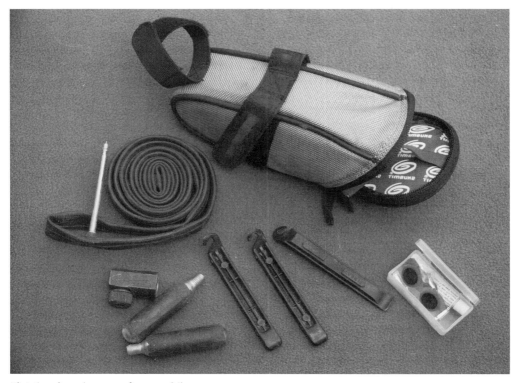

Flat tire changing gear for your bike

take only a couple of minutes once you get it down. While it greatly enhances your relationship with your bike to be able to make repairs yourself, what is critical is for you to be able to recognize problems and then report them to your bike mechanic for repair.

After my first couple of problems on the road, I realized the virtue of understanding a bit about how my bike works. Since I was planning on doing quite a bit of solo riding, I thought I'd better know how to be relatively self-sufficient.

Because I was an ignorant, overzealous, wanna-be mechanic, I decided to learn more about my bike by taking it completely apart and putting it back together (do not do this to your new triathlon bike). Besides taking an entire day, creating a huge mess in my mother's driveway, and being covered in bike grease, I was quite pleased with my accomplishment. I proudly showed the guys at the shop my project. Though I managed to get most of it right, the mechanic had to readjust all cables and put the headset on right side up. They didn't offer me a job at the bike shop, but I was able to walk away with a great deal of knowledge about how a bike operates, realizing that, using some logic, it's relatively easy to sort out.

As a professional triathlete, I always carried a tool kit with me to races. I used it regularly, not only on my bike, but on many of my competitors' bikes when we had mechanical issues or needed to make adjustments while putting bikes together out of their travel cases.

If you pack and travel with your bike, taking off and putting on wheels, pedals, and handlebars are basic adjustments that you'll need to know. If you still have issues with the bike once it's put together at your destination, take it to a shop and have them adjust it for you, so it is race ready. You don't need to know the nuances of tweaking a derailleur or truing a wheel, but you should know how to loosen and tighten the different bolt types on your bike.

Acquire and learn how to use:

- Allen wrenches for all sizes of Allen bolts on your bike plus your shoe cleats
- pedal wrench (always loosen backward)
- all-around bike grease for pedals and other bolts
- chain tool
- chain lube
- a couple of rags (for the sake of triathletes everywhere, never use hotel towels)
- any other wrenches you may need (crank and headset)
- extra flat tire changing gear (tubes, CO_2 cartridge and adapter, tire levers)
- floor pump

Part of learning to love your bike is learning how to take care of it. It's fun! You can become the rider in your training group with the knowledge to help your fellow riders.

BIKE ETIQUETTE, TRIATHLON STYLE

Knowing how to be on your bike on the roads safely and respectfully is called bike etiquette—triathlon style (riding with road cyclists in a large group will require you to expand your knowledge of bike etiquette).

Oftentimes the roads you ride, as well as the specific group you ride with, will further refine your riding process. But in general, if triathletes follow some fundamental guidelines, road time will be much safer and more enjoyable.

Communicate distinctly and often. If you are riding in or near a group of other cyclists, don't assume that they know what you are going to do. Tell them or signal to them. Say, "On your left," when passing, or "Car back," when a car is overtaking your group. Point to obstacles, holes, or problems in the road like rocks or glass, so that the riders behind you are aware. Create a hand signal for stopping and make sure that the riders you ride with understand what your signals mean.

Ride single file when on a road or bike path. Don't give cars any excuse to heckle you or drive too close. It's easy in large numbers to get gang mentality and think you rule the road. But you are required, just like motorists, to share the road. Pull your end of that deal and give cyclists a better name out there.

Ride in a straight line. Be extremely aware of where you are and where the cyclists around you are at all times, but don't assume that others are doing the same. Always ride a straight line and if you plan to deviate in any way, communicate that you are doing so before you do it.

Use reflectors, a light, and a rear blinking light when riding in the dark, at daybreak, or dusk. Assume that you are

invisible in the dark, and use lighting that can be seen by all.

Always carry tools, cell phone, and flat tire changing equipment.

The more comfortable you feel riding around other moving entities on busy streets, the more you'll want to get out and ride. The more you practice these skills and help your training partners to acquire them as well, the more confident your cycling experiences will feel. Ride on!

TRAINING PRINCIPLES FOR CYCLING IN TRIATHLON

There are many skills that you need to learn in order to become a safe and competent cyclist. Some of these include climbing, descending, cornering, shifting, and braking. In order to fine-tune your ability in each area, I recommend that you seek the help of a patient and qualified cyclist or coach who is willing to spend some time with you on the bike. The more skilled you become in each of these areas, the better triathlete you will become and the more you will enjoy riding your bike.

SPIN LIKE A CHAMPION

For several years, two-time Olympic cyclist and former U.S. national champion Bob Mionske would venture out from Wisconsin in the winter to live and train in sunny California. Being a close friend of my ex-husband, Bob would live with us to ride the mountains of Northern California and develop his base of training for the coming bike racing season. Each morning, he would head out on his bike while I was off to my swim, bike, and run training as a triathlete. We'd meet up at the end of the day for dinner and to discuss training and life, but what I remember most about Bob is what he taught me about how to be a cyclist. We talked of the virtues of solo riding to make our minds tough for long hours in our heads in a race. We talked bike gear and training philosophies, and we talked about the importance of spinning.

When athletes get on a bike for the first time, their tendency is to push the pedals at 40 to 60 revolutions per minute (rpms). This low turnover rate is not only inefficient, but it is difficult on the knees and muscles and over time can set you up for injury. To learn to effectively turn the pedals at a natural and efficient cadence, cyclists incorporate spinning into their riding routine.

Spinning is a technique in which a rider turns the pedals around lightly and quickly while in a low (easy) gear, keeping rpms at around 85–100. You can count your rpms, or better yet, use a bike computer with cadence capabilities to determine your rpms. While spinning, you are focusing on technique; speed and power will come later. Similar to your efficient freestyle stroke in swimming, your spin is the basis for all you do on your bike.

During his off-season in California, Bob, who was known for being a huge gear pusher, would do two 6-hour rides each week where he never shifted out of his small chain ring (the smallest of two, or the middle of three, rings that correspond to your front derailleur). He would focus on spinning full circles with each leg. This required him to exert pressure down and then back with one pedal, while releasing the pressure and/or pulling up on the opposite pedal. While spinning perfect circles, he relaxed his upper body as much as possible and focused on his leg and hip activity. His objective was to spin fluidly and quickly while maintaining openness and stillness in the hip area.

As the weeks progressed, Bob continued his work with his spin while adding higher (bigger or harder) gears. His ultimate goal was to combine his perfect spin with a hefty gear in order to create as much power as possible—ultimately taking that power all the way to the Olympics. And he did—twice.

Each gear combination on your bike allows the bike to move forward a set number of inches with one pedal stroke. The bigger the gear, the farther you travel with each revolution. The more power you exert on that big gear, the quicker it covers its corresponding gear-inches. And most important, the more refined your spin with each turn of the pedals, the more chance your power will be transferred flawlessly.

If you are only pushing down on each pedal to generate speed, you are missing a significant component to your pedal stroke, and you most likely will make the mistake of continuing to push down when the pedal is in the recovery phase. In a flawless spin, one pedal should be pushing while the other is pulling up. Since the pulling up phase takes enormous strength and refine-

ment of technique, concentrate first on releasing pressure on the pedal in recovery. Once you have mastered a consistent release of pressure, you can then move into a pulling up motion.

The power from your body to the bike comes predominantly from your quads, hamstrings, calves, and gluteus muscles. With relaxed yet stable ankles, your hip and knee joints flex and extend, but your hips remain basically stable on your saddle. If you are rocking back and forth on your saddle, you either have muscular tightness that is not allowing you to spin fluidly, your saddle is too high, or you need to refine your spin.

Spending time each week to improve your spin technique is time well spent. Use your easy recovery rides or portions of your longer training sessions spinning. Have a friend or bike fit technician videotape you from the front, side, and behind to review your spin and note ways to improve. Slowly increase gears to increase speed and power, but never compromise your fluid spin. Creating the foundation of a good spin will reap dividends in your time-trialing efforts.

PACING

One of the skills of endurance racing is figuring out your fastest pace for a given distance. This takes time and effort and needs to be continually evaluated and refined. The key to gaining your best bike time in a triathlon over a particular distance is to evenly pace the distance while taking into account your post-ride run effort.

If you ride at the highest intensity you are capable of holding for the distance you are riding, you will not only sustain your best possible speed, but you will be the most fuel-efficient for that distance. Scale that effort back a bit on the bike in a triathlon, and you'll hit the mark for your run as well.

Even pacing requires you to have either an understanding of what heart rate range you should be hitting for that distance, or a solid inner pace clock allowing you to target your effort objective. One way to gain knowledge of your inner pace clock is to use the Borg Scale of Perceived Exertion. The Borg Scale is an excellent way to gauge your level of intensity in training and competition without a heart rate monitor.

Using perceived exertion to define your efforts takes some experience in order to become familiar with your ability level for a given distance. Over time you will become accurate at selecting the appropriate effort level for your fitness level. The intensity you choose in a race should depend on your current fitness level combined with your past experiences of speed at certain distances while taking into account the upcoming run.

If you are doing your first international-distance triathlon and your first goal is to complete the distance, you may decide that hitting an effort level of around 12–13 on the Borg Scale would be prudent—especially if you are unsure of your run fitness. If you have done a few triathlons and are using your next sprint-distance race to test a new level of cycling fitness, you may decide to shoot for 16–17, as long as you are fairly certain that your run will hold strong.

I started out in triathlon just like every other non-cyclist—with no clue as to how to pace the bike portion of a triathlon. In my first few races, I sensed that I could ride faster, but I was nervous about doing so and messing up my run split. My fitness increased as I rode longer and harder in training, but I realized the only way to know how hard I could ultimately go on my bike was to do an all-out time trial (TT) sans post-ride run.

Since I had already been doing some bike racing in my off-season, it was a natural to sign up for a 40K TT—bike racer's style. Knowing I didn't have to run after this particular effort, I decided to hang it all out and see how I felt afterward. Being

BORG SCALE OF PERCEIVED EXERTION

6 - 20% effort

7 - 30% effort – Very, very light (rest)

8 - 40% effort

9 - 50% effort – Very light, gentle effort

10 - 55% effort

11 - 60% effort – Fairly light

12 - 65% effort

13 - 70% effort – Somewhat hard, steady pace

14 - 75% effort

15 - 80% effort – Hard

16 - 85% effort

17 - 90% effort – Very hard

18 - 95% effort

19 - 100% effort – Very, very hard

20 - Exhaustion

someone who relishes a really hard effort, I was quite excited about this prospect!

I took it out fast and then narrowed my focus and speed. Continuing to check in with my pace, I was certain I was putting out my best effort on that day. My result was significantly faster than what I had done in triathlon for that distance, and I felt great! In true obsessive triathlete style, I decided to go for a little jog after the TT and noticed my legs were solid.

I started testing out my newfound bike speed in triathlons. As long as my overall fitness was where it should be, I could come off a hard bike effort and still run fast. I did more TTs and bike racing to practice bike-handling skills while riding in tight groups, as well as the type of really tough pre-puke efforts that we love to avoid in triathlon training. The more I experimented with speed, the more in control I felt with these tough efforts. I realized that my body could take what were once extreme speeds on the bike and still run. I just needed some additional race experience to convince the mind they were possible.

As you test your pacing capabilities in training and racing, you will gain a solid knowledge of what you are capable of for a given distance on the bike. This may change as the season progresses and as your fitness increases. While you refine your bike pacing prowess in training, always keep in mind that when you take that skill to your race, you will need to take into account the post-ride run—and your perceived exertion will need to be adjusted accordingly.

Whichever effort level you choose on the bike, the key is to hit it evenly. Riding hard, then easy, then hard will burn up fuel, decrease average speed, and kill motivation faster than riding at a steady, solid effort throughout the event.

TRIATHLON'S VERSION OF THE RACE OF TRUTH

"A time trial is often called 'The Race of Truth' because each rider is racing against the clock, giving his or her best. There is no teamwork. There is no drafting. The winner is the cyclist who can ride the fastest."

Thomas Prehn, author
and U.S. road champion

Triathlons' race of truth is each rider's best effort against the clock for a given distance—after executing a significant swim effort and prior to a tough running endeavor. All triathlons except the Olympics, International Triathlon Union (ITU) events, and other Olympic-qualifying races are draft-free.

A great time-trialist will maintain smooth pedaling technique and an appropriately steady power output while holding aerodynamic position on the bike. In the aero position, you want to take your perfect spin combined with the biggest gear you can maintain with an efficient cadence and turn it over as powerfully as possible for the distance you are riding.

Some wind tunnel tests have shown that about 70 percent of the numbers relating to drag are rider- and rider-position-related (that includes clothes and shoes), and 30 percent are bike-related (frame, bars, wheels, etc.). This means that that really expensive aero bike you just purchased will only account for 30 percent of how quickly you cut through the air—the rest has to come from your body.

How you sit, what you wear, your power to the drivetrain, where your hands are positioned on the aero bars, and how much time you spend in this position determines your speed. In general, you want your back as flat as possible, forearms and hands parallel to the ground, and elbows in front of your knees. Shoulders are low and head is steady. Some bike racers who do time trials use a hands-right-in-front-of-your-face position on their aero bars. But this position is not terribly comfortable for long distances, so most triathletes employ the flat arm/hand position on the aero bars.

If you come out of your aero position often or frequently futz around with your bike or gears, you'll lose valuable time. This means that being in the aero position is a key component of speed, but being comfortable in this position is vital to your wanting to stay there in the first place. Sometimes you have to sacrifice a bit of speed for comfort and a bit of comfort for speed. It takes some time and tweaking of gear and position to find that sweet spot.

When considering clothing and shoes and aerodynamics, you want airflow to hit your body as close to the skin as possible, especially around the hip area. The chest area has also been found to significantly

affect aerodynamics and therefore speed—the smoother the chest's surface, the better (which includes the difference between an open or zipped zipper).

But the ultimate speed of your ride comes from the engine—you. If your body is clothed and in position for optimal comfort, you will pedal your best. Create your set-up so it feels intuitively fast for you—not based on what the numbers say about aerodynamics.

As all great time-trialists will attest, the ultimate race of truth is what happens in your mind when you are riding fast. Though training with other athletes is fun and motivating, make sure you are spending some solo time on the roads refining your self-talk for the lonely act of time trialing (see chapter 9). If you are training for an Ironman, you will be required to ride for 112 miles—solo. If you are not fully familiar and comfortable with the dialog that goes on in your head, race day could become an unwanted struggle. But if you have done some longer solo riding and generated success with your mental talk, you'll be primed to go the distance.

Time trialing is extremely challenging and highly rewarding. There is nothing quite like being successful in a race against yourself and the clock.

RIDE IN A GROUP TO BECOME A BETTER SOLO RIDER

Just as traditional time trialing will help you increase your knowledge of how fast you can go and how much you can hurt, riding in a group of experienced cyclists will help you refine your bike handling skills, ability to deal with distractions, and multitasking while riding fast in tight quarters. The combination transfers to heightened speed.

Ok, let's all admit it—average Joe triathlete has marginal bike-handling skills and is uncomfortable riding near other cyclists. If you haven't noticed this, you are riding metaphorically blind, and that's not a good way to operate on the roads.

When I ride with a group of pure cyclists, there is an ease and comfort in the group while awareness of our surroundings is

heightened, even though we are chatting, communicating about road and traffic issues, and giving each other a hard time, while riding shoulder to shoulder in a pack (or peleton). Sure there are often scary riders in the pack that everyone keeps their eye on, but in general all cyclists know that each is looking out for the others. They are required to trust each other for their own safety and for the safety of the group, and with experienced riders, this trust is taken seriously.

Triathletes who never ride in experienced packs don't give themselves the opportunity to learn these skills, and it shows in their riding style. Triathletes often scatter when they ride together rather than use each other for more efficient pacing. They are less sure of their skills, and it shows in lack of fluid movement on the bike. Pack riding skills teach you how to move on your bike quickly and safely while experiencing countless distractions (kind of like what happens in a triathlon).

You too can ride like a cyclist (minus the biker attitude)! Just like learning to do a flip turn in the pool will help you train to be more streamlined, executing the stop and start, tight quarters pacing that sometimes goes along with pack riding will refine your skill, strength, and finesse on your bike. Get dropped from the pack a few times (like I did countless times), and you'll quickly learn how to take advantage of riding in the middle of the group.

I learned how to descend at top speeds while riding in a tight pack of road riders. I knew I had the skill, I just had to let myself believe it while trusting the other riders. The result was pure riding pleasure.

Practice group riding with a few friends who are willing to teach you the nuances of pure bike etiquette. Listen and trust their experience and engage with it regularly. Be patient with your progress, and if you feel uncomfortable with any situation, release yourself from the pack. Just as it is important to revisit the technicalities of riding your mountain bike on single track, you have to engage with pack riding often to feel comfortable, all the while being smart about what you can and can't take on.

Don't just train to be a better triathlete, train to become a better cyclist! The overall skill you gain will not only keep you safe on the roads, it will pay big come race day while adding pleasure to your riding time.

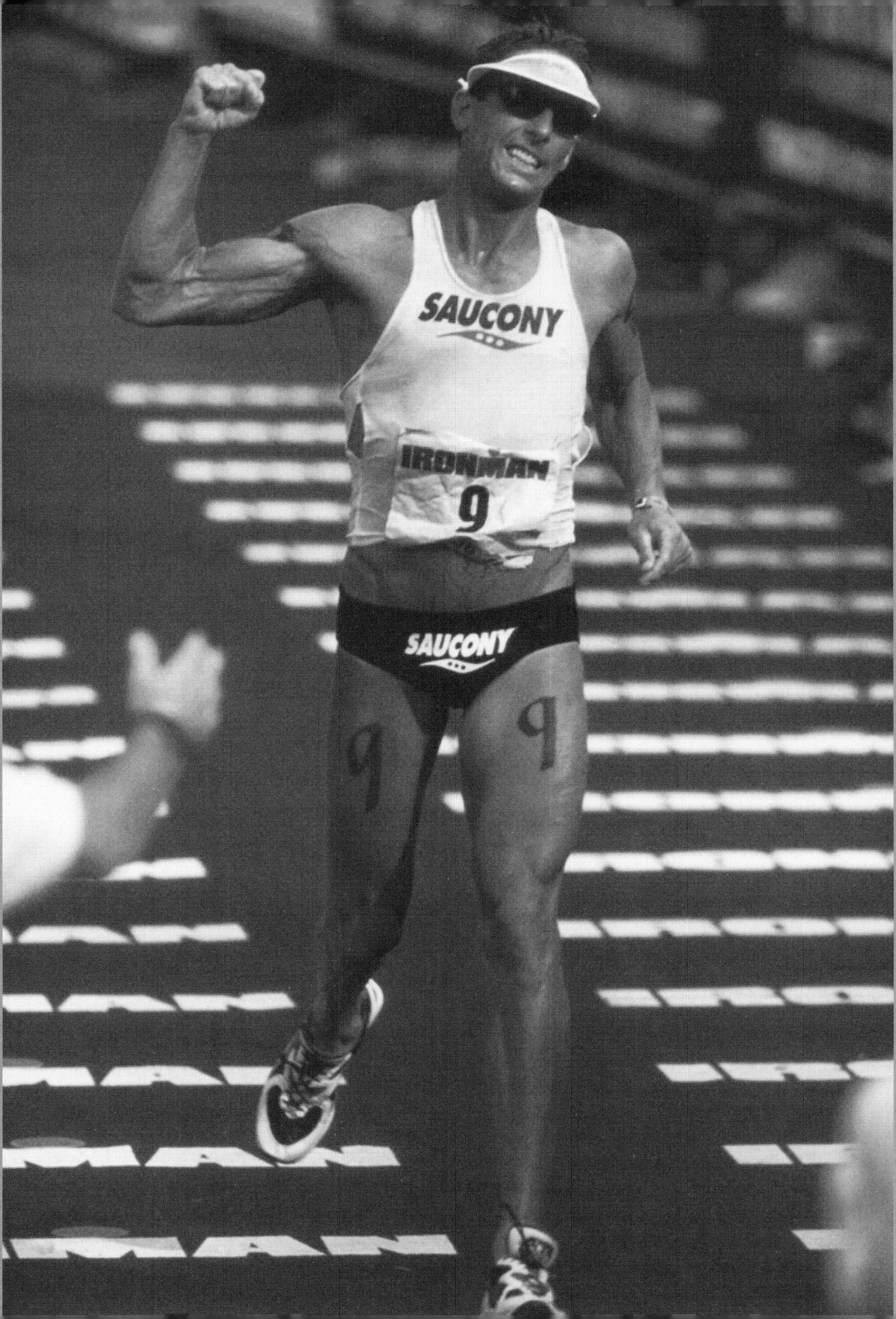

CHAPTER 4

Running in Triathlon

"A lot of people run a race to see who's the fastest. I run to see who has the most guts."

Steve Prefontaine

Running well in triathlon is an art. Infrequently your run is spectacular, occasionally it's really ugly, and most often, with some struggle and a lot of positive energy, you pull it together satisfactorily. In triathlon you run with a perpetual disadvantage—the fatigue you carry from swimming and biking. Your run involves working with this cumulative fatigue to pull out the best overall performance possible—kind of like having to start a painting on a canvas that already contains a few random brush strokes.

Some say a triathlon is won or lost on the run. But just as we can't credit the final three-pointer in a basketball game with winning the entire game, we can't attribute our overall performance in a triathlon to one event. Our result is an accumulation of every moment after the gun goes off until crossing the finish line. What you can peg on your run is how efficiently you've executed your event prior to the run, your overall and running-specific fitness, how well you run off the bike, and how tough you are.

So though your ultimate performance is a complex equation, the run in triathlon can become about "who has the most guts," as Prefontaine so aptly states. Guts can give you a highly satisfying race or get you to the finish line, but in either case, you will definitely find out what you are made of as a multisport athlete in a triathlon run.

Figuring out how to run well in triathlon is a creative and often gut-wrenching experience. Because of its physical and psychological complexity and challenge, a triathlon run that you really nail can offer up a sense of immense personal satisfaction that is unparalleled.

ESSENTIAL GEAR FOR RUNNING

Approximately half of triathletes spend between $100 and $300 a year on running gear for triathlon, and another quarter spend between $300 and $500. Let's take a look at how that breaks down.

Shoes. You can focus your running budget only on shoes and get the job done just fine. In fact, I know a guy who runs naked (at night and with shoes on) in the area where I live. I suspect his gear budget remains quite low.

Shoes are at the top of a very short essential gear list for running, so the type of shoe you ultimately choose is of utmost importance. There is no ultimate shoe or best brand of shoe. The perfect shoe for you is the one that fits your feet and helps keep you injury free. Knowing a bit about your feet and your running style can help you choose that perfect shoe.

Are you heavy or light on your feet? Do your feet pronate (roll inward) or supinate (roll outward)? Do you need a supportive, straight last (foundation) or a neutral or curved, last? With the help of qualified running store staff or a podiatrist, physical therapist, or similar specialist (who is also a runner), you can learn your foot type and running style. Take that information along with your worn-out shoes into a highly reputable running store, and then spend some time trying on lots of shoes. Yippee!

Have the store staff watch you stand, walk, and run, and then try on shoes that suit your feet and foot plant. If you wear orthotics or foot beds, bring those with you when you try on shoes (see "Orthotics or foot beds" later in this chapter). Walk around in each pair, and if the store will allow, run in them outside on pavement. The shoe you choose should feel perfect during your brief trial run at the store—no tight spots, no pinching—only comfort. Fit the shoe to your bigger foot, and always get shoes that give you at minimum a finger-width of space at your toe (more if your

feet tend to swell while running or if you are doing longer or trail races). After you've tried on many pairs, choose the pair that your intuition tells you is the best.

Never choose a subpar shoe because it's cheaper. Your feet are the foundation of your running time, and they deserve the best. Best doesn't always mean most expensive, but if it does in your case, go for it. If you can afford it, get two pairs of running shoes and alternate their use. Your shoes will last longer if they have time between runs to dry and decompress. Changing up your shoes can also help ward off injury issues as you will always be filtering a new pair into the mix.

Most running shoes generally provide cushioning up to 500 miles. Heavy runners or runners who are haphazard about taking care of their shoes find mid-sole breakdown after as few as 350 miles.

Don't wear your running shoes for non-running activities. Not only is that a huge fashion no-no, you will extend the life of your shoes by giving them a rest between runs. Don't leave your shoes in the hot sun or put them in the dryer (I made that ignorant mistake once).

Just as your really great bike and bike fit will mean that you don't think much about your bike when you are riding, your perfect shoes will not enter your mind when you are running—except when you think—"ah, these feel just fine." If you go on a run and forget about your shoes, you probably have on a keeper pair.

Once you get your new shoes, write the date of your purchase in indelible ink on the inside of the midsole of the shoe. This will help you keep track of how long you've had them and therefore how many miles you've logged in them.

Socks. Only use synthetic socks. Any activity-specific sock will work well as long as it is comfortable. Wear your socks of preference when you are purchasing new running shoes. The thickness of your favorite socks will affect your shoe size.

Thinner socks or a double-layer style of socks do help with blister prevention. Toe-socks are excellent if you have severe toe blister problems, but it takes longer to put them on in transition than standard socks. A thinner sock is helpful if you know you will be getting your shoes and socks wet during a race (by pouring water on your head).

Lace locks. Lace locks are mandatory for eliminating frustration and maintaining quick transitions. It is futile with your compromised coordination and mental clarity to try and tie your shoes during a race. Use either a lacing system, such as elastic laces, already set up to lay flush and secure on your shoe or, put your lace locks on your production laces and secure the ends to the laces near the toe area.

Watch. For training efficiency, you need to know how long you are running. If desired, you can also get a watch that tells you how far and how high you went, your splits for each mile, and what your heart rate was at any given moment of your run. But at minimum, get a watch that is comfortable on your wrist and tells you how long you have been running.

Heart rate monitors. These are a useful training tool but are not required in your life as a triathlete. If you do purchase a heart rate monitor, you'll need to shop around to find a monitor you feel comfortable using and that has all the functions that support your training program. At minimum, get a monitor that has heart rate function and time and stopwatch. Any extras will depend on how detailed you wish to become in your training program. Do some research and choose a monitor that will best aid your training program.

Sports bra. Wear a comfortable, supportive (as needed), and breathable sports bra that does not restrict your movement or breathing in any way. If it chafes, you may need a different bra but first try using some lube in the distressed area.

Some sports shops offer sports bra fittings for women. Many find this helpful and informative especially if they need a bit more support. Try on the bra then jump around to make sure you don't bounce. No cotton!

OPTIONAL RUNNING ACCESSORIES

Racing flats. The lighter your shoe, the less energy you expend with each stride. Using racing flats for speed workouts and/or races will help you feel faster and lighter as well as lighten your foot load.

Racing flats tend to have less support than training shoes. If you need significant support while running, it's best not to risk injury such as *plantar fasciitis* by wearing racing flats. But if you are a neutral runner (as determined by a reputable running store) and you have a few extra dollars in your running budget, consider trying a racing flat.

Test them out first in training, then in a sprint- or international-distance race before you wear them in longer events. If you use orthotics or foot beds, use them in your racing flats as well. Racing flats are a fun way to give yourself a significant mental boost on race day while shaving some time off your run split.

Clothing. Wear whatever you feel comfortable in while running as long as it is breathable and not cotton. Cotton shirts will hang like a wet rag once you sweat and can become an anchor on your chest.

For winter, you may want tights and a windbreaker, or more, depending on your winter weather conditions. With the clothing and footwear technology available, there is no reason you can't get out and run in virtually all conditions. Get creative and have fun with your run clothing selections. It's exhilarating to be comfortable in your clothes while out moving in a harsh climate.

Fluid and food belt. If any of your training runs are 75 minutes or longer, you'll need a water bottle and food carrier. There are countless styles and brands to choose from. At the store, try them on and then jump around and jog in them to make sure they won't bounce or shift. Your belt should remain stable on your waist, while not restricting your breathing. Find one that at minimum can hold a small water bottle and an additional pouch for a couple gel packets or a sports bar.

If your long runs reach an hour and 45 minutes or more, you'll want to get a double water bottle belt or a single bottle belt plus an additional handheld bottle. This belt should also include a pouch for carrying food.

Orthotics or foot beds. Running is stressful on your feet and joints and a little help from proper orthotics or foot beds will go a long way. It is rare to find a runner whose foot plant and form are biomechanically perfect or who exhibits no undue torque or strain in any particular direction when their foot hits the ground. The fact that people get running injuries makes sense when you watch most folks run.

In triathlon, your feet and legs are already fatigued when you start running, which can cause compromised running form. Using an insert, such as an orthotic

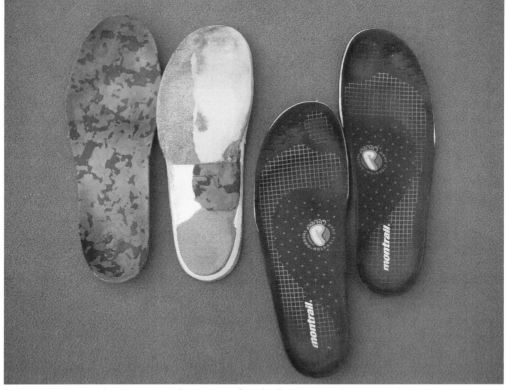

Custom running orthotics vs. over-the-counter foot beds

or foot bed, will give your feet, ankles, and all the joints above them extra support so they won't have to work so hard to maintain alignment.

Before investing in orthotics, start with a foot bed. Get a running-specific foot bed that can be molded to your foot and that feels comfortable and supportive. If you are in need of more support or have had injury issues, get orthotics.

To get running-specific orthotics, you may need to shop around. Go to a podiatrist who will videotape you running. It's a huge plus if your podiatrist is also a runner. He will cast or mold your feet or take a digital measurement, and then order the orthotics to fit you perfectly. But before your feet are casted, ask to look at the type of orthotics he offers. If you are shown orthotics with hard plastic or other rigid materials with no give, go to another podiatrist.

Your running orthotics should be very light and slightly pliable while offering support. Since the orthotic or foot bed replaces the worthless insole that comes with your shoe, make sure that it is full length and accommodates the size shoe you will buy. The orthotic should also be adjustable, meaning that it can be shaved down or reworked to fit you perfectly.

If your inserts create hot spots or blisters, have them adjusted or get new ones. Your orthotics or foot beds should help your running cause, not create more problems.

EFFICIENT DISTANCE RUNNING FORM

When you take off running, you will move in a way that feels natural for you. Though comfortable, your style may or may not be the most efficient. Just as you spend time improving your freestyle stroke in swimming and your spin in cycling, it's important to focus effort on your running form. Running in triathlon is tough enough, why not help your running effort with efficient form?

Working toward proper running form for triathlon won't just help you run your best, it will help you maintain form when the fatigue of your race sets in. Running well in triathlon is about efficiency and strength. If you go into an event having 100 percent efficient form, you may be able to hold on

to about 85 percent of that form when the going starts to get really tough. If you run in a triathlon with inefficient form, you will fatigue more quickly, and there is a better chance that some unexpected (or expected) aches, pains, or cramps will show up due to biomechanical inefficiencies. If you can maintain fluid and smooth running form, you can focus your energy on running faster rather than expending that energy trying to overcome your poor form.

STRIDE LENGTH + TURNOVER = SPEED

To run your fastest, you combine the most efficient stride length for your leg length with your turnover (stride rate), or cadence. To increase speed, you can either lengthen your stride or increase your turnover, or both. To achieve your best stride length, you will need to be flexible in your low back, hips, groin, and hamstring areas. One of the reasons you lose speed when you age is because your stride length shortens as your muscles and tendons become less pliable. To maintain speed, you need to stay on top of your flexibility.

Triathletes, young and old alike, will tighten in these critical areas from bicycling in an aero position. If you look closely, you can virtually see pelvis, groin, and hamstring tightness in runners coming off their bikes in a race. As a triathlete, you must work diligently on your flexibility in these areas in order to maintain running speed because each time you ride, you are shortening the crucial pelvic and upper leg areas that help you maintain your stride length.

Speed work and hill repeats help you to maintain a strong cadence. A lapse in speed work, even for a two-week period, will cause you to lose speed. Just because you did speed work at one point in your life, doesn't mean you will maintain that speed—it's a consistent work in progress. As you age, you lose your quick turnover even if you are diligent in working it. But keep using it to maintain what you can, while accepting the physical changes as they come.

PROPER ALIGNMENT + PROPER FOOT IMPACT = EFFICIENT FORM

There are various schools of thought on effective running form. Some elite distance runners will use a forward lean technique that keeps their center of gravity forward to induce constant momentum. Most distance runners tend to exhibit efficient running form for long distance racing that looks something like this:

- Follow-through of the leg after push-off is relaxed through the hip area, allowing the upper leg, bent knee, and foot to swing through with ease and quickly set up in front of the body.

- The upper leg flexes and then extends while the lower leg follows suit; the foot touches down flat. Yes, flat. The push-off is executed through the big toe area. If you watch an elite distance runner, it may appear that their heel is taking the impact, but actually the full impact of their body is taken by the entire foot at once. This eliminates the possibility of braking and losing momentum (which

a heel strike can cause). It also allows all of the twenty-six bones in each foot to share the impact of body weight. Landing flat spreads out the stress of the impact and helps you maintain your forward momentum while setting you up for toeing off. Very efficient. Landing on your toes over the long haul can create enormous stress on your knees, calves, and Achilles tendon and should be avoided as well.

- When the entire foot is in full impact, a plumb line dropped from your shoulder to your hip to your foot would be in a straight line. The back remains comfortably straight. If your hip is behind your foot at full impact, you are overstriding.

- With the exception of running uphill, your push-off is a natural reaction from your open hips, arm swing, and forward momentum, not a forced motion. If you want more speed, pump your arms, relax your hip joints, and open for a fluid, longer stride or a quicker turnover. Don't push with your foot to try and go faster—this will only generate more tension in your lower body. Open and relax for speed.

- Face is loose, the jaw is relaxed, and mouth open.

- Hands are in a slack, comfortable fist.

- Lower arms are carried with a 90 degree angle at the elbow joint. Your arm swing is generated from the relaxed shoulder joint, and the arm follows the swing while perched in its 90 degree bend. While running long, it is natural for your lower arm to slightly cross the side and front of your body—though your hands should not cross the centerline of your body.

■ Your upper body motion is critical for maintaining and generating speed while running in triathlon. Often in the run, your legs are shot. You can use your relaxed upper body motion to keep your stride relaxed. You can also increase your arm swing to generate a quicker turnover in your legs. Need more speed—pump your arms. Need more power on a hill—pump your arms. Need to increase the cadence on your Iron-man-trot—pump your arms. Your legs will do what your upper body dictates, and in a triathlon run, when your legs have had enough, you can use all the help you can get.

■ Breathing is relaxed and natural as air flows through both mouth and nose. Your abdomen and chest support your spine while remaining open to allow air to move freely. If you feel tense in any area of your body, take an over-exaggerated deep breath while imagining breathing into that tight area. Then relax the body part or muscle on the exhale.

EVALUATE YOUR FORM

If your feet slap when they hit the ground, you may be heel striking. This can cause foot, ankle, and leg stress as well as a decrease in forward momentum. If your head moves up and down significantly when you run, you are bouncing and need work on smoothing out your stride and foot touchdown. Leaning too far forward

or backward can cause undue stress upon impact. If your arms, hands, or shoulders are carried too high, you will generate tension in your upper body that can be transferred to the lower body.

Have a friend or your coach videotape you running at three speeds: 1) slowly, 2) at race speed, 3) while striding out at 90 percent speed. Review the tapes, focusing on:
■ your feet from the front and rear
■ your whole body from the front and rear and from each side

Compare your form to efficient running form described above and note areas to improve. Changing your running form is like changing your swim stroke. It takes time and effort but the changes will slowly come if you are consistent in your efforts.

If you go into your triathlon race with efficient running form, chances are you'll be able to hang on to most of it, while the rest is lost to fatigue. Give yourself the best shot at maintaining form and therefore energy efficiency by continuing to produce proper running form in training.

THE ART OF RUNNING WELL IN TRIATHLON

As you can see from the complexity of factors involved in pulling together a strong triathlon run, being a fast runner outside of triathlon doesn't necessarily mean that you will be a fast runner in a triathlon. But if you are a strong runner coming into the sport or you develop into a strong runner, plus you play out all the other areas of the triathlon equation well, you can learn to run as fast in a triathlon as you do in training.

BECOMING A RUNNER

Running is tough on the body, and let's face it, some people are natural runners while others take a bit longer to ease into the stresses of pounding the pavement. Whichever camp you lie in, you can become a strong runner with smart training and a lot of patience.

One of the biggest mistakes that new runners make is trying to do too much too soon. Don't force your running program! Your body is incredibly adaptable if you give it time. If you are coming from a non-running background, you need to ease into your running program to gain fitness, stay motivated, and allow your body to become accustomed to the activity.

In addition to your swim and bike training, start with a 20-minute walk/run twice a week. Walk 2 minutes, run 1 minute, walk 2 minutes...for 20 minutes. Do it again in two days, this time increasing your run time to 2 minutes. As the days and weeks roll on, continue to increase the total time and running time slowly and methodically.

Continue to progress in this manner, increasing your total time per week and the amount you are running. Even if this feels too easy, stick to it! Patience is important when building a healthy running program. After eight weeks, you will be running well and your body won't even know that you included running into your training program—it will be integrated easily. If you up your running quickly, you are setting yourself up for injury or burnout. Be patient with the process and enjoy your newfound running skills.

WHY YOU SHOULDN'T ALWAYS RUN OFF THE BIKE IN TRAINING

If you are already a runner or have done some running, you are ready to take it up a notch and start progressing toward your best bike/run performances in training and racing. Since a triathlon requires you to always run with fatigued legs, it would make sense that you should always train your running legs while they are tired. Right? Wrong! Some schools of thought believe that you should only run while coming off your bike. Some feel that you should do several bricks (bike/run workouts) a week. I know triathletes who never run unless they have cycled first.

BECOMING A RUNNER: SAMPLE TRAINING WEEKS

	Run Quantity	Walk/Run Time	Walk/Run Strategy
Week 1	2x	20 minutes	2-min. walk/1-min. run
Week 2	2x	25 minutes	2-min. walk/2-min. run
Week 3	3x	30 minutes	2-min. walk/4-min. run
Week 4	3x	30 minutes	1-min. walk/3-min. run
Week 5	3x	35 minutes	1-min. walk/4-min. run

Bricks force you to train your running legs while tired, which is valuable and informative, but if done too much, you'll train yourself to run slower. If you are always training tired, your body will never know what it feels like to run your best. If you want to be a fast runner in triathlon, you need to train like a fast runner.

Running fresh allows you to train proper form, maximal stride and turnover while neuromuscularly implanting positive speed into your running system. If you want to run fast in a triathlon, you need to learn how to run fast while fresh—first and regularly.

Do your hill repeats, track workout, tempo running, and long run as stand-alone workouts so you can maximize your speed and gain the most value for your running. Do your brick workout once a week to tap into the rigors of the bike/run sensation. Every other week in your brick, run the first mile or two off the bike at race pace, then settle into your desired pace for the rest of the workout. If you are training for a half-Ironman or Ironman event and want to know what it will feel like to run after a long ride, do it once a month, but keep your run time to an hour or less.

Ready to move even closer toward that fast run split? Let's look at some secrets to running well off the bike.

RUNNING OFF THE BIKE BY PETE KAIN

Running well off the bike takes time. Most beginning triathletes will say the hardest part of competing in a triathlon is running off the bike. You have already slugged out the swim, hit it hard on the bike, and then have to find some kind of running form on legs wanting to lie down. It is probably the hardest part of any triathlon and takes time to develop, but with training, your body will adapt.

Doing a regular brick workout is key to any triathlete's training plan. It took me about two years of doing triathlons before I felt like I could run well off the bike. It took another couple of years before I could run almost as fast off the bike as I could in an open 10K. Have patience and keep working at it because it will get better. Here are a few ways of incorporating a brick workout into your training plan. This will also help with practicing the transition from bike to run.

1. The following 1-hour bike, 20-minute run can be done indoors on a bike trainer and treadmill or outdoors weather permitting. You can add duration to both the bike and run as fitness gets better.

    Bike 30 minutes: Warm up with 15 minutes nice and easy at 90 rpm. Focus on a smooth pedal stroke, and then increase the pace from 70–80 percent for the final 15 minutes.

    Get off the bike and quickly transition to running shoes and run for 10 minutes. Start out easy and build to about 75 percent effort.

Back on the bike for another 30-minute ride. Start out a bit faster at 70–75 percent effort. After 10 minutes, do 5 x 2-minute efforts at 80–85 percent and 85–90 rpm with a 2-minute easy spin between harder efforts.

Quickly transition to the running shoes and run for 10 minutes. Start out a bit faster, 70–75 percent effort and build to 80–85 percent by the finish.

Do an easy walk to cool down or get back on the bike for an easy spin to shake the legs out. Stretch when finished.

Pete at the Hawaii Ironman

2. Do the above workout, but increase the duration of the first bike to 1 hour, followed by a 30-minute run. You can incorporate a few efforts during the ride, but the key is coming quickly off the bike and into the run. This will get the legs used to the feeling of running directly off the bike. I like to gradually build the pace on the run to finish strong. As you get closer to race day, see how fast you can run the first mile off the bike. Focus on form, as it feels a little off the first few times doing this workout.

3. Running off the bike takes practice. Once a week you should do a bike-run workout, where you set up the shoes as you would in transition and repeat a bike/run sequence. I have our group ride 6 miles, then run 1 mile, three or four times through. I have them focus on a quick transition and try to go faster with each round, so by the third or fourth time through, they are close to race pace. We always finish with a good stretch.

Running off the bike will get better with practice. Incorporate the brick workouts along with your other bike and run workouts for best results. It does take some time for the body to adapt to the feeling of running off the bike. Be patient; it will get better. Be sure to stay hydrated while on the bike. Be quick in transition as well. I call it "free" time. If you take your time, it could cost you the race, even if you are a faster athlete!

Pete Kain (www.KainPerformance.com) is a four-time ITU World Age Group Triathlon Champion and Head Coach of Kain Performance Multi-Sport.

PACING

Pacing your triathlon run carries the same general strategy that you use when pacing the bike portion, with one caveat—you get to hang it all out on the run. Your objective is still to run the fastest you can maintain for the distance you are running, but on the run, you don't have to pull the reins like you do on the bike. On the run, your speed will be scaled back involuntarily from what you can maintain in a run-only event as a result of fatigue. Your ultimate performance will be determined by several factors: how efficiently you've executed your event prior to the run, your overall fitness, your running-specific fitness going into the race, how well you tend to run off the bike, and how much you are willing to throw down for your run.

You can use your run-only efforts in a 5K or 10K as a benchmark for the pace you'd like to hit in a triathlon run. If you are in top fitness, able to maintain form, and have fueled and paced sufficiently up until the run, you may hit close to the mark. But most likely, you will have to rely on either heart rate, perceived exertion, or experience to gain an understanding of your proper run pace. And probably, it will change from race to race and course to course. Running in triathlon is an art; each creation is indeed unique.

If you are new to running and new to triathlon and your first objective is to complete the race, you may decide to start your run at an effort level of 12–13 on the Borg Scale and then try to increase your effort level when you get closer to the finish line. If you are experienced and are shooting for a personal best time, you may decide to shoot for 16–17 on the Borg Scale at the beginning of the run and increase that effort to 18+ once you are within a couple miles of the finish.

It is common on the run for your effort level to increase while your speed either stays the same or decreases. As you become fatigued during the race, you have to increase your strength output to generate the same speed. If you are perceiving your effort as all out for the distance remaining, yet you are simply maintaining speed, pat yourself on the back—that is a strong triathlon run effort.

One of the keys to maintaining pace is to maintain fuel intake. It's tempting to bypass or neglect your eating and drinking program as your body succumbs to race fatigue and as you get closer to the finish line—but giving in to this temptation is a grave mistake. In order to maintain pace to the finish, you need to continue fueling. If your pace slows considerably in the latter stages of the run, you either went out too fast for your fitness level, your fueling program was inadequate, or you are mentally giving in to the rigors of the event. To keep your pace consistent, you need to race smart, fuel to keep your body and mind sharp, and train your mind to be tough.

Practice your desired run pace in training while experimenting with different paces, all the while fueling your efforts with fluids, calories, and mental training.

SECRETS TO A FAST TRIATHLON RUN

I'll bet the word secrets got you excited. These may or may not be secrets for experienced multisport athletes, but they are tried and true methods that have worked consistently for me and for people I've coached to highly satisfying run splits. To run fast off the bike, you need to think and train like a strong, confident runner. Running well after swimming and biking takes strength, stamina, guts, physical and mental toughness, and the belief that you can fight for your pace. There are a few aspects of running off the bike to consider, as well as specific workouts you can do to boost your triathlon running and develop a running state of mind to call your own.

BUILD STRENGTH TO RUN FAST

Most don't think of strength when listing the qualities of a fast distance runner. People tend to think of things like lightness, quickness, and endurance—which are important qualities for elite 10K or marathon runners. If you do think of strength for running, you may think only of your lower body, which is, of course, important. But after swimming and biking and the total stress of your event up to the run, strength

Terri at the Hawaii Ironman

in a triathlon run is a mandatory commodity for a solid performance. Your strength comes not only from your mind and your lower body, but from your upper body and, crucially, from your core.

A good portion of the triathlon run equation is the ability to sustain your effort—to just keep going at a consistent pace. Period. That takes core strength, especially for longer events or events that are longer than what you have done prior. Core strength metaphorically duct tapes all the body parts together to allow you to hold pace when what you really want is to sit on the side of the road and drink a cold Coke. If your core is strong, you'll not only be able to keep moving well, you'll desire to keep moving well. Now that's some exciting stuff.

If you are structurally weak, you will need to build overall and core strength to prevent injury and allow your body to withstand the rigors of a triathlon. If you are naturally muscular, build your overall and core strength to allow it to work for you on race day.

Given my strong build, one would guess that I would not do well at longer distance races. But because of my core strength, I have an ability to run well off the bike and sustain my quick pace. I was able to beat many men and women at Ironman distance who would otherwise kill me at half-Ironman or shorter. My strength allowed me to hit my goal race pace in sprint- or international-distance events right when I touched ground off my bike.

Many people need a bit of time to coax their running legs into doing their job. If you have core strength, you'll be able to tap into

that speed much quicker. Train your strength consistently throughout the season, and you'll be on the right path to a fast run.

RUN CONSISTENTLY AT VARYING EFFORT LEVELS

To run well in triathlon, you need to nail your weekly run workouts consistently at their planned effort levels. If you have been unhappy with your run performances, there is a good chance that if you go back and look at your training log, you'll find inconsistencies within your running program or that you run too fast too often in your workouts. Within your consistent training, your easy runs need to be really easy, so that speed, hill, tempo, or negative split training can be done at strong efforts.

If you are running your scheduled easy run too fast—even 5 percent of max too fast—you may not be able to run your best in your faster workouts. Remember, to run like a fast runner, you need to be able to train like a fast runner and that means using your recovery runs to set yourself up for quality speed sessions.

SWIM AND BIKE TO A FAST RUN

You do swim training so that you can swim, bike, and run well. You focus on your cycling so that you can ride and run solidly in a triathlon. Your swim and bike fitness set up your run performance. Though training to run fast is obviously important, increasing your swim and bike fitness will not only help you run, but run at race pace right off the bike. If you are disappointed in a run split in a race, look back at your run training and evaluate the areas in which you can improve. But also look at your swim and bike training to check for lapses in consistency. Running well in triathlon is about being a strong runner, but it's also about balancing your overall fitness so that when you get to the run, you have the opportunity to do your best.

WORKOUTS FOR A FAST RUN SPLIT

Only experienced or consistent runners should follow as written the workouts listed below because they require a solid running base in order to execute them safely. If you are a consistent but newer runner or currently building your base, cut the workouts in half to start. Then build on the time or distance and intensity as you progress.

Negative Split Running

Objective: To train your body and mind to sustain a realistic and desired race pace in a triathlon run.

One way to prepare for an even run pace in triathlon is to up the ante in training through negative split workouts. A negative split is when you do the latter part of your run effort faster than the initial or middle sections, or when you consistently and gradually increase your pace over the duration of the run. Negative split workouts teach you to strengthen your effort as your workout progresses so that you can either maintain or increase your pace. These workouts also help you mentally lock down on your pace and learn to fight for it.

Start with a mid-week, moderate distance run that is manageable for a hard effort. For example, if on your long run day, you are doing 8–10 miles, and a standard mid-week run is 4–6 miles, run the first third of one of your mid-week runs at a very easy, leisurely pace. For the second third, increase your pace to race pace for your next event or faster. For the final third (before a cool down), increase your pace to faster than race pace. The workout may look like this:

6-mile negative split workout for an athlete who averages a 9-minute-mile pace in an international-distance triathlon:
- warm up for 1.5 miles at 11- to 12-minute pace
- 1.5 miles at 9-minute pace
- 1.5 miles at 8:30-minute pace
- 1.5 mile cool down at 11- to 12-minute pace

When the distance and effort of this workout feels manageable, up the ante to running a negative split in your long run.

Negative splitting your long run may look like this:

10-mile negative split workout for an athlete who averages a 9-minute-mile pace in an international-distance triathlon:
- warm up for 4 miles at 11- to 12-minute pace
- 2 miles at 9:30-minute pace
- 1.5 miles at 9-minute pace
- 0.5 to 1 mile at 8-minute pace
- 2 miles at 11- to 12-minute pace

If your long run is longer or shorter than 10 miles, use the above workout to extrapolate the distance covered at each pace for the distance of your run.

This is a challenging workout. If your current goal is to successfully complete the distance of your long run, don't venture into this workout just yet. If you are comfortable with your current long run distance, try this workout before you increase distance. Only do this negative split workout once a month on your long run. This is a stressful workout, and combined with other weekly track or hill workouts, it will add a substantial amount of high-end aerobic to anaerobic time to your running. Remember, you want to incorporate recovery runs as well as speed sessions into your run training; too much speed in your long run can become negative.

The Sustained Hill Workout

Objectives: To adapt to the unrelenting intensity of a triathlon run, to practice using your upper body in your running, to practice efficient uphill running form while fatigued.

Working the intervals and recovery on a sustained hill will never let you fully recover from each interval. You get enough recovery to push the next tough effort while requiring you to maintain a slightly elevated heart rate and leg effort. Sustained hill workouts give you strength and endurance and allow you to adapt to working with your nemesis in cycling and running—gravity. A hill effort is an exercise in overcoming gravity, and the more you do

it, the easier it will feel—as long as you are running the right types of hills.

For this particular hill workout, choose a hill that is several miles long (if you don't have a hill of this length in your area, you can simulate on a treadmill) and with a moderate grade that allows you to feel as though you can run or jog at a steady pace for the duration. A hill that is too steep will force you to walk or slow your pace, while a hill that is too flat will not offer enough resistance to gain the strength you are going after for this workout.

For example, currently on your long run day, you are running 1:20–1:30, and a standard mid-week run is 40–50 minutes.

45-minute sustained hill workout:
- warm up for 10 minutes at 70% of max on flat terrain
- finish the warm-up at the base of your long hill
- start up the hill for 3 minutes at 80% of max
- 3 minutes at 75% of max continuing up the hill (walk or shuffle jog as needed to obtain this HR)
- 4 minutes at 85–88% of max
- 3 minutes at 80% of max continuing up the hill
- 5 minutes at 85–88% of max
- 4 minutes at 80% of max then 3 min at 90% of max
- turn around and trot easily down the hill for a 10-minute cool down.

If you are still building your run training, cut all the times in half for this workout except the warm-up and cool down. Every other week, increase the intervals by 1 minute.

A sustained hill workout on your long run may look like this:

1:30 sustained hill workout:

- warm up for 20 minutes at 70% of max on flat terrain
- finish this warm-up at the base of your long hill
- 4 minutes at 80% of max
- 4 minutes at 75% of max continuing up the hill (walk or shuffle jog as needed to obtain this HR; 75% is challenging to target going uphill)
- 4 minutes at 85–88% of max
- 4 minutes at 80% of max continuing up the hill
- 4 minutes at 85–86% of max
- 4 minutes at 80% of max
- 3 minutes at 90% of max
- 2 minutes walk
- 3 minutes at 90% of max
- turn around and trot easily down and then onto flat terrain for the remaining time.

If your long run is longer than 1:30, do the above workout in the middle of your long run time, then increase the interval time and effort level as your fitness increases.

This workout will kick your butt (your butt will be sore!). You may need to walk the recovery sections in order to key in on the target heart rates. As you get fitter, you'll notice your HR comes down quicker during recovery. You'll also notice that you'll be able to sustain a jogging effort during recovery.

The Sustained Downhill Workout

Objective: To toughen your quads and train you to run down hills aggressively and efficiently.

Many use the downhill sections of a triathlon to ease off their pace or recover from the flat and uphill efforts. But if you are able to and desire to run a sustained effort for your entire triathlon run you'll need to learn how to run downhill aggressively. This workout will offer some help in that area for the triathlete doing 1:20–1:30 for their long run, and a standard mid-week run of 40–50 minutes.

45-minute sustained downhill workout:

- warm up for 15 minutes at 70% of max on flat terrain
- finish the warm-up at the top of your long hill
- start down the hill for 2 minutes at 10K race pace
- 3 minutes of float running (no effort, just let your legs swing through easily)
- 3 minutes at 10K race pace
- 3 minutes of float
- 4 minutes at 10K race pace
- 3 minutes of float
- 2 minutes at 5K race pace
- trot easily down or on flat for the remaining 20-minute cool down.

Do this once a month or every three weeks.

Play with downhill intervals on your long runs as well, but keep these focused downhill sessions dedicated to shorter run sessions. Unless you are training for an ultrarun on trails or the World's Toughest

Triathlon, you don't need to thrash your quads more than the above workout. You will be sore after the first couple times trying this workout.

Tips for downhill running

To gain speed on the downhills without a lot of effort, slightly pitch your upper body forward from the hip. This will give you momentum by directing your body weight downward and letting gravity do its job. At the same time and in order to maintain control, bring your pelvis underneath you by elongating your lower back and tucking your tailbone underneath you. This position allows your legs to remain under and in front of your torso, rather than flailing out of control behind you.

The tailbone tuck can be slight, but in doing this, you'll notice an instant shift in downhill control. Do your faster intervals in tail tuck position while memorizing this feeling for future reference. If you have a sense that you are in control on a downhill, you will feel more comfortable increasing your speed—the tail tuck will help.

One of the many years I did the Wildflower Half-Ironman, I had a monumentally crappy bike split. My swim was reasonable, but I just couldn't pull it together on the bike due to my lack of adequate bike training. While riding, angry at myself for lack of cycling fitness, I kept in the back of my mind that my running fitness was on par. So I maintained pace and bided my time.

Once I hit the run, I was on fire. I brought to mind the challenging up-and-down hill training I had done and decided it was time to pull out the stops. I got aggressive—fueled by my poor bike split. On the flatter, rolling sections of the run, I sustained my goal race pace (on a flatter course) for that distance, and when I hit each up- or downhill, I aggressively pumped my arms and pushed strongly.

I could sense that if I ventured into anaerobic land on each uphill, I would be able to recover on the flats due to my heightened run fitness, so I went after the hills strongly. When I came to a downhill, I didn't just float down, I tucked my pelvis, used my arm position for balance, and ran fast with a slight edge of float for recovery.

My overall performance at that race was lackluster because I was not able to push the bike, but I had a bit left over for the run. So I took advantage of it and was able to come away with a 1:28 split on one of the toughest half-Ironman run courses around. In the end, I got to really test my hard-trained running skills on a challenging course. And I learned even more about my ability as a hill runner. I also learned that you don't pull off an overall best time at a half-Ironman race without doing proper training for all of the swim, run, and bike.

The Track Workout

Objectives: To learn pace, and adapt to the unrelenting intensity of a triathlon run with sustained pacing.

There are many track workouts that you can do to quicken your triathlon run. This one teaches you to know pace by shifting gears quickly from one pace to another as well as challenging you anaerobically. I loved this workout—thrived on it. In many ways, it highlighted my life as a triathlete and runner because it asked me to draw on several running virtues: to know my pace, to sustain my pace, to lock into and fight for my pace.

Track workout for Ironman training:

- 1.5 mile warm-up at 70% of max
- 10 minutes of stretching
- 8 strides (100 yards striding or building speed up to a sprint; 100 yards easy jog)
- 2 x 2 miles: within each 2 miles, alternate between a 400 at a pace 1 minute-per-mile slower than your 10K pace and a 400 at 10K race pace. Recover with 5 minutes of easy walking and repeat. For example, I would run my first 400 at a 7-minute-per-mile pace, the next 400 at a 6-minute-per-mile pace, and repeat this pattern for 2 miles.

If you are training for a sprint- or an international-distance triathlon, try starting out with 2 x 1mile as your main set executed in the same manner described above. Over time increase to 3 or 4 x 1 mile. Always end this workout with a 1–2 mile cool down at 70 percent of max.

As your fitness increases, challenge yourself by decreasing the pace over time. Learn to love this workout by starting out at a reasonable pace for the faster quarters.

This workout requires you to know your goal paces—rock solid. Know the pace you are able to and desire to run, and train it. Memorize it. Know it in your sleep. Training for pace is about fine-tuning your inner

running clock. Using a heartrate monitor to develop this ability is a good idea. This skill is invaluable, and this workout helps you dial in that clock.

This was a benchmark workout for me prior to an Ironman race. When all of my other training was in place and I nailed this workout while feeling completely in control, I gained huge confidence knowing I was on target to run a strong Ironman marathon—and most often I was correct. The benchmark was not in obtaining pure speed but in sustaining the overall effort and hitting my pace right on.

In order to sustain your pace in a triathlon, you first need to know what pace you want to sustain! Track workouts are about learning pace as well as learning to run fast with efficient form. When you start the run of a triathlon, do you know what pace you are running? If not, you should work diligently on this process. Integrate pace into your mind as well as your body and remember what each pace feels like.

The Long Speed Play Run

Objectives: To learn pace, gain confidence to sustain your pace over the long haul, and learn to run tough when you're tired.

Your long run helps you build strength, stamina, and mental tenacity. It also gives you confidence to know that you can go the distance on race day. If you are new to running or in the process of building your running, continue with your easy to moderately paced long run for now. This run is the stepping-stone you need to acquire the confidence to sustain your race effort, so continue to build your long run slowly. But if you've developed a solid run base and are looking to up the ante on your long run day, try incorporating speed play into this workout.

If you are doing 1:20–1:30 for your long run, your speed play workout will look like this:

- Easy warm-up at 70% of max for 20 minutes
- 15 minutes at half marathon race pace, or 10 minutes at 10K race pace (depending on the distance of your next event)
- 15 minutes at 70% of max
- 15 minutes at half marathon race pace, or, 10 minutes at 10K race pace
- remaining time at 70% of max

If you are training for an Ironman, incorporate speed play into your longer run once you feel solid with the distance of this run.

While training for an Ironman, I would do a 2:30 speed play workout like this:

- 30-minute warm-up at 70% of max
- 30 minutes at PR marathon race pace
- 30 minutes at 70% of max
- 30 minutes at PR marathon race pace
- remaining time at 70% of max

In addition to your other speed work for the week, adding this workout can be quite stressful and should only be done once a month. Learn your race pace so you can practice it with these sustained efforts on your long run. This workout will mentally tax you and is an excellent time to prac-

tice your positive or rational self-talk (see chapter 9). Picture yourself in your race, running well, holding pace, feeling strong and confident.

If you start this workout and the higher intensity levels feel over-the-top tough, back off the pace or the length of time for each higher intensity effort. You want to walk away from this workout with a positive mindset about your long run. Challenge yourself while setting yourself up for a feel-good experience.

To put yourself physically and mentally in a race setting (pace and self-talk), do this workout solo. The intensity change-ups and the mental training will give you something to focus on, and before you know it, you'll be ready for your post-run latte with friends!

When placing these workouts into a weekly running plan, make sure that you are doing no more than one or two high intensity runs per week. That may include a sustained hill workout plus some speed play in your long run. Or a track workout plus a sustained hill effort in your longer run. Or a hill workout or track workout combined with a slow, steady long run. Remember, too much of a good thing can be a bad thing. Build your running distance slowly, while cautiously incorporating speed and strength running into your program.

The Running Pace Chart (in Appendix A) will help you gain an understanding of pace and how you can expand your per mile run pace over various distances.

THE MENTAL GAME OF RUNNING

Training your body is one aspect of having a strong triathlon run. The most important element of your run creation is your mind. What happens in your mind is the foundation of your run effort. The mind drives the engine, and it's more powerful than you can possibly imagine.

NEGOTIATING YOUR RUNNING FORM

A triathlon run can become a constant exercise in deal-making if you are paying attention and willing to go after your best effort. When the legs start to rebel or the mind starts to whine, change up your running form by negotiating your effort like this: "I'm going to lengthen my stride to the next aid station, then allow myself to shuffle jog through the station to eat and drink. Once I get to that next tree past this aid station, I'm going to ease back into my longer stride length again." Or, "Chop your stride and run on your toes up this hill while pumping your arms. Once you get to the pink house at the top of the hill, ease back into your natural stride." Or, "For the next 5 minutes, I'm going to shorten my stride and increase my turnover; the next 5 minutes I'll lengthen my stride and decrease my turnover." Or, "Run for 2 minutes and recover jog for 30 seconds, alternate for the next mile and see if you can increase overall speed slightly within the next mile."

Make a deal. Then stick with your deal. Then make another deal. Offer yourself rewards for keeping your deals—that cold beer at the finish, the new wetsuit you've been eyeing, or acknowledgment of your excellent effort. This is all a form of rational self-talk discussed in chapter 9.

These intermittent negotiations help you change up the mental and physical stresses of the race, keep you present to your race process, and keep your mind out of the negative pity pit you can fall into when under physical duress. You can change your stride length and arm swing, the way your feet hit the ground, or the tilt of your head, all the while planning where and when you will do which.

Don't forget to recognize your efforts post-race by reflecting on your negotiating efforts. You don't need euphoric race experiences to warrant post-race celebration. Staying present to your race process, in a positive or rational manner, is celebration enough and will lead you closer to that rare euphoric experience.

RACE SMART—NO, RACE REALLY, REALLY SMART

Racing smart means creating a plan, carrying it out, and adapting it when the rigors of the race, the environment, or your body are requesting a change. Your plan includes logistics for before, during, and after the race as well as plans for gear, fuel, pace, and mental training. Write down your plan, and be willing to abort or change it when it's not working for you or your body is needing something different.

Having a strong run requires that you race smart—not just during the run itself but during the entire race. If you pace yourself poorly or forget to eat and drink, you may be able to get through the swim and bike, but your run will suffer. Your run performance is dictated by what you do during the swim, the bike, and the run.

ACCEPT THAT IT'S TOUGH, ACCEPT THAT YOU'RE TOUGH

Running off the bike is tough. Accept it. Don't try and skate around it or pretend it's not—just face it head-on. It's tough and you know it and the sooner you accept it the better you'll run. It's ok that it's tough. See your strength, accept your tenacity, and let these qualities shine come run time.

The other thing you know (even subconsciously) is that you are adaptable and you are bigger and smarter than the pain of a triathlon run. You can run your best race if you train and race smart and if you let yourself run your best. Your mind can trip you up. If you spend a lot of run time talking negative, defeating your efforts, or being delusional about the challenges at hand, you will prevent yourself from running well. Accept that it's tough. Accept that you're tough, adapt to the stress of the race, then go after your run.

NEVER, NEVER, NEVER GIVE UP

Anything can happen over the course of a race—especially if you are racing long. You never know how you'll perform each segment until you start swimming, biking, or running. So race smart and never give up because right around the corner could be the performance break you're reaching for.

If any leg of your race is not playing out

Terri en route to third place in Kona

well, get rational and stay present to your pace and fueling plan—and never give up. Endurance racing can be one big mood swing. One minute you feel solid and the next you think you can't take another step. As long as you are hitting your plan, you can pop back from a tough spell at any time. Eat and drink well, pace properly, and your race will fall into place.

How much are you willing to work for it? Are you willing to never give up? Get aggressive in your mind. Go after that run you trained for. You deserve it. Show yourself you believe this by never giving up.

I remember running in third place coming out of the Natural Energy Lab at the 1990 Hawaii Ironman. I had a decent swim and strong bike and was running reasonably well until the Natural Energy Lab sucked the oomph out of my legs. At the Lab turnaround I realized that the fourth place woman was making serious time on me. I hit the highway and with about 10K to go I was hurting—badly.

So I got aggressive.

I spoke out loud to myself, "You want this. You want this more than she does! You worked for this. It's yours. Go after it!" My sole objectives were to keep fueling the body and hang onto my pace—for dear life. I convinced myself that third was mine, but I knew that I'd have to dig deep to hang onto my pace and effort. I believed I could, I put my mental hooks in that belief, and my result followed suit.

Never give up. Even if your day is not playing out well, if you perform your best every moment, you can walk away with the satisfaction that you gave it your best shot.

CHAPTER 5

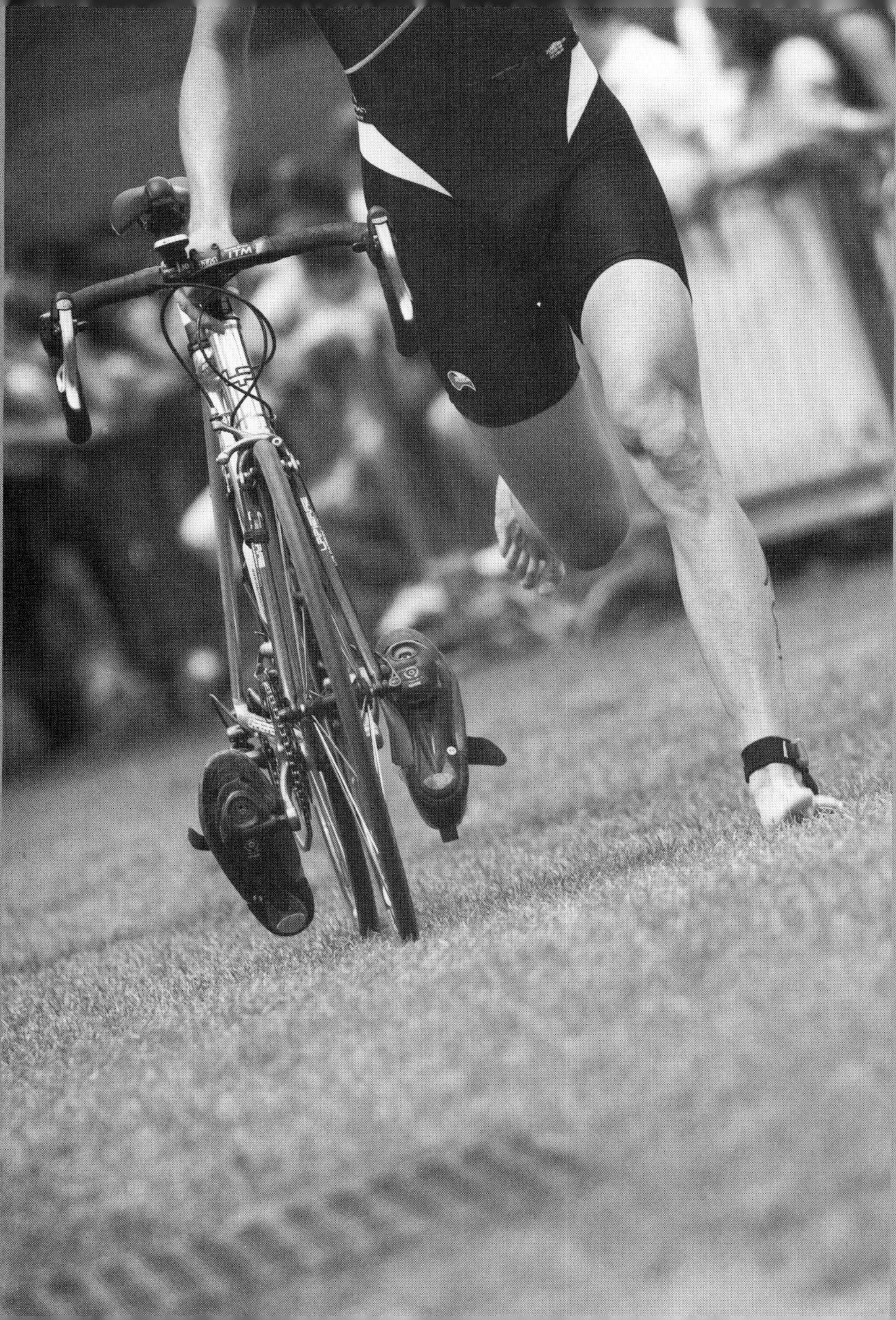

Transitions and Race Warm-Up

"If I spend minimal time in the transition area, I can run a bit slower and still win."

Mark Allen

The transitions between each sport in a triathlon are an exercise in efficiency. The goal is to effortlessly prepare yourself for the next event while recovering as much as possible.

TRANSITION AREA GEAR

Well in advance, create a gear list for everything you might need for the race. Your

transition preparation starts while you are at home organizing your race gear using your gear list. Arrange it in your transition bag by categories: swim, bike, run. Keep all the items you will be using before and after the race in a separate bag.

ESSENTIAL TRANSITION GEAR

Bike
Bike seat pack with spare tube, CO_2 cartridge and adapter, tire levers
Towel
Helmet
Sunglasses
Cycling shoes and optional socks
Race belt with number attached
Running shoes with lace locks, optional socks (powdered and rolled)
Race fuel and water
Electrolyte tablets

ADDITIONAL TRANSITION GEAR

Some of these items will not be laid out on your transition towel come race start:

Hat or visor
Bike pump
Bike tools
Lube (for body)
Powder
Stool (placed on or next to towel)
Pre-race food and fluids
Water bottle or tub for rinsing feet

YOUR TRANSITION AREA

Lay your folded-in-half bath towel next to your racked bike. You may need to fold the towel into thirds if you have less space between bikes in the transition area. Most likely the race will have a space for you in the transition that corresponds to your race number. You must use this space.

At the back of the towel, place your running shoes—laces open—and your socks—open and powdered—on top of each shoe. If you opt to wear socks, putting powder in them and rolling them open will help with ease of entry. You will either wear your race number belt under your wetsuit and over the top of your race clothes, or it will be next to your running shoes on the towel waiting for you. You can also pin your race number on a shirt to be worn on the run, though some events require you to wear it on the bike. Put your run hat on top of the running shoe scenario.

In front of your running shoes are your bike shoes, socks, and helmet with sunglasses placed open and inside the helmet. Another option is to place your shoes on your pedals (I'll go over this later) and perch your helmet on your handlebars with sunglasses inside. My preference is to put all bike gear in one place (on the towel), out of reach of getting bumped by other athletes, so my swim to bike gear-putting-on activity will happen in one location.

Water bottles are placed on the bike, and you have your bike food either in a pouch on the bike or in your clothing in an easy to reach pocket. You can also mount gels and bars on the bike itself with tape or stick pieces of a bar directly onto the bike (this works with some bars but can get a bit messy).

Once you have placed your race gear on the towel and bike, take everything else out of your transition area. Either put it in your post-race gear bag and give the bag to a support person, or put it in your transition bag, zip the bag up and place it out of the way of your and everyone else's transition areas.

Do not leave extra stuff on your towel with the intention of deciding during the race whether you will use it. Decide what you'll use before the race; given too many options, your brain will spend time making decisions when it actually should be executing what's already been decided. The goal in transition is to get to a point where your brain does not have to consciously think. You automatically perform your transition while your mind gets to take a break. Eliminating any impromptu decision-making will help this cause.

Here's a checklist of how your transition set-up may play out:

TRANSITION PREP

- Place race fuel—bars, gel, liquids—on bike or in pockets.
- Lay out transition towel while being

mindful of your and your neighbors' allotted space.

- Roll and powder socks (if you are going to wear them), or lube the inside heel of your running shoes.
- Powder running shoes.
- Put bike shoes with socks on top (optional) on pedals or towel.
- Lube the inside heel of your bike shoes.
- Put on race number belt, or place it next to your running shoes.
- Check tire pressure. You can pump your tires while at your car or in your hotel prior to the race, or bring your floor pump to the transition area.
- Check gear on the bike. Make sure your seat pack with flat changing gear is in place.
- Put on heart rate monitor (optional).
- Put on sunscreen. I recommend putting on sunscreen first thing in the morning prior to putting on your race clothing. Apply more sunscreen in the transition area before the race start.

After Your Bike/Run Warm-Up

- Place all non-race clothing and gear into your transition bag or post-race gear bag and place it outside of your towel area.
- Put on wetsuit lube.
- Put on wetsuit, cap, earplugs, goggles.
- Make sure that your bike is in a gear that will allow you to pedal easily away from the transition area.
- Do a final transition check.
- Memorize where your bike is in the transition area. Count rows or note landmarks outside of the immediate area

that line up with your bike so you can reference its location.

- Go to swim start in time to carry out a swim warm-up (20–40 minutes).

Be Organized

Your goal on race morning is to focus your mental and physical energy on your upcoming event, not to dig through drawers looking for your cycling shorts. Plan to do the organizing, packing of car, and prepping food and fuel on the day before the race. On race morning, allow yourself to set up your transitions, do your warm-up, stretch, and have some solo time to get psyched about your race.

Being organized isn't just about knowing that you have all you need, it's about easing your stress level so your mind has some latitude to prepare for a really hard effort. To this end, take into account your race travel time, checking in and getting through transition area security, minutes spent standing in line, and getting your race number marked. Think through race morning in total, and then build in some additional time so you don't find yourself rushing to the start line. You'll have plenty of time to drive your heart rate and anxiety level up during the race—no point in starting early.

Be Respectful

I remember a woman who got a couple of penalties in races for having a messy transition area. She would fly through the pro racks, knocking over bikes and disrupting others' transition towels while sending gear flying. It was scary to imagine what was going on in her brain while she negligently stormed through our transition space.

As an endurance athlete, you have a dichotomous responsibility when you race. You need to be accountable to your race process to be singularly focused on performing your best, while at the same time acknowledging and being respectful of the fact that all of the other people around you during the race are doing the same thing.

Every once in a while you'll come across people who firmly believe that the entire triathlon universe revolves around them and that you should too. These are the people who will disrupt your gear, move your bike over, or be verbally inconsiderate of others before a race. Don't be one of those people. Organize your gear well while being respectful of others' space as well.

If you are unsure if you are encroaching on someone or if you need to move your or someone else's gear in a way that will affect others—say something to your neighbors. Don't assume they will be okay with it or that they will understand why you made a move—communicate. Communicate, be respectful, and everybody is happy.

Be Present

While setting up your gear, taking your neighbors into account, be present to your process. Notice what you are doing and why you are doing it. Place items where you want them to be and know why you put them there. Being present gives you confidence that when you get back to your transition area after swimming or biking your stuff is there and in the correct place.

And that you haven't forgotten to leave anything out and ready.

The transition can be a social place pre-race; it is part of the fun of a race. But within your chat time, make sure you take a moment to review your set-up and transition prep to make sure it's spot-on before you head to the water.

RACE WARM-UP

Once you have set up your transition, it's time to warm up for your race. The quantity of warm-up you do depends on your goals for the race, your level of fitness, and the distance of the event. See chapter 9, "Creating Your Pre-Race Zone," to learn to prep your mind pre-race. This is an important piece of your pre-race groundwork.

If your goal is to complete the distance of the race, then you'll want to warm up enough to feel rested, confident, and mentally prepared going to the start line. This may mean getting in a good stretch, then jumping in to get used to the water and warm up your upper body for swimming.

If you are fit and racing a sprint- or international-distance event, and your goal is to get a personal best in your race, you'll want to toe the line lubed and ready to rock when the gun goes off. A rule of thumb is the shorter the race, the longer the warm-up. Higher race speeds require you to be fully warm and sweaty with an open vascular system so you can hit your pace right off the line. You want significant blood motion prior to asking your body to move quickly.

A complete warm-up for a fit athlete racing a sprint- or international-distance event might look like this:

■ Start your warm-up with an easy spin on the bike. This may last 10, 20, even 30 minutes if you are very fit and looking for a fast race time. Spin easy for the first third of your warm up, then throw in three to six 30-second jumps in speed—standing out of the saddle to get up to speed, then sitting for the last 15 seconds. Spin easily back to the transition, making sure that you rack your bike in the gear necessary to easily start your ride out of the transition area.

■ Do a light stretch of key tight spots before you head out for your run warm-up.

■ Jog easily for 5, 10, or 15 minutes, throwing in three to six 30-second strides within this run time—building your speed up to race pace or faster within each stride. Finish your run warm-up with some easy jogging back to the transition.

■ When you get back to the transition, you should be sweaty, lungs open, feeling loose, and ready to go.

■ You can either take some more stretching time now, or put on your wetsuit, head to the shoreline, and stretch there before you hop in the water.

- Get to your wave start with time to get in the water and do a swim warm-up. If the water is cold, give yourself a few more minutes to submerge. Swim easily for several minutes then do three to six 30-second surges in speed, before an easy couple more minutes of swimming. Hop out of the water and you are ready to rock.

- If you are racing an event that does not let athletes in the water prior to the swim start, and there is no other swim location in the immediate vicinity in which to warm up, then do a swim warm-up on land. Start with some light upper body stretches—triceps, chest, side stretches (see chapter 8). Then starting with the right arm, swing the arm in front away from your body and then behind you in a half circle. Let the arm swing back and forth like a pendulum for a minute, then switch to the left arm. Come back to the right arm and swing in full circles forward, then backward a few times, and then switch to the left arm. Swing both arms in the same or opposing directions at the same time. Do some jogging on the beach and a few push-ups. The idea is to get a solid blood flow to the upper body before you ask it to work for you.

Remember, in prepping your mind and body for the stress of an event, your body may react with a flight-or-fight type response. You may get sweaty palms or a nervous stomach, or you may be spending much more time than usual in the Port-a-Potties prior to the race. Your heart rate will increase, and you may even have an anxious feeling in your chest.

Practice and execute your mental training prior to a race, and use these physical responses in your favor. Accept the physical responses, but learn how to control and channel them effectively (chapter 9).

Whether you are racing a sprint- or international-distance race, perform a warm-up similar to that described above. If you are racing a half-Ironman for a personal best, take the above warm-up and cut all the times and distances in half, or less. For all events, including Ironman distance, stretching, prepping your mind, and doing a swim warm-up are the minimum you should do prior to a race. Anything less will not allow your body and mind to be ready to perform your best.

Warm-up is also a great time to take a moment to thank the people at the race supporting you as well as to thank yourself for all your hard work and training. Celebrate getting to the start line ready to express yourself in a way that you love—an endurance race. This can be an exciting, emotional time.

TRANSITIONS IN TRIATHLON

A well-organized transition area and a well-prepared body and mind can make a big difference in your overall race performance. Methodically transitioning from swim to bike and bike to run builds on that preparation and will contribute to your overall race success.

SWIM-TO-BIKE

Keep your swim-to-bike transition simple. Take off your wetsuit as soon as you come out of the water—at the shoreline. While you are running out of the water, unzip your suit and peel it down to your waist. As soon as you touch land, move to the side of the other exiting swimmers and stop and peel off the legs of your suit. You may need

Taking your wetsuit off at the water will save time in transition

to help the suit over your heels with your thumbs. It will peel off easily since there will still be a thin layer of water in your suit. If you wait until you get to the transition area to take off your wetsuit, the water between you and the suit will have drained out and the neoprene will therefore suck onto your skin.

If you feel nauseated or dizzy when you come out of the water, sit down and take a break or start walking slowly up to your bike until you feel more settled. You'll come around with a bit of time.

Even if you don't feel dizzy, it is common to feel out of sorts when you come out of water onto land and ask your body to move quickly. You are swimming in a horizontal position with limited visual stimulus, and then you force blood into your legs as soon as you leave your cocoon of water. It may take a few races until you have your bearings about you when you hit land.

If you feel anxious or your heart rate is high when you come out of the water, take off your wetsuit and walk to the transition. If you are feeling comfortable with your effort level, jog with your wetsuit slung over your shoulder. Once you get to the transition, take a few deep breaths while you are putting on your bike gear. Take control of your breathing and heart rate. Imagine your heart slowing down. Relax your mind and your heart will slow.

The lower your heart rate in each transition, the more quality your recovery. Even 30 seconds of a lower heart rate will go a long way in setting you up for a strong bike and run effort.

MORE FROM PETE KAIN: NO SHOES?

I had one pretty unique experience happen to me during a race back in the late '80s. I was having a great race at an event in Santa Barbara, coming off the bike in second place overall. I was confident in my run and was ready to challenge for the overall win! I came into transition, racked my bike, and could NOT find my shoes! I was in a full panic, when I just thought to myself, well, it's only a 4-mile run, I guess I'll just run barefoot! No joke, I just figured I could run 4 miles barefoot! Well, it started out nice, on a long stretch of grass, then hit pavement and ouch, ouch, ouch! I realized it wasn't going to be that easy. I came up to a race volunteer and yelled, "What size shoes do you wear? He yelled, Nine, why?" I said, "Close enough, take off your shoes." (I wear an $11^1/2$). I promptly put on his shoes and promised to return them after the race. I never caught the guy leading, but I did hold onto second overall in the race! I finished with some black toes and a few blisters but did return the shoes to the generous volunteer.

Put your wetsuit toward the back of your towel out of the way of your other transition gear. Don shoes, helmet, glasses, and then grab your bike and walk or jog briskly out of the transition area all the while paying attention to the location of other athletes around you.

Do you need socks? No, but you may want them. Do you need gloves? No, unless you want them. If you don't use socks or gloves, you won't realize during the race that you don't have them. Keeping your transition simple allows your mind to focus on more important things like biking and running. And as they say in adventure racing, "If you don't have it, you don't need it."

If you have practiced in training, you may want to attach your bike shoes to your pedals and put your shoes on as you are rolling away from the transition area. This saves time only if you can do it seamlessly and safely. If you are spending a lot of time riding slowly in order to get your shoes on, or if you crash while trying to get your shoes on, the time you may have saved will be for naught.

To practice this maneuver, put your bike shoes on your bike at home and leave them there. Each time you get on to ride in training, put your shoes on while rolling forward. When you return from your ride, take your feet out of the shoes while riding and leave the shoes on the bike for your next ride. Only try the shoe-on-pedal set-up in a race if you feel very comfortable with it in training.

BIKE-TO-RUN

Several minutes before heading into the transition area, put your bike into an easier gear. Spin lightly and start to focus on your next transition experience. If you are going to leave your shoes on your pedals (recommended), unfasten Velcro or laces, and either flatten the heel of the shoe (like a mule) so that your foot can slide out easily or take your foot out of the shoe and place it on top of the shoe to pedal in.

Your final minutes on the bike are valuable in setting up your recovery from bike to run. Take some deep breaths and imagine your heart rate coming down. This will give you several minutes of an easy effort prior to your run. Take this recovery time while you're moving forward, spinning easy on your bike, rather than in the transition area. By the time you hit the transition to dismount, you will be relaxed, your mind clear. You are ready to take on the last portion of your race.

Unless you have no interest in your time for the race distance (which is just fine), there is no reason to spend more than a minute in the bike-to-run transition. Leave shoes on the pedals and unclip your helmet once your feet touch the ground. You may already be wearing your race number belt and sunglasses. The only tasks ahead are racking your bike and putting on your running shoes. Grab your run hat and you're outta there! If you need more recovery leading into the run, walk-jog out of the transition area for a quarter mile, and then

assess how you feel. As the distance progresses, add in more jogging.

If you go sockless, lube the inside heel of your running shoes and powder the inside of the shoes and your foot will slide right into your lace-locked shoes. If you opt for socks, use the same socks you use on the bike, or roll and powder your run socks so they slide on quickly.

Whether you stand or sit in transition is a personal preference and may be decided by your ability to balance during a race. If you feel unstable, even with practice, consider getting a small stool to sit on. If you struggle with momentum or motivation going into your run, remain standing to keep your energy dynamic.

Bike-to-run transition should be easy. Keep it simple and you can shave minutes off of your transition times.

CHAPTER 6

Building Your Finest Training Program

"The fight is won or lost far away from witnesses—behind the lines, in the gym, and out there on the road, long before I dance under those lights."

Muhammad Ali

Now that you've defined the amount of time you can devote to training each week, reviewed the important variables involved in creating your best training plan, and gathered some information on swimming, biking, and running for the sport of triath-lon, it's time to pull it all together into a detailed training plan.

Appendix B provides several sample training programs to help you create your own detailed program. Here we'll cover guidelines for choosing your first race, plan-

ning your race season, and the importance and relevance of tapering for a race as well as the best means for acquiring knowledge, support, and coaching for that carefully planned season of fun.

CHOOSING YOUR FIRST TRIATHLON

Some choose to jump into their first race on a whim, and that is certainly a fine way to come into the sport, especially if you enjoy spontaneity and don't mind severe fatigue, muscle soreness, or injury post-race. Not to say that all spontaneously born triathletes will have a physically negative experience,

but it is highly probable you will to some degree. You don't train just to do well in a race, you train so you can come out of your race experiences healthy and can come back for more. If you are looking at triathlon for a long-term lifestyle change, a more user-friendly means to jumping into the sport is to look forward and choose a race that looks interesting and fits into your projected training time frame.

■ Does the event location, course, and overall feel of the race sound enticing to you? Why do an event in Timbuktu, if you don't enjoy spending time in Timbuktu? Especially if you wish to combine an event with some fun leisure time,

CONVERSATIONS WITH HEATHER FUHR: RACING AND SELF

Terri: In what way do you find that your racing efforts make you a better person? Make the world a better place? Have an effect on others—if any?

Heather: I don't race because I want to make a difference in the world, nor do I do so to have an effect on others. I race because I enjoy the process involved in getting in shape for a race and competing in a race. I do feel, however, that racing and being an athlete has made me a better person. I am a more confident person than I would otherwise have been. I also believe that the discipline that comes with training and racing then crosses over to all aspects of life.

Heather finishes strong at a local 10K.

choose a race location that appeals to you. That may be your hometown—definitely a user-friendly place to do your first race.

■ Do you have sufficient time to train for this event? Again, if you are new to triathlon but you have the basic skills needed in all three sports, consider an eight-week training program leading into your first sprint race. If you are new to swimming or running, you may want to give yourself a few more weeks in order to gain proficiency.

■ What distance race should you shoot for as your first race? An obvious choice is a sprint race. Why not get your feet wet and allow yourself to walk away with the odds of a positive experience? But if you wish to hop into an international-distance event for your first race, increase your projected training time by a few weeks.

PLANNING YOUR SEASON

Part of planning a race season involves revisiting your athletic goals for the year (see chapter 9). You may decide to stick to shorter events for the whole season or your whole career and continue to refine your speed and skill base. Or you may decide to hit your goal of finishing a sprint race early season, then plan to take on a longer distance event in the fall with an ultimate goal of doing an Ironman next season. In any case, planning your season starts with looking at your long-range goals, then sit-

ting down and making a race wish list.

Your wish list will include the dates, names, and distances of all events in which you are interested in participating. In addition to triathlons, include 10Ks, century rides, a backpacking trip with the family—anything that requires time, is physical in nature, or may affect your consistent training program. All of these activities will affect how you race and should be reviewed in total.

Then categorize each event on your wish list into the following:

A races. These are the most important to you when it comes to performance. You want to get a personal best or have a peak performance. Usually an athlete will have one to three A races a season. These are the ones you want to prime for.

B races. These are important but not enough to generate a complete taper for or plan your season around. You want to be relatively rested for a B race, but not necessarily in peak form. B races are excellent events to use as benchmark events—to test your fitness, try a new fuel plan, new bike, or race pace.

C races. These are events you want to do for fun, camaraderie, and as a diversion from training, but you are willing to train through them if needed to shoot for a better performance at an A or B race.

Now take a look at whether the events in total complement your ultimate goal of doing well at your A races. This means that you have weeks before your A races to generate some solid cycles of training and to be best set up for an effective taper.

Can you race too much? Yes. There is a school of thought that regular A races are just the kind of training you need in order to hit peak form. I disagree. Events are an excellent means to test your fitness in a strong physical, mental, and emotional effort, but in order to race really well in at least a few events each season, you need some recovery time prior to each race. If you push hard in an A race, you need some recovery time post-race as well. Recovery time ranges from a few days to a week or more (for longer events) when you are diminishing the volume and intensity of your training in order to prepare for or recover from an event. If you do this too frequently—even twice per month consistently—you will lose some fitness.

If you are willing to train through (sticking to your build cycles pre- and post-race) some of your B and C races in order to keep a positive training progression, you may not lose fitness but you might be adding too much stress to your training regime.

Some like to race frequently because they enjoy the ambiance of the triathlon

community, and it gives them motivation to push hard. Those are excellent reasons for putting your money down. But if you desire one or two peak performances in your season, you are better off choosing a couple of A races in each season, then throwing in B and C triathlons with some other form of training events added for spice. Another solid option is to do one or two triathlons a year and then devote your time to other fitness areas. Look at your goals and then create a plan that addresses them.

The sample event calendar gives you an idea of how you might put together a full triathlon season. This athlete's season goals are to peak at his A races and complete his first half-Ironman event, while adding some additional non-triathlon-specific events to refine his skills and keep the season interesting and fun. Before the season and in between events, he is building his training toward his most important season race—his half-Ironman—only taking full taper and recovery before and after A races.

SAMPLE EVENT CALENDAR

April

Date	Event	Category	Additional Goals
1st weekend	10K run	B	test fitness
3rd weekend	100K ride	C	fun ride, train through

May

Date	Event	Category	Additional Goals
2nd weekend	sprint tri	B	test fitness, practice transitions
3rd weekend	1 mile swim	C	test fitness, train through

June

Date	Event	Category	Additional Goals
2nd weekend	intl tri	A	personal record on course
4th weekend	off-road tri	C	fun race in the location of my next endeavor

July

Date	Event	Category	Additional Goals
1st week	backpacking trip with family		
4th weekend	sprint tri	B	test fitness

August

Date	Event	Category	Additional Goals
3rd weekend	intl tri	B	test new bike/fuel plan

September

Date	Event	Category	Additional Goals
2nd weekend	half marathon run		
	100K ride	C	training events on one weekend

October

Date	Event	Category	Additional Goals
2nd weekend	half-Ironman	A	finish strong!

TAPERING FOR A RACE

Tapering before an A race is as important as training. It allows you to set yourself up for your best performance by resting your body and your mind and eliminating any cumulative fatigue gathered during the building of your training. The length and amount of your taper will depend on the length of the race and how important the race is to you.

If you are preparing for an A race, maximize your taper time for optimal rest and recovery—lean toward a twelve- to fifteen-day taper. If your upcoming race is important but more of a fun race or a training race (B or C), then your taper can be shorter, or you can decide to train through the event and eliminate a taper altogether. The longer your event, the longer your taper (up to three weeks for an Ironman). This assumes that if you have done proper longer training for a longer event that you need more time to recover from the cumulative physiological and muscular fatigue from many hours of training.

All taper programs will include a change in total training volume, frequency, and intensity. Use the guidelines in appendix B, but remember that it is usually better to do a bit less volume than too much. Don't get greedy—don't panic train! Your training adaptation is complete at this point and trying to force a higher training effect this close to an event will only hurt your race effort. If you want to train more because you think it will psychologically help you in your event—let go of that thought. It will only make you more tired on race day.

- For a twelve- to fifteen-day taper, cut your initial volume by 30 to 50 percent, leaning toward 50 percent for longer events.
- On the front end of a two- to three-week taper, maintain frequency of workouts per week while cutting back on the duration of each workout.
- During the last week of your taper, cut frequency and duration an additional 50 percent from week 1.
- For a two- to three-week taper, maintain intensity in your workouts while decreasing duration of higher intensity bouts.
- Even in your last week of taper, maintain very short duration intensity bouts (up to 1 minute) while cutting duration and frequency.

The two-week Sample Tapering programs in Appendix B take all the above factors into account. A person who might use these sample programs has trained to a level in which they feel very comfortable with the distances and intensities in these workouts. If you are not comfortable with this level of training, this would not be an adequate taper for you. These sample schedules are meant to be a guide to help you create your own personal taper.

GAINING KNOWLEDGE AND SUPPORT

HOW TO FIND EVENTS
The internet provides the easiest way to find events, clubs, local masters swim programs, or training buddies in your area.

‍

THE SPIRIT OF TRI COMMUNITIES

We belong to various "communities" throughout our lives, and as our interests grow and change over time, our communities may change up as well. Some are transient and some are enduring. Sometimes you are fortunate enough to connect with a community of people who become a part of your life in a way that impacts you forever.

I don't know exactly when I decided to do a triathlon, but I do know it was sometime toward the end of a weeklong organized bike ride. While I was contemplating how good it was going to feel to not be riding almost a hundred miles a day for six straight days, the thought of some different means of motion sounded appealing.

I returned home and started reading websites and race calendars and stumbled across a local "tri for fun." So I signed up and jumped in with both feet, literally and figuratively. It was interesting and intriguing and confusing, all at the same time. I knew how to swim, I knew how to bike, but I felt like I was a horrible runner and the process of going from one discipline to the other was mind boggling.

Clearly there were secrets to be learned that everyone else knew about except me, so I decided to seek out the local triathlon club. Joining the local club was a real enlightenment

for me on several levels: yes, there were things to learn that made everything much easier, but even better, there were many involved and committed athletes who would actually take the time to talk to me and show me things I didn't know. This was a solid change from other clubs and sports that I had been involved with. I found out that the community of triathlon had a very unique spirit.

As my experience level grew and improved, I started to travel for races and found that every race, club, and community involved with triathlon was just as open to teaching, coaching, cheering, and overall support as my own. Most important, it didn't seem to matter whether you were a competitive winner or someone whose main goal was to meet the challenge of finishing. All support was created equal.

I embraced this community just as it embraced me. I became active in our local club, eventually serving as president. In addition, I became active in our national association for triathlon, which provided me with an even broader perspective and opportunities.

But my embrace of community didn't stop there! Perhaps one of the biggest changes within the community of triathlon came when I decided to leave a very comfortable paycheck and start an event production company of my own. The energy and spirit of the sport have become so fulfilling to me that this is my way of giving back to the community of triathletes. Besides, now that I don't work a "regular job," I'm supposed to have more time to train for my own races, right? I'm still looking for that time. I know it must be under the piles of race bibs and registration forms all over my desk. But if I don't find it there, I'm certain I'll find it in the motivation gained from the great folks in my own tri community.

Penni Bengtson is the owner of Finish Line Productions, a multisport event production and timing company. She is a USA Triathlon Certified Race Director and an active triathlete and runner.

From internet searches, you will start to gather information about websites and local periodicals or publications that list events. Pick up these publications at your local running or cycling stores—they often are free. While you're at the shop, talk to the athletes who work there, they are an excellent resource.

Consider joining your local triathlon club, where you'll gain instant training partners as well as organized training sessions. Through clubs or organized workouts, you can network for more information on what is available to you in your area.

GAINING SUPPORT

Some regions are more favorable than others for year-round training and support. If your area does not seem to have many resources available, a good place to search is USA Triathlon (www.usatriathlon.org), which lists all of the sanctioned clubs in the country as well as many other sport resources. Triathletes are friendly people who love their sport and are more than happy to share useful information with anyone who is interested in listening. Meet a couple of local triathletes or an enthusiastic running store employee and the sport will unfold before you.

COACHING

Training effectively for triathlon is a complicated process. Just because you are an accomplished person in your life, career, and family, as well as a solid athlete doesn't mean that you know how best to fit triathlon into your life. Some people will read books like this one to gather information to put together a program. But most will start that process with good intentions and then walk away due to decreased time or interest in the process.

If you are passionate about your sport but you are not passionate about figuring out how to do your sport—you're in good company. No one said you had to be an expert at creating the perfect triathlon program. But what you do owe yourself is a means of generating the best program for you. If a haphazard program is causing you to be over- or undertrained, injured, or underperforming, and you don't have the time or interest in gaining the knowledge to create that optimal program, enlist a coach.

Many people who come to me for coaching already train in some manner, but they may not train properly for their ability level and time constraints. They may be reinforcing bad habits, training at ineffective intensity levels, or most likely they are the on-again, off-again athlete who has difficulty remaining consistent. These are very human issues and ones that can be easily rectified with a bit of guidance.

HOW TO SELECT THE PERFECT COACH FOR YOU

A coach-athlete relationship is critical in that your coach now and then reflects pieces of yourself back at you. You need to feel comfortable within that intimate process. I've worked with many adults who have been scarred for life from bad youth coaching experiences. They were not able to realize in adulthood that the inappropriate comments made to them as children were the coach's interpretation of them and not necessarily reality. They carried the scars with them through their adult athletic life, or worse, didn't have an adult athletic life.

Triathlon is a lifestyle sport that brings joy and pleasure to people's lives in so many ways. Hiring a coach should in no way end the positive feeling you have for the sport. Your coach should enhance your training process by challenging you to bring even more of yourself to the sport—in a caring, human way.

Yet in this age of virtual coaching and dime-a-dozen certifications handed out to fitness professionals, selecting a coach can be as challenging as financing a home in the San Francisco Bay area. When considering acquiring a coach, it is first helpful to address what you want out of your coaching relationship.

- What are your goals for your sport and what do you wish to learn from your coach?
- Is there any ancillary training knowledge you wish to gain from this person?
- How involved do you want your coach to be in your training, your everyday life? Do you only want a guided training program or additional hands-on or phone time with your coach?
- How are you best motivated by others?
- What personality style do you think would work for you? Write down qualities in a coach that would be favorable to you.
- What is the background of the coach (race experience, education, etc.)?
- Has the coach participated extensively in the sport in which you are to be coached? Is this important to you?
- Are you interested in working with someone new to coaching or do you want your coach to have more time in the sport?
- What level of athletes has the coach worked with? Having worked with elite athletes doesn't necessarily make someone a solid coach. Many coaches who prefer to work with elites have poor people skills in coaching middle- to back-of-the-pack athletes. Coaching athletes of different ability levels requires a variety of skills because the mindset of each is unique.
- What is your budget? There are many inexpensive generic training programs you can purchase on the internet, but they will be just that—a generic training program. If you desire a customized program and human interaction, you'll have to pay a bit more.

With your answers to the above in mind, research available coaches and interview those who appear to fit the bill. Be proactive in the interview process, and use the above questions to guide you. Your coach is your teammate in your training and racing process. You need to feel solid about having this person on your team.

Below are some additional qualities that I believe should be present in a quality triathlon coach. A quality triathlon coach:

- Guides you in making your own decisions. A smart coach does not force-feed your process. He facilitates your evolution as an athlete.
- Guides you in learning more about yourself through the sport.
- Sees and acknowledges the different needs of male and female athletes as well as elites and beginners.
- Speaks to your personality type. Does she talk to you in a way that you can understand? Or is she continually talking over your head or down to you?
- Knows how to give positive reinforcement when it is warranted, but doesn't play perpetual cheerleader.
- Shows you your strengths on a regular basis as well as how far you have come in your training, especially when you forget to see this for yourself.
- Can safely point out areas that need work, while acknowledging that most athletes are sensitive to criticism.
- Teaches you how to coach yourself during races and during the off-season.

- Teaches you how to execute an event without having to vicariously hold your hand.
- Teaches independence in the athlete and supports the relationship as one based on growth.
- Mirrors the healthy ways in sport. He practices what he preaches; he is someone you respect.
- Has extensive experience doing triathlon.

She has been there and can relate to your experience on all levels.

- Allows that your program is the most important thing to you and treats it as such.

Ask for references and find out what other athletes say about how he operates. Set yourself up to select a coach who will shift your training to a positive light. And in doing so, don't ever settle for less.

Nutrition for Training and Racing

"Food is an important part of a balanced diet."

Fran Lebowitz

What athlete doesn't want an edge, an elixir, or a magic formula for training and racing faster? But the plain truth is that unless you're willing to gain that edge via illegal or unethical substances (don't do it!), your "edge" ultimately consists of your dedication to the components in your sport that are right under your nose on a daily basis—nutrition practices, strength and flexibility programs, and mental training. If you want an edge on your competitors, including yourself, home in on these aspects of sport. You'll be one up on most folks out there, and you'll enjoy triathlon even more!

Though this chapter will focus predominantly on nutrition for training and racing, I'll also comment on daily nutrition needs for the endurance athlete. See Resources at the end of the book for more information on refining your daily nutrition practice.

PAY ATTENTION

These days you can find high carb, low carb, and no carb diets, as well as programs that focus on specific food groups, liquid only,

fruit only—you name it, it's out there—but when it comes to the finest performance nutrition program for you, there are no shortcuts or ideal diets. When creating your daily nutrition plan, there are no absolutes. You are unique, you are a nutritional work in progress, and your dietary needs should be addressed accordingly through sound practices.

Read available literature, experiment with reputable programs, talk to nutrition professionals. Most important, pay attention to how you feel when you eat different foods. Log your diet and take notes on how you perform each day in training. Compare the feelings you notice in your training to your diet. Do you see common denominators?

On some days you may crave more protein and some days more fat. Honestly listen to what your body needs. Focus on eating like an athlete. While there is no shortage of people claiming to have the perfect formula for what to eat when, you still need to find the perfect formula for yourself and that means experimenting and learning about your body's needs. This takes effort and thought.

You can get very precise with your program by consulting a nutritionist to guide you or by learning what to eat during certain cycles of your training process—these are valuable learning processes. But ultimately, unless you can afford to have someone do all the figuring and number crunching for you (and then make your meals), you'll need to pay attention.

THE CARB-PROTEIN-FAT CONUNDRUM

Most people respond well to a diet consisting of 55 to 65 percent carbohydrates, 12 to 20 percent protein, and 15 to 25 percent fat. The percentages in each area that are most effective may change up depending on who you talk to, but ultimately they should reference what works for you. This

is where refining the paying attention part comes in.

Once you've started to fine-tune the quantity of carbs, protein, and fats needed to run your engine smoothly, focus on keeping it simple. Eat whole foods and food that is fresh and unprocessed. When it comes to day-to-day eating, experiment a lot, pay attention, and keep it simple.

TRAINING AND RACING FUEL GUIDELINES

Too often triathletes blow what should have been a positive race experience because they did not follow through with an effective eating and drinking plan for their event. This aspect of your racing is as important as making sure there is air in your tires before you ride your bike. No air, no ride. No calories, no forward movement and no effective brain function. Do not underestimate the importance of this aspect of your training and racing. It will make or break an otherwise well-thought-out training or race experience.

What follows are guidelines that will help you to refine your nutritional process for training and racing and for the hours leading up to, during, and after the workout or race. Experience and intuition go a long way, and in this case you are the expert.

PRE-EXERCISE NUTRITION BASICS

- Replenish carbohydrate stores and fluids lost while sleeping.
- Use foods that sit in your stomach well

and are satisfying and comforting physically and emotionally.
- Keep it light.
- Only consume foods or fluids that you have already experimented with.
- Eat foods that will help you perform at your best.

PRE-EXERCISE NUTRITION GUIDELINES

- For those with a sensitive stomach, liquid calories often go down more easily. Experiment to figure out what works for you. For example, a protein shake with a banana or berries or a liquid breakfast drink mixed with soy milk.
- Try to avoid eating a lot of fiber the morning of a race. Empty your bowels pre-race and be done with it. Excess fiber can keep your colon more active than you wish.
- Use caffeine only if you are used to taking it prior to exercise, but use it sparingly during training and racing (experiment before using).
- Many experts recommend eating a meal of 300 to 800 calories or more 2 to 3 hours before a race, long run, or workout. This should be mostly carbohydrates, but there are benefits—feeling satisfied as well as settling a nervous stomach—to eating some protein as well as a bit of fat along with your carbs. Modify this to suit your lifestyle, palate, and stomach. Specific quantity in total depends on your body size and the length of your event.
- Use foods that will keep you stable by avoiding huge influxes of blood sugar

and subsequent insulin responses (dizziness or excessive hunger). Experiment with different foods to figure out what works best for you. For example, oatmeal with a banana and apple juice or wheat toast with butter and an egg.

- Drink 14 to 22 ounces (400 to 600 ml) of water or sports drink 2 hours before an event. Play with quantities and types of fluids.

- Hydrate well several days prior to your event, especially for training or events done in hotter climates and lasting longer than 4 hours.

- Eat an additional 100 to 200 calories an hour before your training or event. The calories will help support glycogen stores and prevent body proteins from being sacrificed for fuel.

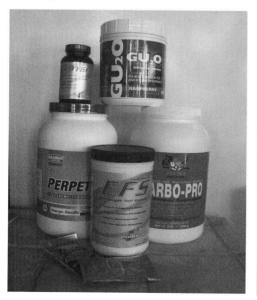

For example, 2.5 hours before race start, eat wheat toast with butter and an egg. On the way to the race, sip water or your chosen sports drink and continue to sip as you prep for the race. One hour before the race, drink half of a protein shake or eat half of an energy bar along with more water or sports drink.

I've had countless conversations with athletes who did not perform up to par in an event. If they are able to rule out inadequate pacing or race strategy as problem areas, the finger usually points to their nutrition plan, or lack thereof. If they don't recognize the mistakes as taking place immediately prior to or during their event, the problem is usually found several days prior to their race.

Given all of your time spent training, you deserve to spend a few more minutes planning your pre-race nutrition program. It's easy to believe you can rest on the laurels of a well-trained body, but that body will not perform well if you do not feed and water it well. Think through your plan, and then pay attention to performing it.

DURING-EXERCISE NUTRITION GUIDELINES

Having a very specific eating and drinking plan when heading to the start line or out the door for a long day of training is just as important as knowing your pacing plan for the ride or what type of socks you'll wear to prevent blisters on your long run. This is critical stuff and can take many training sessions to solidify. Walk through this information with your next race in mind. Come

CONVERSATIONS WITH HEATHER FUHR: NUTRITION

Terri: Do you do anything special with your day-to-day diet in order to perform at the top? Do you have any nutritional guiding principles?

Heather: I try to eat a balanced diet, nothing extreme. When I am in a heavy training cycle, I will make sure that I get in a good balance of carbohydrate, fat, and protein. I have never been so strict in my eating that I have denied myself something—I believe that anything in moderation is fine.

up with a nutrition plan for that event and most important, follow that plan.

There are three key components to a training or event nutrition plan: calories, fluids, and electrolytes.

The following guidelines will help you create your nutrition plan while keeping these components in check:

- Most endurance athletes need 150 to 400 calories per hour during activity. Consider factors such as exercise intensity and duration, fitness, and body size when determining how many calories you need to consume for a given workout day. With practice you'll be able to come up with an exact number that works for you to start a race, and then you can adapt during your event as needed.
- The carbs you use should come primarily from glucose. It doesn't matter how you get the carbs—from drinks, gels, or bars. Figure out which type or combination works best for you, and then consume the correct amount of calories in whichever form suits you. Drink plain water with your gels or bars.
- Eat or drink your calories steadily, not in one big gulp. Avoid taking in large

quantities of calories infrequently as your body will not be able to assimilate more than 50–100 calories at a time. The result can be stomach problems or a bonk as the food remains in the stomach. Take in 50–100 calories along with some plain water every 20–25 minutes during a race or training. Do this consistently. Some people need to set their watch alarm to remind them to eat at regular intervals.

- During exercise or an event, drink 6 to 12 ounces (150 to 350 ml) of fluid every 20 minutes. Don't wait; start drinking shortly after you begin. Personalize this quantity—the recommended amount may be too much or too little for you. Experiment with types and quantity based on stomach comfort, body size, and absorption, but make sure you are taking in plain water in addition to your chosen calories for optimal assimilation of calories from the stomach.
- Select sports drinks that include sodium or eat foods containing sodium such as pretzels, chips, salty soup, and take electrolyte tablets.
- Sports drinks should be 6 to 10 percent carbohydrate concentration for optimal

absorption. This is a much lower concentration than is advised on the package of most drinks. If, like most people, you enjoy it more concentrated, make sure you are cutting your sports drink with a couple swigs of plain water.

- Carbohydrates are your best source of fuel for events lasting 1 to 4 hours, but I have noticed that the majority of the people I have coached desire some sources of protein and fat—especially in events lasting longer than a few hours (this can be specific to an individual). Too many carbs can be harsh on the stomach or palate. A bit of protein or fat can help settle the stomach and give you a sense of satisfaction (see "Nausea" under "Special Nutritional Considerations"). Don't force-feed a carb-only race diet if it isn't working for your stomach or your psyche. Experiment and allow yourself to come up with a protocol that works best for you.

- Eat what you like based on the above

guidelines. Make sure that you really, really like the foods you are planning on eating in your event. Even if you start out really liking them, there's a good chance they will be marginally palatable once you've been out there for several hours. Experiment and give yourself options on event day.

■ Electrolyte tablets with potassium and sodium are known to aid in electrolyte balancing during prolonged exercise. Use electrolyte products as recommended on the package. Adjust quantities based on body size and weather conditions but definitely use them—they may be your lifesaver.

Got Electrolytes?

If there is one thing that goes in your mouth that could single-handedly balance your total nutrition program while racing, it could be your electrolyte tablets. I'm not talking about the electrolytes in your sports drink or gel packets; these don't provide the quantity of electrolytes needed to keep you fully in balance in longer events and in extreme conditions. I'm referring to electrolyte tablets that include a combination of sodium and potassium (not salt tablets).

A while back I was trotting along in a 100K trail race in the Marin Headlands and engaging in a likely ultra running activity—chatting. Yet this particular chatting experience was unique in that I was actually being "outchatted" by a gentleman who worked in a think tank for cancer research in Texas.

He told me about recent breakthroughs with his work, his running, and his predisposition for memorizing certain categories of things in life—like music and wine. I passed the time trying to baffle his photographic memory by throwing down random questions like: "Which appellation grapes are used in David Bruce's award-winning 1997 Pinot Noir?" Or "Who wrote the theme song for Gilligan's Island?" Despite my efforts, I couldn't stump him.

Then all of a sudden he became quiet. I glanced over to notice he was white as a sheet and laboring. The coach in me had been noticing out of the corner of my eye that he had been eating and drinking adequately the last few hours, so I didn't suspect a calorie or water bonk. I asked him how he was feeling and he confirmed, with a few expletives, my observations.

I swung my fanny pack around and pulled out my running "drug bag." I grabbed three electrolyte tablets, and as we jogged along I extended my hand, "Here, take these." Without so much as a grunt, he snatched the tablets and downed them with a swig of water. Though a gentleman of such refined intellectual property, he didn't so much as ask me what I was pushing.

A half hour later, he caught back up to me. "Man, what did you give me back there? I feel great!" After commenting on how I thought it was a bit odd that he unquestioningly took unknown tablets from a complete stranger, I offered him further information on the least touted yet one of the most critical ingredients to successful endurance racing—electrolytes.

I'm going to go out on a limb here, as I don't know of any specific research that will back up a personal observation. As with my Marin Headlands running buddy, I have noticed that taking electrolyte tablets in really long events can be the duct tape that holds the blood sugar–hydration scale at a balance point. There are obviously many variables involved in keeping this critical race balance, but I have noticed that if some calories and fluids are present, the electrolytes can help pull them into balance to keep you moving forward adequately.

My Marin running companion went on to beat me in the race while becoming another electrolyte convert. We kept in

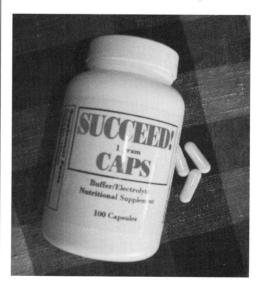

touch—he to tell me how this slight change in his race fuel plan continued to positively affect other races down the road. And I to reassure him that I was continuing to practice electrolyte pushing in my coaching and racing.

Brain Function and the Bonk

Have you ever felt sleepy a few hours or more into a race or training? Mentally and physically out of sorts? Lethargic? Or, have you slipped into a really bad mood during an event and subsequently spent some solid time bashing your abilities as an athlete or perhaps why you as a human exist on this planet at all? If you answer yes to any of these, there is a good chance you have been on the edge of or in the throes of bonking. Bonking is general fatigue resulting from muscle glycogen depletion. When your stores are severely threatened, your brain function is impaired.

It can come on slowly like a vague, edgy feeling of impending doom. Or it can hit you suddenly—one minute you're moving okay, the next you're irritable and feeling as though someone pulled the plug on your energy stores. Someone did pull the plug—you! At that point without attention, the mind can spiral downward into the black vortex of negative self-talk.

Some people working through a bonk can keep going by basically shutting down their brains and plowing forward. It's not pretty to watch—and generally makes for an experience you wouldn't wish on your worst enemies. One objective in creating a nutrition program that works is so that you never get close to the bonk. Keeping your fluid, electrolyte, and glycogen levels in balance will not only help you perform physically at your best, it will ensure that you remain mentally focused.

There is a difference between feeling tired muscularly and bonking. Take note of these differences and store the information away. You never want to get close to bonking, but if you know the signs, you can catch it before it hits you hard.

If you start to bonk while cycling, slow your pace or pull over and ingest a couple hundred calories along with some fluid. If you are running, walk or slow to a jog and do the same (chances are you are probably already walking or jogging, or have stopped on the side of the road). Your stomach may struggle a bit to assimilate this large intake, so slowing your pace or stopping will help. But if you don't catch the bonk, it will progress rapidly. You can definitely prevent yourself from bonking if you note symptoms and address them quickly.

POST-EXERCISE NUTRITION GUIDELINES

Nutrition is an important aspect of an adequate recovery. Let's take a deeper look to help you decipher the best program for you.

▓ Eat and drink within 20 minutes after exercise. Muscles can be empty and blood flow is still high—capitalize on that time. Fluids are usually the most convenient way to immediately replenish post-workout; they have the added benefit of helping you rehydrate and can be consumed quickly and easily.

Use a recovery drink that has a 3:1 or 4:1 ratio of carbohydrates to proteins and is easy to drink and palatable. Make sure it is available right after your workout. Your recovery carbohydrate needs are based on your body weight and training schedule. It's important to replace carbohydrate stores to speed recovery of your muscles and get you ready for your next workout and/or the rest of your day.

▣ Carbohydrates are the key to glycogen repletion and the key to replenishing glycogen stores in your body. Glycogen replacement and quick recovery helps prevent fatigue and increase endurance, speed, and agility by replacing muscle glycogen stores—kind of like putting high quality gas back into the tank of the race car. Adding protein can be helpful for muscle protein repair and in helping absorption of carbs.

▣ Keep in mind that a perceived high exertion in your workouts corresponding with poor performance can be directly related to muscle glycogen stores, or the lack thereof.

▣ If you have a particularly sluggish feeling for a few days or longer while

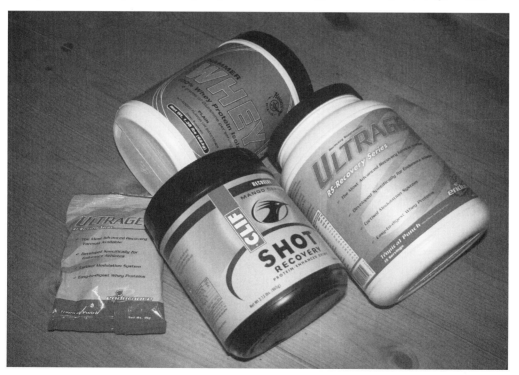

training, you may be partially glucose- or fluid-depleted.

Below are some examples for post-exercise replacement based on a 140-pound person. *Note:* These are consumed immediately following workout; an additional meal should be eaten within an hour:

Moderate-intensity workouts (less than or up to 1 hour): 220 calories
Example, energy bar and water or the equivalent in a recovery drink
High-intensity workouts (1–2 hours): 300 calories
Example, energy bar and banana or the equivalent in a recovery drink
Endurance (3 hours or more): 400 calories or more
Example, energy bar and bagel with sliced turkey or the equivalent in a recovery drink

SPECIAL NUTRITIONAL CONSIDERATIONS

PRE-RACE CARBO BOOSTING

■ For events lasting more than 3 hours, it can be beneficial to take in several hundred more carbs than usual 24 hours to several days prior to your event in combination with a few very short bursts of higher intensity training. Liquid sources of carbs work well for this and will not overload your intestines.

HYPONATREMIA

■ Extremely rare but possible in events lasting 4 hours or less.

■ More readily seen in events lasting 8 hours or longer because glycogen depletion is ensured and there is more time to create an imbalance in electrolytes versus fluids versus calories. There is also more time to become mentally unfocused on your eating and drinking plan, which can contribute to the above issues.

■ Prevention requires a sharp focus on balancing fluids and calories continuously during any activity in your training and racing.

SOME CAUSES OF NAUSEA

■ Imbalance of fluids to calories
■ Dehydration, or lack of adequate *plain* water intake
■ Incorrect foods or fluids for your body or lack of proper absorption of foods and fluids
■ Nervousness
■ Salt- or lake-water ingestion
■ Too many carbs (with an absence of protein, fat, or plain water)
■ Improper pacing (i.e., going out too fast or sustaining a pace that is beyond your current fitness level)
■ Doing an event longer than 12–15 hours. The longer your race the more you will need to fine-tune your nutrition plan as stomachs generally become unhappy over extended periods of time. Experiment with different fuel types and pay attention.
■ None of the above
■ All or some of the above

SOME CAUSES OF CRAMPING

- Dehydration
- Imbalance of electrolytes
- Imbalance or inadequate amounts of calories and/or fluids
- Imbalance of flexibility or strength in a given area, inducing cramping with a sustained workload
- Inappropriate pacing
- Hyper-fatigue, relative to the length and difficulty of the activity and your fitness level (i.e., going out too fast or sustaining a pace that is beyond your current fitness level)
- Hyper-fatigue in a specific muscle group due to compensation issues in biomechanics
- Hyponatremia
- General inefficient biomechanics (neuromuscular strain or central nervous system fatigue)
- Burning protein for fuel in the absence of carbohydrates (refer to imbalance or inadequate amounts of calories and/or fluids)
- None of the above
- All or some of the above

It is vital to spend some time refining your nutrition plan, especially if you suffer from some of the special considerations listed above. If you tend to cramp or get nauseated during events, you are in good company, but you need to figure out why. Use this information to help you sort out why these are problem areas for you. This process will take time, but every athlete I have seen who puts in this time has reaped the rewards with a cramp- and nausea-free event.

SUPPLEMENTS

One of the million dollar questions in sport is whether you should supplement your diet with vitamins, or minerals, or other. I'll give this question a million bucks because it is complex and the vast array of opinions on this topic can be confusing. In short, my opinion is yes.

After studying and discussing eating habits with many athletes and non-athletes as well as being a shopping cart voyeur, I can categorize myself as a healthy eater. I tend to stick to whole, fresh foods, a lot of veggies, fruits, whole grains, and lean cuts of beef, chicken, and fish. I rarely venture down the frozen food aisle unless I'm looking for the occasional ice cream fix—but even that purchase tends to be unprocessed and "natural." I frequent farmers markets, shop organic, and hit up the yacht harbor or fish market for the fresh catches of the day. I take full advantage of these privileges year-round.

But despite my food selections, I am still not getting all the nutrients I need as an athlete because in general the food we eat these days is not 100 percent packed full of what it is supposed to be packed full of. So to ensure I am getting all I need to function optimally without having to eat thousands of calories to get it, I take a full-spectrum or multi-vitamin supplement.

To add a few more cents of opinion into this million dollar question, in addition to full-spectrum vitamins, there are many supplements on the market that may or may not give you an edge athletically. Can you go faster, recover better, and get stronger from legal supplements? Maybe. If you try a product and you feel it is working to your advantage, then it probably is, and I would recommend you continue taking it. If you don't notice any change, keep your money in the bank. Supplements can be expensive and may or may not help you. Experiment with different products and pay attention— all the while making sure you are keeping your daily nutrition regime fresh and whole.

A full-spectrum vitamin can go a long way in this era of subpar food production. Additional performance-specific supplements may also help your endurance; if you feel they do not, save your money for that new racing wheel set you've been eyeing.

THE FOURTH DISCIPLINE OF TRIATHLON: NUTRITION BY KIMBERLY MUELLER

Whether you are gearing up for your first triathlon or are a seasoned athlete, staying on top of your race-day nutrition will contribute to a more enjoyable experience and allow you to reach your performance peak.

SIP FLUIDS LEADING UP TO RACE START.

Unless you plan on swallowing the lake or ocean you are swimming in (not recommended), it is essential to be properly hydrated going into the swim leg, especially in Ironman competition where total time without fluids and the consequent risk for dehydration—the number one performance inhibitor among endurance athletes—are greater. Aim to drink 8 ounces of fluids every half hour leading up to race start. Athletes racing in hot environments should be sipping a salt-containing beverage like a sports drink; sodium ingested pre-workout has recently been shown to delay the onset of muscle fatigue by as much as 20 percent.

TRANSITION ONE IS NOT TIME FOR A BUFFET.

Overconsumption of solid calories like energy bars, highly concentrated drinks, or energy gels in the first transition can be detrimental to cycling performance. Many triathletes will exit the water a little bit in the hole with respect to hydration, which makes absorption of solid calories tough leading into the bike leg and may even contribute to premature muscle cramping since fluids ingested will be directed to the belly to aid breakdown of the solid calories rather than lubricating your "dry" muscles. Furthermore, with blood and oxygen also being diverted to the belly to aid in digestion, you may feel dead-legged, and your pedal

Kim fuels well to finish fast at the Big Kahuna.

stroke efficiency and power output may diminish. When hydrating in transition one and during the initial stages of a bike leg, focus on fluids containing no more than 20 grams of carbohydrates per 8 ounces to aid rehydration after the swim and promote optimal absorption of calories.

DON'T TRY TO REPLACE 100 PERCENT OF THE CALORIES YOU ARE EXPENDING ON THE BIKE.

Sometimes I am amazed at the strategic placement of food on the bike with my most hysterical observation being when a female triathlete pulled a chicken drumstick out of her sports bra. Many triathletes, especially during long-course training, admit that they are scared of running out of energy on the bike and consequently they consume an immense amount of food only to find themselves with serious stomach issues on the run. For most triathletes, a calorie replacement regimen of 150–300 calories for every hour beyond 60 minutes of racing is ideal. Be sure to take account of all calories ingested including bars, bananas, sports drinks, gels, and so on.

PRACTICE DRINKING "ON THE RUN."

As your race progresses, body heat continues to rise as does the sun, which means sweat rate is generally at its peak during the run leg in a triathlon. As many seasoned triathletes know, race performance can spiral downhill pretty fast during the run leg, especially when dehydration rears its ugly head. Make sure to become very efficient at drinking on the run. Some techniques that may need to be practiced as means to promote hydration include minimizing spillage when grabbing the cup at aid stations (try pinching the cup) and carrying hydration devices such as fuel belts, Camelbaks, and water bottles. On average, athletes require approximately a liter of fluid per hour, although sweat rates can vary immensely.

BE WARY OF SOLID CALORIES DURING THE RUN LEG.

Stomach sensitivities are heightened during the run, partially due to dehydration but mainly to the jarring nature of running. In my practice, I have found symptoms such as nausea, diarrhea, side stitches, and cramping that arise during the run leg are more prevalent in athletes trying to ingest primarily solid calories (gels/bars/fruit/cookies) rather than focusing on sports drinks that contain an optimal carbohydrate concentration for absorption. If you choose to use solids on the run, make sure you consume water as well to ensure optimal absorption. For every 20 grams of carbohydrate (the average for most gels) ingested, aim at consuming 8–12 ounces of water.

Kimberly Mueller, MS, RD, is a Registered Sports Dietitian, competitive endurance athlete, and owner of Fuel Factor Nutrition (www.Fuel-Factor.com), a company dedicated to customized meal planning and race nutrition coaching.

CHAPTER 8

Strength Training and Flexibility

"Strength does not come from physical capacity. It comes from an indomitable will."

Mahatma Gandhi

When I was a young runner, I was fortunate to have a smart, forward-thinking coach who believed in the benefits of strength training for endurance athletes. I learned early on how amazing it felt to be fit and strong. I recall my endurance and speed while leading my high school girls' cross-country team to many victories, but mostly I remember my strength. My team used to have regular pull-up and bench press contests. The coach crafted the competitions to make them fun. We enjoyed showing off by flexing our young muscles for photos—we were tough and unbeatable and we thrived on our strength.

Even though I heard many voices as a young girl warning "your uterus might fall out if you run too much," or "don't let your muscles get too big or you won't be able to get a date," I solidly knew that my uterus never faltered from a hard workout, and that the really cool boys loved the girls with muscles—and the confidence that came with them.

I went on to run in college before I got hooked on triathlon. Though I continued to train in swim, bike, and run post-graduation,

my strength training was hit or miss for several years, due to time constraints. During one winter of base training leading into my fourth Ironman race, I started getting up that extra hour earlier to include some core strength and resistance training into my program. I went into that early season race in New Zealand making no significant changes to my training program except the inclusion of consistent strength work two times per week. The result: I blew the doors off what I thought I could do at that race distance with a 30-minute improvement in my run split alone (from 3:45 down to 3:15).

But even better than the time improvement, I felt amazing during the race. I had a deep reserve of strength I had never felt prior. I kept asking myself at various points during the run, "Can you go faster given X miles to go?"—the answer was always yes, and I'd open myself to a bit more speed and stride. That event showed me a strength I didn't know existed and offered me the confidence to go after even faster times in my career as a triathlete.

As an endurance athlete, strength

Terri enjoying a solid Ironman finish

training helps you maintain muscular balance and power, as well as prevent injuries by offering stability to joints, tendons, and ligaments. Gaining muscle increases your metabolism, which helps you burn fat and aids your sport-specific workouts and performances. It also offers you an opportunity to get in touch with the weak spots on your body and focus a bit more effort toward those areas to balance your power. And most important, your physical strength helps your mind get behind your mental strength. If you believe you can believe, you will believe. Strength can give you that.

THE NUTS AND BOLTS OF STRENGTH TRAINING

- Strength training helps prevent injuries by establishing a foundational strength base.
- Strength training creates a sense of stability and balance that in the long run will allow you to stress your body further, therefore creating a more solid training effect going into events. In short, you'll get more from your workouts.
- Strength reserves help you mitigate any fatiguing effects from prior efforts (swim and bike) during your race or event.
- Strength training gives you an extra edge toward the middle to end of races. You have more strength reserves to draw from and, therefore, can hold pace better when it comes down to the wire.
- Depending on how strength training is specifically incorporated, it can help

with speed, endurance, and power in your training and racing.
- Strength training promotes muscle growth, which promotes a quickening of the metabolism.
- More strength allows you to improve your swimming, biking, and running as well as the combination of the three.

STRENGTH TRAINING GUIDELINES

- Lifting three times per week is optimal; two times per week is effective, and once a week can be basic maintenance.
- Three sets per exercise is optimal; two sets per exercise is effective.
- Strength-building training generally involves heavier weights and fewer repetitions (reps) per set (6–10). This is effective for pre-season base training to establish a solid foundation.
- Endurance-building training involves circuit training, super-sets, or training in which you use lighter weights and more reps per set (12–18). This is valuable for endurance-based athletes during their season.
- Power-building training involves a more explosive movement within an exercise. The weights and reps depend on the kind of shape you're in and your experience with this type of training. Power training is generally reserved for sports with explosive movements such as sprinting but can be quite helpful for cycling. If you consider adding power training, consider consulting with a strength training professional, as

proper form is key to getting results and remaining uninjured.

- I generally recommend super-sets with any of the above training types. Super-sets group two to three exercises together and alternate them until all sets are complete before moving on to another group of exercises. For example, combine lat pull down, bench press, and upward row. The main advantage of super-sets for triathletes is that it is very time efficient and allows for an active recovery between sets. You can move through your workout with virtually no downtime while still gaining adequate recovery for each muscle group.

- Warm up with some light cardiovascular activity before picking up the weights. I like to do my weights after I have completed my other workouts, so I have more to give in my swim, bike, and run workouts.

- Make sure you stretch after the entire workout.

- You may feel a bit tired in your other workouts from your weight training, but remember, the big picture is the event. The fatigue you endure now will pay off in the long run.

ADDITIONAL THOUGHTS ON ADDING A STRENGTH TRAINING PROGRAM

Weight training is a valuable tool in enhancing your performances as an endurance athlete. However, I realize that as athletes with jobs, families, and other responsibilities, your time is limited. You need to decide whether it is feasible to add an additional 2–3 hours of training time onto your week. Here are some options.

Better than nothing. Start weights during the winter base training period, and only lift for three to four months. As the race season begins, drop the weights completely.

Better option. Start weights three times per week during the winter base training period, and continue lifting once or twice a week during the season. Eliminate weights completely the week before big events.

STRENGTH TRAINING COMPONENTS

Your strength training program should include the right balance of the following ingredients:

Strength training (weights): To help promote the recruitment of the desired muscle that is being exercised.

Reps: To help develop muscle endurance and improve neuro-pathways to the muscles.

Perfect form: To optimally use the desired muscles and prevent injury.

Eccentric control: The lengthening portion of the muscle contraction (lowering the weight back to the starting position) helps the body adapt to gravity in the weight-bearing position. This is needed in running and provides balance in all activities.

Best option. Start weights during the winter base training period, and come racing season, continue a program of consistent strength training, offsetting your gym time with a home program of plyometrics (see Plyometrics for Endurance Athletes later in this chapter) and core strength.

BASIC STRENGTH TRAINING EXERCISES

Below is a list of exercises you can use to create a complete strength training program in a gym facility. To give you some options, I list several exercise options for one muscle group, but it is only necessary for you to do one exercise for two to three sets within each muscle group.

If any of these exercises or machines are unfamiliar, consult a trainer at the facility where you work out. If you have never lifted weights, hire a personal trainer for one or two sessions to help you with form and equipment. Ask the staff at your fitness club for a recommendation.

ABDOMINALS/CORE

1 Ab crunches

Four positions on bench. 1) Knees bent with feet on bench, arms crossed at chest, use abs to lift head and shoulders off bench. 20 reps. 2) Knees bent with feet on bench, hands behind but not holding head, elbows out, use abs to lift head and shoulders off bench. 20 reps. 3) Left knee bent with foot on bench, right leg extended with foot turned out and elevated 6 inches off bench, hands behind head with elbows out, use abs to lift head and shoulders off bench and twist toward the right leg. Raise the right leg 6 inches while you crunch. 20 reps. 4) Repeat 3) with left leg raised instead. 20 reps.

2 Hanging ab curls

Hanging from an elevated straight bar with your upper arms in straps, bend your knees as you lift them toward your chest. Prevent

your body from swaying after each rep by using your core for stability. 3 sets of 10.

3 Push-ups/extensions using an exercise ball

A) Lay over the ball on your stomach and walk your hands out until your knees, shins, or ankles are on the ball and you are in push-up position (walk your arms in closer to the ball to lessen the challenge). Do five push-ups. B) Stay in push-up position but bring your hands right under your shoulders. With straight arms roll the ball and your bent knees toward your chest. Your pelvis will naturally rise into the air. Do this five times. C) Walk your hands back until your abdominals are on the ball. Extend your legs straight up and behind you. Do this five times. The three exercises above are one set. 3 sets.

4 Push-ups

Do full-body push-ups only if you can comfortably keep your entire spine straight and hips even with your spine, while moving into the bent arm position of your push-up. If this feels too challenging, place your

3A

3A

3B

3C

knees on the ground and execute a bent-knee push-up with a straight spine (commonly referred to as women's push-ups). If your knees don't like the pressure of the bent-knee push-up, do a full-body push-up with your hands on a stair or even the curb on your street or the back of your car. The angle lessens the difficulty and allows you to maintain correct form. 3 sets of 15.

5 *Chair sitting while rowing with stretch band*

Use a stretch band with handles and anchor the band around a stationary object that won't move when force is applied (i.e., a

machine at the gym). A) Walk backward from the anchor point until you feel a firm stretch on the band. With your arms extended, slowly come into a squat position—as if you're sitting in a chair. Be sure that your knees do not extend over your toes. B) Pull the band until your elbows are bent at a 90 degree angle while squeezing your shoulder blades together as though you're rowing. 3 sets of 10.

6 *Back extensions with Roman chair*

Enter the "chair" with the pad supporting the front of your upper thighs and locking the lower leg (typically at the ankle) and

bend forward at the waist. Your head will hang close to the ground. Use the muscles of your lower back to straighten your body, extending your upper body upwards. Do not hyperextend your back. 3 sets of 10.

HIPS/PELVIS

7 *Standing hip flexors*

Use a machine with a cable attachment low to the ground that is attached to a weight stack. Attach an ankle strap to the cable and your right ankle. Step away from the weight stack several feet. Stand on your left leg with your back to the weight stack and

bend your right knee up and toward your stomach (as if you are doing a high knee running motion). Work up to doing this exercise without hanging onto anything for stability; this will help you work balance in the opposing leg. 3 sets of 10 on each leg.

8 *Standing hip extensors*

Using the same machine as above, face the weight stack, and attach an ankle strap to your right leg. Start with your feet together, then push the right foot back and up (in the running motion) behind you. Push as far as you can while staying upright. Again, work up to doing this exercise without hanging onto anything for stability. 3 sets of 10 on each leg.

9 Adductors

Using the same machine as above, stand a few feet away with your right side to the machine. Attach the ankle strap to your right leg, and stand on your left leg with a slight bend in your knee. Pull the right leg across the front of your left leg. Hold onto the machine for balance. 3 sets of 10 on each leg.

10 Abductors

Using the same machine as above, stand a few feet away with your left side to the machine. Attach the ankle strap to your right leg, and stand on your left leg with a slight bend in your knee. Let your right leg cross the front of your left leg to start. Pull the right leg back across the front of your left leg and then out to the right side as far as you can lift it. Hold onto the machine for balance. 3 sets of 10 on each leg.

QUADRICEPS

11 Leg press

There are many variations on the leg press machine. Look at the instructions on the machine that your gym has available. Do a set of presses with your left leg only coming down to a 90 degree angle, and then do a set with your right leg only. 3 sets of 10 on each leg.

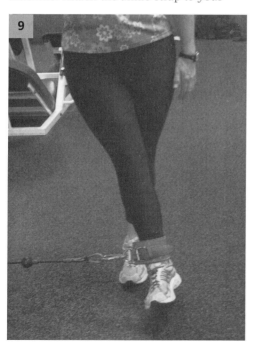

12 Smith rack squats

Stand with your feet slightly wider than shoulder-width apart and rest the bar on your upper back and rear shoulders. Grip the bar with your hands spaced evenly apart and un-rack the weight by pushing the bar up and twisting the hooks. Begin the movement by bending at the knees and squatting toward the ground with your back straight. Continue to lower yourself until your thighs are parallel to the ground. Once you reach the bottom, drive the weight back up until you are in a standing position. 3 sets of 10.

HAMSTRINGS

13 Leg curls

Lying facedown on the bench with the pad behind your ankles, bend your legs to curl the weight up. Do a set of curls with your left leg only and then your right leg only. 3 sets of 10 on each leg.

GASTROC/SOLEUS

14 *Calf raises*

You can use the calf raise machine or find a platform or stair step and stand on the edge so the balls of your feet bear the weight of your body. Lower your heels as far as you can and then raise yourself up onto your toes. That is one rep. 3 sets of 10.

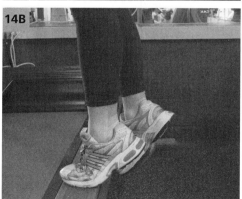

LATISSIMUS DORSI

15 *Lat pulldowns*

Sit facing the machine and grasp the bar above you. Pull the bar down to your chest. Change the position of your hands—wide, medium, and narrow grip—on the bar for each set. 3 sets of 10.

16 *Pull-ups*

Start in a dead-hang and grasp the bar with an overhand grip. Pull your body up until your chin clears the bar, and finish by lowering the body until arms and shoulders are fully extended. As needed, use a pull-up-assisted machine for this exercise. 3 sets of as many as you can do.

PECS

17 *Dumbbell press*

Standing with a dumbbell in each hand, swing them up to your chest and hold them there while you sit and then lie down on the bench. Once you are in position on your back, bring the dumbbells to the front of your shoulders, palms facing your feet. Press the dumbbells up above your chest keeping your shoulders down and palms facing your feet, and then lower them back down to the start position. That is one rep. 3 sets of 10.

18 *Bench press*

While lying on your back on a flat bench, lower a straight bar with weight attached to the level of the chest, then push it back up until the arm is straight. 3 sets of 10.

DELTOIDS

19 *Slightly bent-arm flies*

Standing with feet shoulder-width apart, bend your knees slightly and lean forward slightly from the hips. Hold the dumbbells in front of your quads with your palms facing your body and your elbows slightly bent, lift your upper arms to the side of your body until your elbows are even with your shoulders—the dumbbells will follow and remain slightly lower than your elbows. Return to the start position. That is one rep. 3 sets of 10.

20 *Shoulder press with dumbbells*

Sit straight up on a bench with back support holding a dumbbell in each hand. Bring dumbbells up to rest on the top, front of your shoulders. Extend your arms and press the dumbbells up to touch above your head. Lower them back to shoulder height. Repeat. 3 sets of 10.

BICEPS

21 *Curls*

Use dumbbells or attach a straight bar or curl bar to a cable system low to the ground. Grasp the bar with both hands at each end with palms facing the machine, and stand with arms extended so the bar is in front of your thighs. Curl the bar up to your chest area. Lower to the start position. That is one rep. 3 sets of 10.

TRICEPS

22 *Tricep extensions*

Attach a straight bar or curl bar to a cable system high off the ground. Grasp the bar with both hands with palms facing the ground, and stand with your elbows bent by your sides and the bar in front of your chest. Leaning slightly into the weight stack, extend your arms to straight then return to the start position. That is one rep. 3 sets of 10.

23 *Tricep extensions with straight arm option*

At the end of a set of tricep extensions, move right into the straight arm option— take one step back from the machine and extend your arms overhead. Pull the bar down to your thighs with straight arms. That is one rep. Do 5 reps within each set of your tricep extensions.

Here is an example of how you can implement this program in total:

Ab Crunches plus super-set the following groups of exercises:

- leg press, leg curl, calf raise
- lat pull down, dumbbell press, bent-arm flies
- tricep extension, bicep curl
- hanging ab curls, push-up extensions using an exercise ball, chair sitting while rowing with stretch band
- standing hip flexors, standing hip exten- sors, abductors, adductors

THE POSITIVES ON NEGATIVES

Eccentric or "negative" strength training is a technique that is often used in the rehabili- tation and prevention of injuries, and many feel it can be a key to strength training for endurance athletes looking for benefits over long-duration events.

Each strength training exercise has a lifting (positive or concentric) phase and a lowering (negative or eccentric) phase. For optimal growth and response, your muscles actually need both. Most athletes empha- size the lift portion of their weight training and let gravity do the work of lowering the weight. By moving slowly through your range of motion during both phases of the lift, you are working the muscles eccentrically as well as concentrically and thus optimally for endurance sports.

For negative-emphasized reps, the lift should take two to three seconds, followed by a controlled three to four seconds in the negative or lowering phase. You may experience more muscle soreness with eccentric training, especially if you solely do negative-focused exercises.

If you are strength training two times a week, do one session of positive-focused lifting, and one session emphasizing the negative of each exercise. This is a sure way to see optimal results for your gym time.

PLYOMETRICS FOR ENDURANCE ATHLETES

In the 1970s, plyometrics was credited for the growing number of Eastern Europeans winning international track and field events. Coaches and athletes around the world rapidly became aware of them as exercises aimed at linking strength with speed through a full range of motion to produce power.

Plyometrics can help maximize power in the stretching and shortening cycle of a muscle or muscle group. They also promote reflex power through a broader range of motion than that which most endurance athletes experience. The balance-strength aspect of the movements allows for the development of optimal efficiency within a muscular range. These exercises also train

an athlete to absorb shock better and therefore define and redefine resiliency in the joints and soft tissue.

Plyometrics can also help train the aerobic system to better train the anaerobic system. If you take an already aerobically fit athlete and implement plyometrics, the potential is to expand their anaerobic base. It's like strength training for the aerobic and, therefore, the anaerobic system.

These exercises should be combined with a sport-specific training program and should be done only twice a week on nonconsecutive days. An optimal training situation is to combine plyometrics with a standard resistance-training program and a cardiovascular program. Healthy, uninjured, and fit athletes should take on a plyometric program only as a supplement to an established training program. A program starts with just a couple of exercises and builds on those each week. If done properly, you will get sore your first couple of weeks!

Here are a couple basic plyometric exercises to get you started. Using the guidelines above, start with 2 sets of 10 reps for each exercise.

24 Walking lunges

These are considered a warm-up or drill for the more dynamic exercises. Step out with your right foot far enough in front of you so your knee is bent at a 90 degree angle and over the heel. Lunge down with your left leg slightly bent behind you, until your left knee almost touches the ground. Lift your

body up and over the right foot, without pause, then step out and lunge in the same manner with the left foot. Use your arms as needed for power and balance while focusing on the quads and glutes. For those with knee weakness or issues, modify by only bending the knee to a 30–40 degree angle to start.

25 Side-shuffle lunges

The motion in this exercise is similar to skipping sideways. A) Step to the side with your right foot so your feet are slightly wider than shoulder width and go into a full squat as if sitting in a chair, your arms will naturally want to move to the front of your body. B) In one dynamic motion, extend your legs while shuffling your right foot to the right, shuffling your left foot to where the right foot was, and placing the right foot so your feet are slightly wider than shoulder width. Squat again, extend, and shuffle to the right and

repeat the motion. A full set is a continuous motion of squatting, extending, and shuffling. Alternate leading legs on each set.

Combining plyometrics with some upper body and core strength work will round out a full body home exercise program.

SAMPLE STRENGTH TRAINING PROGRAM YOU CAN DO AT HOME

If you just can't get yourself, your pocketbook, or your schedule to accommodate consistent gym time—no worries—with a few choice pieces of gear, you can maintain solid strength in the comfort of your living room, backyard, local park, or hotel room.

Equipment: Exercise ball, stretch band with two handles.

Exercises:
- Push-ups: 3 x 15.
- Ab crunches: 100 total. 4 positions, 25 reps each position.
- Ball push-ups/extensions using an exercise ball: 3 sets of 10.
- Chair sitting while rowing with stretch band: 3 sets of 10.
- Walking lunges: 3 sets of 10.
- Side-shuffle lunges: 3 sets of 10.

The following is an example of how you can implement this program in total:

Ab Crunches plus super-set the following groups of exercises:
- walking lunges, side shuffle lunges, push-ups
- ball exercises, stretch band exercise, ab crunches

25A

25B

FLEXIBILITY FOR RECOVERY AND PERFORMANCE

Stretching not only allows you the range of motion needed to optimize the power in your muscles, but it feels great—kind of like taking care of an itch that needs to be scratched. I'm a believer in the adage "use it or lose it," especially as you age. For middle-aged and older athletes, the "use it" part isn't just about endurance and strength, it's about flexibility as well. As you can see, it is important to stretch.

STRETCHING FOR ENDURANCE ATHLETES

Let's take a look at a few basics to learn how to do it safely as well as a bit of motivation to do it consistently.

Why Stretch?

Stretching is useful for injury prevention, injury treatment and maintaining range of motion, as well as getting in touch with your body daily. If done properly, stretching increases flexibility, and can translate to reduction of injury. A muscle tendon group with a greater range of motion when used passively, as in stretching, will be less likely to experience tears when used actively, as in running. Stretching is also thought to accelerate recovery and can enhance athletic performance.

How to Stretch

There are three general methods of stretching: static, ballistic, and proprioceptive neuromuscular facilitation (PNF). Static is the method recommended for the majority of athletes since it is the least likely to cause injury, and it can be done solo. Ballistic (bouncing) is ill advised, and PNF stretching is probably best reserved for those who are experienced with its use. This section will focus on the static method.

To get the most benefit from your static stretching routine while minimizing injury, stretch in conjunction with your workout after warm-up exercises. The warm-up increases blood flow to each muscle, which enables you to then stretch more easily and with less risk of injury. In static stretching, you slowly move a joint toward its end range of motion. You should feel a gentle "pulling" sensation in the targeted muscle. Hold this position for 40–60 seconds. Do not stretch to the point of pain, and do not bounce. Within a session, each subsequent stretch of a particular muscle group gives progressively more flexibility. Alternate between agonist and antagonist muscle groups (e.g., quadriceps and hamstrings) and alternate sides, right to left.

Stretching should also be done after the workout or in the evening at the end of your day. The post-workout stretch is thought to aid in recovery from the workout. Consult a health care professional or your coach before stretching an injured area.

Why Am I So Tight?

There is considerable variation in baseline flexibility between individuals. There may also be variation within a given individual (e.g., flexible shoulders but inflexible hips or flexible right hamstring but tight, inflexible left hamstring). Genetics, injuries, and asymmetrical biomechanics all play a role in these differences. One shouldn't try to make big gains in flexibility in a short period of time. Stretching should be increased gradually over weeks or months and then maintained to prevent slipping back toward inflexibility. Some people will enthusiastically embark on a stretching program but then quit two weeks later because they haven't seen any benefit. Be patient and consistent. It takes a long time, but the rewards are worth it.

Relax

It is very important to relax during the stretching routine. It should not be a rushed event. Some athletes employ mental imagery while stretching or use breathing to enhance a stretch. In this relaxed state, the athlete visualizes proper form and deeply inhales and exhales while moving deeper into a stretch.

How Do I Find Time to Stretch?

It's easy to neglect stretching due to time constraints, yet it's just as simple to fit it into a down moment in your daily life. Consider stretching while you are on the phone, hanging out with family, or while relaxing and reading. Stretching is an excellent way to wind down your day, relax, and put you in the mood to gain solid sleep.

STRETCHING ROUTINES

26   *Tricep and side stretch*

Grab your elbow with the opposite hand and gently push the elbow up and behind your head until your hand reaches down your back. Gently nudge your elbow to guide your hand down your back as far as it will comfortably go, stretching your triceps and shoulders.

27   *Standing side stretch*

Stand with your feet shoulder-width apart. Clasp your hands overhead while maintaining a straight spine and hips. Stretch toward the sky and bend from the hips slightly to

29 *Chest stretch*

Stand with your hands clasped behind your back. Keeping your hips and spine straight and your shoulders down, slowly raise your hands behind you.

the right. With arms continually extended, move through center and bend to the left.

28 *Upper back and shoulder stretch*

Grab your right forearm or wrist with your left hand and gently pull your arm across your body and in front of your chest. Keep your shoulders down and spine and hips straight. Repeat with left arm.

30 *Lying spinal twist*

Lie on your back with your arms out to the side and legs straight. Bend your right leg toward your chest and then over to the left side while keeping your shoulders on the ground as much as possible. Place your left hand on the outside of your right knee to further the stretch and turn your head to the right. Repeat on left side.

31 *Low back stretch*

Lie on your back with your knees bent and hug your legs into your chest.

32 *Low back extension*

Lie on your stomach with your legs straight and your hands next to your shoulders. Keeping your hips on the ground and your shoulders down, press yourself up with a slight arch in your lower back.

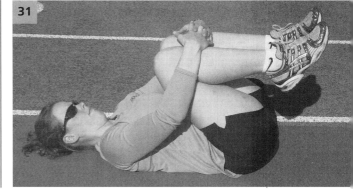

33 *Standing spinal twist*

Standing and holding onto a tree, fence, or wall, slowly turn your lower body to the left, away from what you're holding while maintaining your upper body position. Keep your spine straight and long. Do the same on the right side.

34 *Sitting spinal twist*

Sit on the ground with your legs straight out in front of you. Bend your right leg and cross it over the left so your foot is on the ground near your knee. Place your left arm on the outside of the right knee to accentuate the stretch and place your right hand behind while looking to the right. Change legs and repeat.

35 *Standing or sitting groin stretch*

Standing with your feet wide (3–4 feet apart), fold your arms at the elbows, or place your hands on your quads, and with a straight spine, bend forward from the hips. For back support, keep your hands on your upper quads. To enhance the stretch, let your arms and hands move toward the ground. You can also do this stretch while sitting with your legs spread apart. In both variations, keep your spine straight and bend from the hips.

36 *Seated groin stretch #2*

Sit with the soles of your feet together. With your elbows on the inside of your knees and your spine straight, gradually lean forward from the hips and gently press your knees toward the ground.

37 *Lunge for hip flexors and psoas*

In a lunge position with your right leg straight behind you and your left leg bent at a 90 degree angle, place your hands on the inside of your left leg. Hip flexors and psoas are stretched by keeping the toe of the trailing leg pointed straight down as you drop your knee to the ground and tuck your tail bone under. To enhance this stretch, move your torso into an upright position, keeping your hips and spine in straight alignment, and raise your arms overhead. Repeat with opposite leg.

38 *Lying hip stretch*

On hands and knees, extend your right leg back. Pivot and rotate the left leg underneath you. Slide the right leg farther back while keeping your hips level. Move onto your hands, forearms, or chest, whichever allows for a safe yet effective stretch. Repeat with opposite leg.

39 *Hip stretch #2*

Sitting cross-legged on the ground, lift your right leg so the knee is pointing up and cross it over the left, which should remain bent. Keeping your spine tall, hug the right leg to your chest, or place your hands on the ground behind you for support. Repeat with left leg.

40 *Standing quad stretch*

Stand on one foot, with a hand on an object for balance if needed. Hold the top of your foot with the opposite hand and raise the heel of the lifted foot to the buttocks (or as close as comfortably possible) to stretch your quadriceps. Keep both knees close together and your spine and hips in a straight line throughout. Repeat with opposite leg.

41 *Sitting quad stretch*

Sit on the ground with your legs crossed. Lift your right bent leg and rotate it outward so that it is lying on the ground and your right knee is touching the bottom of your left foot. With a straight spine, place your hands on the ground behind yourself and lean back to stretch your quad. Repeat with left leg.

42 Lying hamstring stretch

Lie down on your back with your right leg
straight up in the air and the left leg extended and flat on the ground. Loop a towel
or strap over the arch of the right foot, and
gently pull on the towel until you feel a
gentle stretch in your hamstring. Repeat
with left leg.

43 Standing hamstring stretch

Place your right foot on a raised object. The
height of the object will depend on how
flexible your hamstrings are. Only raise
your leg to a height that allows you to feel a
gentle stretch. Keep your pelvis in a straight
line with your spine. You may feel the
stretch while remaining upright. If so, continue standing upright. If you need more of
a stretch, lean slightly forward keeping your
spine long and straight. Repeat with left leg.

44

44 *Calf stretch*

Stand about three feet from a wall or fence, feet shoulder-width apart, toes pointing forward. Put your hands on the fence with your arms straight for support. Lean your hips forward with a soft bend in your knees to stretch your calves. You can also do this stretch one leg at a time for a more focused effect.

45 *Standing calf stretch #2*

Stand on a curb or step and drop your right heel just to the point of tension while relaxing your calf. Repeat with left heel.

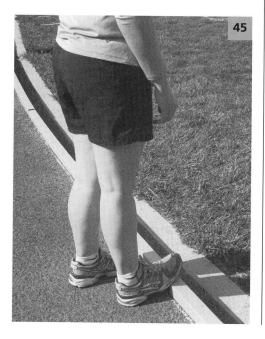

FULL STRETCHING ROUTINE

Done in total, the Full Stretching Routine covers all the major muscle groups and should be done in some part at least once per day. To shorten this routine do one stretch per muscle group. Hold each stretch for 40–60 seconds.

- Tricep and side stretch
- Standing side stretch
- Upper back and shoulder stretch
- Chest stretch
- Lying spinal twist
- Low back stretch
- Low back extension
- Sitting spinal stretch
- Standing or sitting groin stretch
- Seated groin stretch #2
- Lunge for hip flexors and psoas
- Lying hip stretch
- Hip stretch #2
- Standing quad stretch
- Sitting quad stretch
- Lying hamstring stretch
- Standing hamstring stretch
- Standing calf stretch #2

SHORTY STRETCHING ROUTINE

This routine covers all the major muscle groups and can be done before, during, or after a workout. Hold each of these stretches for 40–60 seconds.

- Standing spinal twist
- Standing side stretch
- Standing hamstring stretch
- Calf stretch
- Standing quad stretch
- Standing groin stretch

I SUCK AT YOGA BUT I KEEP DOING IT ANYWAY

If there is an activity for which I'd definitely get picked last for a team, it would be yoga. After spending most of my life in a forward plane of motion, I have come to terms with my partially frozen hip joints and virtual lack of lateral rotation in my spine. But at the onset of my triathlon career, in an attempt to put a chisel to the solidifying body parts and in order to gain speed and range of motion, I started doing yoga.

Of the various types of yoga practices, I gravitated toward Iyengar yoga. Not only because it focuses on precise body alignment, balance, and spinal extension, but because I didn't want to be in motion—or sweat—any more than I already was in my training. For me, Iyengar yoga offered a means to gain an intimate understanding of my body as connected to my mind in a different medium than swim, bike, run. I used the time to visualize my open, fluid body in a race as well as become more in tune with the nuances of how my body was feeling.

Though my yoga instructor (whom I privately labeled the "Yoga Nazi") tried diligently to convert me to full time yoga practice, yoga always was and still is an excellent means to an end in my endurance life. I will never come close to even a partial half lotus pose (my top knee sticks up almost vertical), but despite my inadequacies, I continue to show up because yoga keeps me in the game I love—the world of endurance sport.

I'm pretty sure body parts would have started to fall off a long time ago without even my irregular yoga practice. I may get laughed off the yoga team, but perhaps we can learn something from each other.

CHAPTER 9

The Mental Game

"The essential nature of the mind is pure and untainted by negative emotions. Since negative emotions are not intrinsic, [there is a possibility to eliminate them] and purify the mind."

His Holiness the Dalai Lama

In mastering "the mental game" in endurance sports, you come to realize that there is no such thing as "potential" for a long-time endurance athlete. Potential implies an ending place. Engaging in the mental game in sport teaches you that your intellectual and emotional growth as an athlete is limitless. Your body may age and slow, but if you train your mind, you can choose to enhance and find satisfaction in your endurance life indefinitely.

There are many facets to developing your mental game for triathlon. This chapter will show you the possibilities of how mental training can play out with a real life story. You'll see the unparalleled role that confidence plays in your mental game. Putting your mental training in practice, you'll learn about developing a relationship with your goals as well as highlight the possibility of stretching beyond your goals. You'll identify how to use self-talk and imagery in your mental game, as well as address a particular sticking point in endurance sport—creating your best pre-race mental plan. Later in this chapter there are samples of mental training plans you can use for guidance.

MEETING THE MENTAL GAME

A few months before the 1992 Hawaii Ironman World Championships, I pulled my calf muscle while racing the Germany Ironman. En route to a PR (personal record) at the Ironman distance and a blazing run split, my leg came up lame with 5K to go. Despite the pouring rain, I was on fire and too stubborn to let the injured leg stop my race, so I hopped and skipped to the finish, still getting that PR (9:09) and fast run split. I went home to rehab the injury and figure out how best to alter my training plan to accommodate for the downtime in running. All the while I considered the ugly, twisted effect on my psyche that this serious injury imposed, juxtaposed to the looming biggest race of my season. In short, I had been unwittingly thrown, mid-season, into the biggest game in sport—the mental game.

WHEN IN DOUBT, THINK

While dealing with the injury—increasing and refocusing my swim, bike, and strength training and incorporating deep-water running into my program to offset my lack of road running time—I pondered my injury frustration. In light of the compromised leg, was I doing everything I could to get myself to Kona ready to race?

Prior to this injury, over many races and countless hours of solo training, I realized I was someone who naturally paid attention to what was happening in my head during training and races. I observed that on days when my attitude was either positive or rational, I had much better performances than on days when I mentally beat myself up. I had sensed that as humans in the throes of physically brutal endeavors we could guide our thoughts—direct them to orchestrate fine race experiences. So I played with this concept over the years while out there breathing hard and sweating. Now with an injury and a big race looming, I decided it was time to put that theory to the test.

It seemed rational to me at the time that if your brain can learn, then you can teach yourself to direct your thoughts under physical duress, rather than unconsciously open your mind to the whims of your random, sometimes unconstructive internal chatter.

Through trial and research, including observing of a lot of crazy head dialog by myself and others, I developed a mental training program using goal development, self-talk, affirmations, and imagery. I incorporated these regularly into my weekly training program. I thought through my pre-race routine and implemented a mental training program that addressed my nervousness and need for solo time to get my mind wrapped around the task at hand. Most important, I lived my plan daily, weekly, and monthly. While my body was healing, my mind was growing stronger each day.

THINK, SEE, FEEL FOR SPEED

I came up with three word cues I used in training—patience, strength, and flow—and partnered each with a visual and a feeling to personalize a complete experience of patience, strength, or flow. These were words that came to me in my training, words I was naturally attracted to and moved by in some way. Over time they just stuck. I said them to myself when I desired to be in each particular frame of mind. For instance, if I was struggling a bit or felt tight, I would think "flow" and at the same time, picture myself moving in my body in a relaxed and open manner. Each time I thought "flow," I would concentrate on my breath—seeing it as a white light moving through my body. When I said, "flow," the breath initiated the feeling of relaxing for more speed. Focusing on my breathing and the white light, I would sink deeper into my body to generate a feeling of speed with less effort. Using

this type of imagery took some time to fine tune as well as a lot of tough training days in which I had to convince myself blindly that the effort would bear fruit.

Each morning and before I fell asleep at night, I would read several cards on which I had written affirmations for my race. "I am a strong, powerful cyclist" or "I want it more than my competitors" ran through my head each day. Some days I struggled to believe these phrases. I just couldn't feel their meaning, so I'd say them anyway—repetition, repetition, repetition. Repeating these affirmations trained my mind to accept them as truth, and over time I noticed the essence of the phrases entering my thoughts naturally.

In addition to developing my race word cues, I practiced quite a bit of imagery about specific pieces of my upcoming race, especially my finish. With the advantage of having done the race several times, I placed myself on the course during the swim, bike, run, and each transition. While training in open water, on the bike, or in my deep-water running sessions, I pictured myself in the heat and wind of the lava fields, conjuring the feelings I sought: strength, patience, and fluidity. I trained myself to attach the race reel in my mind to the feeling I desired. Over time the visuals and feelings started to transfer into performance. I knew from experience that I couldn't beat the course. We don't win over nature. I was teaching myself to move with the brutal, renowned elements on the Kona coast.

Opposite: "Flow"

HAVE MENTAL TOOLBOX, WILL TRAVEL

Even though I was only able to run on land for several weeks prior to the race, I felt tougher than ever with my fresh, focused mindset. By the time I got to Hawaii, the words "patience," "strength," and "flow" had become instant cues for the frame of mind I wanted to conjure up at any given moment—tools for the mental toolbox I would carry through my race.

The week before the race in Kona, I spent time on certain sections of the run and bike courses, leaving patience, strength and flow vibes and visual cues in the lava fields to connect with as I moved through on race day. The year before, I had struggled immensely in an area of the run called the Natural Energy Lab. The stillness, heat, and placement of this section of the course made it a formidable mental obstacle to the finish line. I spent some time a few days before the race in the Lab area, sitting calmly, feeling the energy there and leaving mine. My motive was to meld with the Lab area, to eliminate struggle and perpetuate flow with the natural environment. With white coral on the black lava, I drew the rune symbols for strength and flow at the turn-around and on the climb out of the Lab.

My place was set. I was ready to take on my race.

Be in the Moment and What Follows Will Follow

My swim and bike were solid. With favorable wind conditions, I clocked 5:02 on the bike and it felt effortless (patience and

Terri en route to a PR

strength). For some reason, my watch had stopped working on the bike, so during the run, I paced myself by intuition and the drive of my newfound tools—patience, strength, and flow.

I observed that my self-talk was either positive or rational throughout the entire event. If I felt a struggle or even the thought of a negative attitude creep in, I would say, "STOP!" and replace that thought with "patience," "strength," or "flow." I checked in with my body constantly, asking, "Can I go faster given the distance remaining?" and answering, "Yes, you have more to give." And I would open up my stride, just a bit, for speed and then lock down on my pace. The more I stayed present to my process, the less I thought about the outcome of the race. If I were in the moment executing at my best, then my best would be my best.

As I rounded the corner just before the finish line on Ali'i Drive, I had no idea what my overall time would be. My motive on the run had been to remain present, hydrate, eat, and use my mental tools to negotiate the tough spots.

A photographer caught me running at the instant I saw my time on the clock and raised my fist in the air for triumph. What I saw was my best time on that particular course (9:29) and that I had wrapped up fourth place in the women's division. Not bad coming off an injury.

These tangible rewards and the paycheck that came with them were a huge perk, but the real treasures of that race were my newfound ability to use my mental tools while remaining present to my race process the entire day. This showed me that as an athlete I had graduated to a new level of maturity, and the growth process was limitless. If I learned one vital piece of info to carry forward it was—never underestimate a trained, potent mind.

SEEKING "IT"

The trained mind is the adhesive that holds together all the aspects of your training and racing life—planning, organizing, and experiencing to create a clear picture. You can try to take the intellect and emotion away from your physical life, but they relentlessly find ways to sneak back in. As an athlete needing to remain motivated, you are also required to think, examine, and ponder the hows and whys of your place in this sport. "Is it possible for me to complete this race?" "Why am I putting so much time and effort toward triathlon?" Trying to separate the mind from the body is like taking away the bonding agent that shapes the theme on a mosaic—without this foundation, the image will never come together clearly.

As you've noticed over the course of training, you have a lot of workouts that feel physically mediocre. You have an additional handful that feel pretty good, and you have that infrequent session that really positively brings together body and mind—you nail it. "It," or this supreme workout experience, feels great physically— maybe effortless, maybe strong, maybe fluid. Though that specific physical feeling disappears once your workout is over, the essence of it lingers in your mind. The memory of it helps motivate you to get out there and put in the time. You continue to seek the same feelings you got from that really amazing workout. This may be a similar sensation that you get from other really great stuff that happens in your life: falling in love, getting a promotion, or winning your age group in a triathlon. All

can make you feel as though you can take on the world.

You may have felt capable in your body on that zenith workout day, but the mental rewards of it extend well beyond your feeling of increased fitness. A peak workout or race offers you a strong sense of efficacy, or belief in your abilities. Repeated experiences can offer you confidence and satisfaction that your hard work is paying off—you start to see yourself as a viable athlete. You may like your body a bit more on that day, and that may lead to a brightening of the attitude you share with others. On that day, you may subconsciously think, "I'm capable and tenacious and others surely can see those qualities too." The chances are they do.

The flip side to the peak workout experience is how your physical life is affected when tile pieces are misplaced or have fallen off due to inadequate mental adhesive. Have you ever had depression or severe trauma shut down your athletic life? Death of a loved one, divorce, or getting fired from a job can literally immobilize a person temporarily. You spend some time on the front end of the misfortune, staring into space until a bit of perspective allows you some breathing room.

Your desire to train comes from the same place as the motivation to live life: a healthy mind. Tenacity, toughness, aspiration, confidence, focus, and more are mental qualities needed to keep playing out your training game. A healthy mental and emotional state is not only necessary to get you out the door in the morning, it is the reason you engage in sport to begin with. Seeking to nurture your mental state is what keeps you in the game. The mental game is the total game, and all of us have the capacity to engage in that game regularly.

In your mental game, are you interested in being the one who calls the shots? And not just on some random or unknown day, but every day? Or are you okay with letting your mental state remain the victim of whim or random chatter driven by past experiences? Do you want to be in charge not just for a sprint triathlon or a track workout, but for the long haul—long training days, the Ironman, or longer? You can. Make time to address your mental game. It will be the highest quality time investment you will choose for your athletic life and your life in total.

THE ELIXIR IN SPORT

I lied when I said there is no such thing as a secret elixir in sport. Motivation, intensity, and focus are all necessary in endurance sports, but there is one asset that is the ultimate driving force for an athlete—confidence. Confidence is the elixir in sport and an extension of your respect for self. But just like many things you strive for in your athletic lives, confidence and authentic self-respect need to be earned, which requires a focused, dynamic course of action.

As an athlete, you can gain confidence by preparing and hitting your training goals, gaining support from others, taking on adverse conditions in your training,

using your self-talk, taking time to enjoy your successes, and regularly acknowledging your strengths as well as your choice to tackle your weaknesses.

You can train your body to complete an international-distance triathlon in under 3 hours, but if you don't believe you can complete the race in this time frame, there's a good chance you won't. If all skills and fitness factors appear equal among two triathletes in a given event, it is the one who has the confidence to come out on top who will.

The true tests of your confidence-building development are the challenges and road blocks you encounter along your confidence-gathering path. There are many experiences that may defy your belief in self. They can be anything from a disappointing day of training, a negative comment thrown out from a friend, a strategic error in a race, to a deep-seated question about your abilities. Developing your confidence in sport and acknowledging the challenges you face in this process is a dynamic game.

One challenge to your confidence comes in the form of voices from your past (or present). Something like, "You'll never amount to anything," or, "You're too old (or too young) to do a triathlon." All athletes are faced along the way with words that don't meet their needs. These voices can test your belief in self.

In encountering this type of roadblock, it's important to remember that others' words are their interpretation of you. Not an accurate representation of your reality. You can hear these voices and choose

CONVERSATIONS WITH DAVE SCOTT: OVERCOMING OURSELVES

Terri: You mentioned that your work ethic helped you as an athlete but sometimes would bite you in the ass as well. Was there anything else that you had to overcome on your way to becoming a top athlete? Mentally, physically, or emotionally?

Dave: The biggest thing always for me is that emotional fine line of being an athlete. At what level can I be an athlete and what are the expectations, or my perception of them, on the outside. When I step off a plane to give a clinic or a talk, I decide that I'm on. I never let my guard down and just be a normal person. I think the public has an expectation, and I have always put that pressure on myself to perform at a certain level. In preparing for races, I needed to uphold that supersonic stature, which is really kind of silly, but I've built it myself.

Dave on his way to another triathlon win

Mentally I could always push the buttons and say, "I want to do this," and I would just do it. It was that willingness to not have to wiggle around. I could say, "If I want this, I'm just going to go after it." The most difficult part for me was not the physical preparation. When people ask me today what I like to do, I still tell them, "Swim, bike, and run." I still get gratification from it.

And I still like to play mental games when I exercise. I swim now with these twenty-year-old race horses, and I never lead my lane, but I still like to stick the needle in them and make sure that they know I'm there. I like the game of looking at the clock and pushing myself, or trying to hang on a ride with a bunch of fast guys. I still enjoy that mental part.

to react to them with a few options: own them as yours, hear them but deflect their meaning, or acknowledge that they do not represent who you are and let them go.

Two additional barriers to gaining confidence are fear and frustration. Fear can cause frustration, and frustration can cause fear—they can be powerful partners. Both can set you into a vicious cycle that will prevent confidence from growing. Facing fear head-on can often force you through the pain and discomfort that may threaten to keep you stuck. If you are deeply gripped, you may even lose a certain level of awareness of your level of confidence. When this happens, come back to what you know, what you have control over. Experience teaches that referring to your current skill level when you are afraid can effectively combat fear.

Choosing to walk through fear and come out on the positive end can be the ultimate

CONVERSATIONS WITH HEATHER FUHR: HITTING THE TOP

Terri: Do you think elite athletes are found or made? Did you wake up one day and say, "I want to be an elite triathlete," or was it something you progressed into?

Heather: I believe that elite athletes are both found and made. I never in a million years thought that I would make a living being a triathlete. It was not something that I set out to accomplish. Having said that, I have been an athlete my entire life, and while I never made the conscious decision to one day be a professional triathlete, being the best athlete I could possibly be was always a goal. An athlete must have that underlying discipline and drive necessary to be a top-level athlete, but then through a lot of hard work, an athlete can be made.

Terri: What happened in your career that allowed you to believe that you could be at the top of the sport?

Heather: Many people believed that I could be at the top of the sport of triathlon before I did. I just kept plugging away and slowly got better and better results. It was really only once I believed myself that I could compete at the top that I then started to actually compete for the top positions. There was not any one event that spurred this, just the confidence that is gained from having good races.

in confidence building. Using your mental training program will help you negotiate your fears and past voices so that you can engage in the challenges you desire. One of the beauties of this process is that once you walk through a fear—running your first 10K, your first open-water swim, signing up for your first triathlon—you need never go back to your existence before you took on that fear.

Fear prevents many people from accomplishing grand experiences in their lifetimes. Facing your fears and completing that first race or ocean swim can give you an overwhelming feeling that you accomplished something great. In standing down fear we gain something that eludes many men and women in their time on earth—a solid sense of self.

MENTAL TRAINING IN PRACTICE

You've learned what mental training and confidence can offer you as a triathlete. This section looks at the nuts and bolts of how to implement your mental training tools through goal development, self-talk, and imagery.

DEVELOPING A RELATIONSHIP WITH YOUR GOALS

In discussing goal development, I'm going to start at what might be your desired goal-setting effect, and then move backward. I'd like to plant in your mind the most important concept of this section—how you can develop an optimal relationship with goals in your life—and then discuss a means to expanding that relationship as a triathlete.

Let Go of the Outcome

It may seem odd to discuss letting go of the outcome when we're talking about obtaining an outcome—a goal. If you have an objective, say, a finish line in a race, you typically have zeroed in on the finish line as your defined outcome goal. Mid-race you may even continue to try and mentally place yourself at the finish when you still have quite a ways to go.

But if there are six aid stations between your current location and the finish line—stations three through eight—then your immediate focus is to get yourself to aid station three as efficiently as possible. What if you let go of the outcome goal for a moment and focus on performing your best to aid station three—checking in with your pace, making sure you are eating and drinking, using word cues to keep you on track in your mind. Executing your best with each step given how you are feeling on that day. In being in each moment to aid station three, you are remaining present to your race process.

Before you get to aid station three, plan what you will do when you arrive—grab water, sports drink, a gel packet, slow your pace to take it all in—then hop back into your race pace once you are past the aid station. After you have performed that plan, continue this planning-performing process through each moment of your race. Trot along, eating and drinking and checking in with your body and your pace, all the while looking forward to your next oasis—aid station four. Create a plan for aid station four, perform it, and keep moving while planning for the next fuel stop. If you are performing your best at each moment, then what happens at the finish line will be your best outcome for that day of racing. Period.

By letting go of the outcome and bringing the process of the race to the forefront of your mind, you are allowing your arrival at the finish to reflect your best performance. Your objective—a positive finish line result—will authentically represent your best shot. The predetermined goal of finishing needs to be present in this process in that it has a healthy relationship to your motivation to finish. Your finishing goal is related to all of your intermittent race process goals, but it does not define your ultimate race experience. The journey is the experience—good, bad, or mediocre. The finish is a moment of that journey.

GOAL GUIDELINES

In letting go of your outcome, you can obtain your best outcome. If you develop a healthy relationship with your journey goals, they can direct you in your training and racing process and keep you on track. These goals can assist you in maintaining focus and attention in all areas of your training process. Within that focus, your goals can continue to set you in motion when your motivation wanes. Keeping that motivation tool in place, here are some initial guidelines to keep in mind when creating your goal-setting groundwork.

Process goals build to outcome goals. Process goals are the stepping-stones to your desired result. The best way to reach a particular outcome goal—like finishing—is to focus on the process. Let go of the outcome and the outcome will come. Process goals also help you stay focused on the skills and race strategy that will help you reach your ultimate goals.

Race process goals might be starting the swim near the front of your wave, consistently executing your established nutrition plan for your race, or checking in on your race pace and adapting on the fly.

Goals should be challenging, but realistic. People thrive on challenge, and many athletes flourish with challenge in their lives. They want to set goals that will stretch them, yet over time, are attainable. Goals that are easy to hit will not give you that sense of satisfaction you gain when really testing yourself, but goals that are unrealistic can be self-defeating. Put your goals out there, but keep them real.

Challenging but realistic goals might be doing an international-distance triathlon after you have completed a sprint, or deciding to do an Ironman after you've completed your first long-course race. You may structure your training to beat a past race time, or you may add some training sessions that are longer or more challenging than you have completed to date.

Set specific goals. Studies shows that specific goals produce higher levels of performance than either lack of goals or just-do-your-best goals. Specific goals can be measurable—hitting a certain time or going a desired distance—or they can involve nailing your weekly training sessions, such as doing all three of your prescribed run sessions for the week as planned. Measurable goals give you a tangible focus and result.

When setting specific goals, look at what you have done historically, make sure the goals are challenging but realistic, and give yourself an adequate amount of time to attain them. For instance, if you just started in triathlon and your goal is to complete an Ironman distance event, you may need a year or more to complete this goal (depending on your background). Or if you are planning to run an off-season marathon and your best time after several tries is 5:15, it may be futile to choose 4:00 as your next time goal.

Focus on how many of your goals you achieve, rather than absolute goal attainment. Though you may not reach all your goals, you will almost always reach a portion of your goals. By reflecting on the degree to which you have reached your goals, you can acknowledge your improvement and success.

If your weekly training goals are to run three times, bike three times, and swim three times, but you only have time in a given week to get in two of those bike rides, don't fret! You are still three runs, two bikes, and three swims closer to your fitness goals. Congrats! Since there are so many variables in your triathlon life, it is quite challenging for all your goals to fall into place in any given week or race. Shoot for absolute goal attainment in your training and race journeys, and reflect regularly on the gains you actually make—all the while knowing that your competitors are most likely just as challenged as you in this regard. Do what you can, then cut yourself some slack.

Goal developing and goal reaching are dynamic and fluid. Goal-setting is a continuous process. When one goal is achieved, reach for another. When you miss the mark on another, adapt and change it up, and then strive again. When a goal isn't motivating or you realize it is unattainable due to time constraints or your physical abilities, redevelop your relationship with that goal. Review your goals regularly, not only during training but during a race. Compare them to your actual progress, and adjust them as needed so they can remain vital

motivation tools. Just as you have trained yourself to be adaptable to the dynamics of your sport, your goals must be adaptable.

Prepare a written contract. Research suggests that goal-setting is most effective when you create it as a contract for yourself. Having your goals on paper keeps you accountable—just like signing up for a race helps you motivate to train. Adjust goals as needed, and log all adjustments. If you are motivated by being accountable to someone else, share your goals with your coach, your training partner, or your spouse.

Take the "Types of Goals" outlined in this chapter and create a contract for each. Date each goal, as well as each revision. Review this information regularly and be open to changing and revising it as needed to keep you present to your real-life journey. Goals are there to help you in your processes, not to instill defeat. Write your contract knowing it is amendable from the outset.

Keep a training log or journal. It is very motivating to spend a few minutes each day writing down your actual daily training. This also helps you develop an honest relationship with your progress, or lack of progress. The log does not lie and can give you critical information as to how you have hit your goals, or why you haven't.

Your log can be your most important training partner. You can look back on the weeks or months before a race in which you were particularly pleased with your result and use the log as a guide to creating a training program for that same event. Or you can look back on your training for an event that didn't go as well as you had hoped. If you journaled about how that race played out, you may be able to see what you could have done better and devise a new race strategy accordingly.

Training logs can also show you why you got injured. Perhaps you overtrained, ramped-up your training too quickly, or waited too long to replace your running shoes. If you log your diet as well, you may be able to see patterns in your performance compared to your food or fluid intake. Your training log is a valuable tool in your goal-developing process, and it helps keep you honest about your efforts and time constraints.

Create action plans for reaching your goals. An action plan tells you specifically how you might go about achieving your goals, giving you specific guidance in this process.

If your goal is to become a faster open-water swimmer, you can create an action plan to include swimming in open water

at least twice a month during the season, taking an open-water swim clinic, getting coaching specific to learning open-water technique, or creating pool swim workouts that can simulate the stresses of open-water swimming.

Behind each goal create a process to achieve that goal. In that development, you are refining your relationship with that goal by integrating it into your life.

Prioritize your event and training goals. You may have time goals, feeling goals, placing goals, and more going into a specific event or training session. Prioritizing goals helps you to keep the most important ones in focus when the going gets tough in a race. You may prioritize them like this: (1) finish the race, (2) finish feeling strong yet spent, (3) execute eating and drinking plan as laid out, (4) get a PR, (5) beat Bob. If you are having a tough race, you may need to zero in on the first goal just to get the job done. If things are going a bit better, you can reach for some of your deeper goals or the ones a bit farther down the list. Prioritizing also helps you keep your racing in perspective—finishing is top priority, beating Bob is a secondary perk.

If you have that weekly training goal of running, biking, and swimming three times a week, you may need to prioritize these workouts if time constraints keep you from completing them all. If swimming is your weakest link and you need to drop a workout, you may choose to drop a bike workout in favor of getting in the water three times. Prioritizing can be defined ahead of time but will also need to work on

a dynamic continuum, just like all other goal processes.

Keep the above guidelines in check as an active part of your goal-setting. You can more specifically define your goals by using the guidelines from the section, "Types of Goals." By categorizing and defining your goals in detail, you are formulating a plan of action for your life as a triathlete. I can't stress enough that this is a dynamic process.

Goals can keep you on track while you refine your training program. They can be that friend that motivates you to be consistent in your weekly training process. And they will teach you to adapt as an athlete when you realize that changing up your goals is sometimes the healthiest process for your training progression.

THE NUMBERS PITFALL

Society is hardwired to have definitive goals and aspirations. Many of these goals involve numbers, and in the sport of triathlon, these numbers can represent a distance covered in a certain amount of time, heart rate, pace over a specified distance, and more. Number goals are important in that they give you tangible information on progress in training and in a race.

For some people, number goals can define how they do their life daily. I believe that aspiring to hit certain numbers is important for athletes. They keep you motivated, organized, and challenged, and these are important qualities to being a successful endurance athlete. But I have seen many athletes, myself included, get sucked into

The Numbers as the fixation that defines the sport experience. If you fixate on numbers when the numbers aren't boding well for you on a given day, you may be ineffective and stress-ridden in trying to hit your goals.

All goals—numbers goals and others—have a dynamic relationship with your race experience. You may get lured into a fixed method of using goals, thinking you are being tough and focused, but you are selling your athletic experiences short and you can end up generating more stress come race day.

For example, if Lori has been training on the bike at an event heart rate that challenges her at an average of 16 mph, she may decide to create a goal to hit that speed in her next sprint triathlon. She locks into this goal and heads to the race only to find that the hills and wind are more than she bargained for. She gets out of the water and heads out on the bike and after a few miles notices that she is only averaging 14.5 mph and her heart rate is at her race rate for that distance.

In assessing her 16 mph number goal mid-race, Lori has a few options:

1. She can give up her cause of hitting her goal speed on the bike and give in to the challenges of the course.

2. She can panic, struggle, and fight with the fact that she is not hitting her goal speed, and in the process eat up a lot of quality energy.

3. She can note that the heart rate she is maintaining is her optimum heart rate for that distance, and that her average speed is down because of the hills and the wind. She can check in on her effort level to see that she is honestly giving it her best, eating and drinking positively, and then let the numbers go.

If Lori chooses option three, she is wisely realizing that her original goal of 16 mph may not happen on this day. She is better off focusing in on the journey of the race and letting her bike split be what it may at the transition. In this she has adapted her relationship with her original goal to meet the demands of the race—she has to let go of the numbers.

I've seen many athletes mess up their races because they become too locked into their number goals and they are not able or willing to adapt and further develop their relationship with their goals on the fly.

Goals can guide you. They can be a strong tool that you use to negotiate pain, motivation, fear, nervousness, and all of the other challenges you face en route to your finish line goal. If you keep in mind that you have a fluid, dynamic relationship with all aspects of your goals, including your number goals, then you are on your way to playing out each moment of your athletic experience in an adaptable, stress-free manner.

TYPES OF GOALS

Long-term goals represent what you ultimately want to achieve in your training and fitness program and in your life as a triathlete. Examples include finishing a race, increasing race distance, or improving race times. You may wish to use your long-term triathlon training to gain fitness, lose weight, or increase health. As you progress through your triathlon career or change up your life priorities, it is important to adjust your long-term goals as well so they remain motivational.

Yearly goals are what you want to achieve in the next twelve months. Many people create these goals at the beginning of a calendar year. It is helpful post–New Year's to create a wish list of yearly goals, which can be a reflection of your long-term goals, or you can fine-tune them as you gain more experience. Once you've hit your goal of finishing a race, you can decide to take on a longer distance event or work more specifically in a particular area, such as getting in open water to train two times a month during the season. In any case, revisit your yearly goals often so you feel reassured that they are working for you, and continue to examine them as you roll through the season.

Event goals are anything you wish to strive for during your race and can range from winning your age group or finishing a race to completing a long-course triathlon or getting a PR. When creating event goals, it is important to remember the guideline of creating challenging but realistic goals that reflect your skills, fitness level, and experience, while challenging your abilities in these areas.

Feeling goals represent how you want to feel in your training or an upcoming event. You may wish to feel comfortable in your race or like you are pushing the edge in your next cycling hill workout. You may want to feel happy during your entire race or satisfied and tired at the end of a long training day. Feeling goals are the essence of your relationship with your goals; they incorporate heart and meaning. It is critical to check in regularly with your feeling goals and make sure you are offering yourself the real meaning of why you race and train.

Training goals can be a type of action plan for specific areas of your training. They not only keep you progressing toward refining your abilities as a triathlete, but they help keep your training creative, interesting, and fun. You may create a goal of doing more concentrated hill training on the bike in order to gain strength in your cycling or take swim stroke lessons to refine your freestyle technique. You may pinpoint which workouts you'll use to practice your word cues or create a run workout that will help you concentrate on proper pacing. You can have training goals for each workout as well as training goals for an entire month as well as everything in between.

Lifestyle goals can set you up to accomplish your training and event goals. Lifestyle goals can be getting 8 hours sleep a night, paying attention to your diet so that your daily intake is optimal for your training process, scheduling time to stretch each day, or ways that you can integrate your spouse or family into your training process. Refine these goals as you learn how to best incorporate training into your schedule; they can help take the stress out of your training life.

Achievement goals reflect your vision of success in your training and racing. They help you keep the dream of what you wish to accomplish in focus and facilitate you in nurturing your belief in self. These goals might be increasing challenge in your life through racing, learning to run, gaining confidence in your athletic life, or aspiring to specific race success. They may be lofty or realistic yet challenging, but they reflect your dreams and how you wish to see yourself as a triathlete.

STRETCH BEYOND GOALS

Why stop at prescribed goals? Why not broaden your athletic life by raising the bar of what you think is attainable? Why not go after being remarkable or dreaming big? Defining success by preconceived notions will limit you to what others identify as valuable. Stretch beyond your goals—aspire for vast depth and you'll find the motivation will be there. You are what you dream.

You want to do a triathlon? Choose a race, prepare, then enjoy the newfound confidence waiting for you at the finish line—but don't stop there. You want to run a marathon? Do an Ironman? It's yours. The only limiting factor is your mind. If you see beyond the immediate goal and dream big, that vision will pull you forward.

I have seen amazing feats of human

endurance. I've seen grown men sob in a blundering mess then pick themselves up and move forward because their vision of self was bigger than their physical discomfort. Sometimes completion of an event is solely due to the human mind digging deep for sustenance. That potent fuel is present in your mind—open the door and take a look.

These aspire-driven experiences transcend the concept of challenge to a deep stretching of self. A "stretch" experience tends to lie on the extreme of what has come before in your athletic life—something you start without perhaps having the ability to fully visualize the outcome. A stretch requires full concentration each moment of the journey—acknowledging that the immediate difficulty surpasses solid formulation of the ultimate goal.

If you choose to really stretch, you can be launched into the fringe of how you view yourself as an athlete, as a human. For some this can be a scary place. For others it represents a fresh starting point without the need for a conclusion. Stretching shows that your growth in this process is limitless.

SELF-TALK

What do you say to yourself when you are having a positive race experience? Or when you are negotiating whether you should get out of bed for that early-morning swim

THE MENTAL GAME OF A LEGEND BY MARK ALLEN

At some point every athlete gains an understanding that the numbers in the logbook are only part of what will make a great performance. Often the deciding factor between a good race and one that is a lifetime memory is what takes place between the ears. We all acknowledge this, but few actively do anything to develop their mental game. Most just hope that they will have what it takes up top to have the day of their dreams when it counts. But going into a race without mental prep would be like never swimming, biking, or running prior to the starting cannon and just hoping that somehow you will have the physical fitness to win your age group, set a PR, or any other definable goal. Here are a few tips to develop mental strength for triathlon.

DESIGN TOUGH DAYS

Put a few workouts into your training program that are going to be huge stretches for your level of fitness. These should be workouts that are longer or faster or done on terrain that is more extreme than anything you will encounter on race day. This recalibrates your body's perception of what tough really is. If, for example, you need to run a 7-minute mile in your

race, then do some running at 5:30 pace, even if it's only 400 meters at a time. Then when you get in the race and have to sustain your 7-minute mile, even though it can be tough, your body knows that it is nowhere near its real limit of speed.

USE IMAGERY

Imagery is the most basic technique for getting where you want to be on the day that counts most. Find a time when you can just relax, then in your mind, play out the ideal scenario for your event, associating key words or phrases that go with the pictures that you are seeing. Do this over and over. On race day, it is like you have practiced and done your ideal race so many times already it becomes just a matter of going through the physical motions to make it happen.

KEEP QUIET

Keeping quiet means developing the ability to quiet your mind so that judgment is suspended and thoughts cease to take place. It takes tons of energy to think, which means it takes tons of energy to tell yourself how good you feel or want to feel. But if your mind is quiet, you have all of that extra energy available to drive yourself forward in an incredible fashion. In every single workout, try to find that place where you just become the motion of your sport. This is especially important to practice when you are not feeling great, as this is also going to be the point when you need to call upon this technique most in your race.

BREAK IT DOWN

Often in endurance racing the toughest part is handling the distance between you and the finish line. At times it can seem absolutely unfathomable how you are going to make it there. In those moments, break the distance down into small enough chunks that each one of those is at least manageable. In training, make a deal with yourself when it gets tough. It might be saying you will go hard for the next 5 minutes and then you can back off. There may be many of those 5-minute blocks ahead of you before the workout is over, but at least making it to the next one is something doable.

BE GRATEFUL

When things get tough, we often want a way out, an excuse to slow down, to do something else, skip a workout, or drop out of a race. The opposite of this is to go to a place within yourself where you become grateful to even be searching for your ultimate fitness or best race. For every person who attempts to do their best in sports, there are millions who would never even dare dream such a grand thing for their lives. So be grateful that you are one of a select few, and then see how your entire workout or race will change!

Mark Allen (www.markallenonline.com), six-time
Hawaii Ironman Triathlon World Champion

workout? What does your head-chat sound like when you are struggling or having a tough day of training?

You Are What You Think

The way in which you speak to yourself can define your perception of self. If your internal dialog is positive, rational, or effective, you may have a realistic sense of who you are. If you regularly speak to yourself critically or negatively, you may struggle with your belief in self. Whether you are aware of it or not, your concept or perception of self is a mediator to all that you do in sport, from training consistency to effort levels to desire to dig deep in races. As an athlete, it is vital to develop a self-perception that allows you to perform personally successful training and race experiences.

Triathletes tend to be high achievers in many aspects of life, and they bring this valuable quality to their training and racing life. Unfortunately, what often comes with that wonderful drive is a critical voice that can evaluate your performances as inadequate. Feelings of inadequacy can come from many places, such as false perceptions of self and interpretations of events from your past. But if you make choices to reshape your current self-talk, you can also

make choices to let go of interpretations of your past that no longer serve you in your life as a triathlete. You are today what you choose to think today.

Although triathlon is a sport packed full of incredible support and mutual respect, negative self-talk is common among triathletes. If you are feeling negative about yourself, you may have a human tendency to put others down as well. If triathletes spend a moment looking inward when they find themselves being outwardly critical, they may notice that the person they are really criticizing is themselves.

Take all that enormous drive and mutual respect and channel it inward in a positive and effective way, and restructure your thought processes. Just like you train your legs with repetition to withstand the stresses of running long distances, you can train your mind to withstand the rigors of training and racing and in the process rework and evolve your perception of self. With training, your mind can be reset. If you are what you think, train your mind to think positively or rationally.

Think Yourself to Success: Positive or Rational Self-Talk

Self-confidence, self-perception, optimism, and self-efficacy, which is the belief that you can execute a required task successfully, are the mental keys to successful physical performances. A technique used frequently by sport psychologists to aid athletes in cultivating these mental attributes is positive self-talk, often referred to as "the key to cognitive control."

Here's how it works. You engage in self-talk any time you carry on an internal dialogue with yourself via instruction, encouragement, interpretation, babble, and so on. This internal talk can be positive, neutral or rational, or negative in nature. It has been determined that athletes who practice positive self-talk perform better, and that the positive self-talk is beneficial regardless of task complexity or duration of activity. In short, it works anytime for any sport.

Negative self-talk is especially detrimental when it defines your performance or attaches a label to you as an athlete or person. This behavior can reinforce that negative self-concept. Can you think of a time when your mental chatter slid quickly from judging a race performance as "bad" to labeling yourself as a "bad athlete"? Yet you are not your disappointing races; they are events that you experience. Your healthy self-perception can mediate how you place yourself within the context of your race. Self-talk can teach you to evaluate your events from this mediated perspective.

To race well, your mind must be present to the possibility of racing well. To set yourself up for this possibility, you have to train your mind to believe in your ability and to remain positive or rational. This must be trained consistently. If you only train your body right before an event, you are significantly limiting your possibility as an athlete. Maximize the value of your training and races by working your mind with your body daily. Repetition, repetition, repetition.

Self-Talk in Practice

In addition to shaping your self-perception and general self-talk in endurance sports, self-talk can be used specifically for the following:

- Skill acquisition: Learning new techniques, pacing, skills of a sport.
- Changing bad habits: Making your unconscious, ineffective habits conscious, and changing them to be effective habits.
- Attention control: Being there now.
- Defining mood or attitude: Eliciting a feeling or outlook.
- Defining effort: Maintaining pace, acceleration, continuing forward motion.

One way to tap into all of the areas above is by putting self-talk in motion. The following is an example of how you might access your self-talk:

Step 1: Identify the self-talk you currently use. The key to step 1 is to determine what words or phrases set off negative or ineffective self-talk. This process may take some time and effort but is an important first step toward reshaping your self-talk.

Write down your answers to the following questions.

- What do I say when I talk to myself before, during, and after competitions?
- What thoughts precede or occur during successful performances?
- What thoughts precede or occur during disappointing performances?
- During training or a race, do I call myself negative names or talk to myself in a defeatist manner? If so, how?
- During a race, how much do I tend to stay present to my race strategy?
- How much does my mind wander to things outside of triathlon?
- Do I worry about my competitors' or friends' reactions to my performances?

In examining your current self-talk, now look at your dialogue in a couple of areas. First, is your chat internally or externally focused? For example, are you concentrating internally on your race strategy, or are you thinking externally about your competitors or what color you are going to paint the bathroom next weekend? You have no control over your competitors, so why spend energy worrying about them? Focus on what you do have control over—your own race.

It is important to be aware of what is happening around you in a race, while focusing internally on your body, mind, and race process. You can then set yourself up to generate optimal self-talk. If your internal focus is your direct line of sight, external stimulus is your peripheral vision.

The more you generate self-talk that references your own training or race goals, the more you will learn to internalize an essential self-concept.

Second, examine whether your self-talk is predominantly positive, neutral or rational, or negative. In gaining the desired effect on your performance, your self-talk should remain in the positive to rational range. The objective with self-talk is to generate a sense of confidence, self-efficacy, and efficiency in yourself and your training and race processes. After you determine what your self-talk sounds like, you can come up with strategies to reshape or change the internal dialogue to work toward improving your experience.

Step 2: Manage negative self-talk. The key to step 2 is to change your negative words or phrases into positive or rational self-talk.

■ While executing all areas of training and racing, pay attention to your negative self-talk.

■ When you hear negative self-talk creep in, intercept it by saying, "STOP!" This process is called "thought stopping."

When you are under severe physical duress and generating negative thoughts, it is very challenging to change them up! You can try to negotiate a change or grab hold of something different to say, but before you can implement a change, you need to break the loop of negative thought that you are spinning within.

If you try to stop negative talk in a "nice" way, it usually won't remain gone. "Don't think that—try and be positive," or, "I really am a good athlete," just doesn't hit you over the head hard enough when you are spinning negatively downward. The detrimental thoughts will find a way to creep back into your chat. You need to aggressively slice the negative thought from your mind with an abrupt statement. STOP!

Step 3: Turn your negative thoughts into positive or rational thoughts. The key to step 3 is to develop positive or rational replacement words or phrases and use them often in the following way:

- Choose words or phrases that resonate with you and have them ready to replace the negative thoughts.
- After you say "STOP!" immediately replace the negative word or phrase with something positive or rational.

Here's an example:

Thought: "Legs are feeling heavy, slow."

Thought stopping cue: "STOP!"

Replace negative thought with: "I am light and strong," or one-word cues such as: "light" or "strong."

Just like your physical training, practicing your self-talk consistently will produce results. Revisit step 1 on a monthly basis, and use steps 2 and 3 regularly in your training. Because it is quite challenging initially to train your self-talk while in the throes of tough training, start your self-talk process while you are doing easy swim, bike, or run workouts.

As you become more natural with your self-talk process, start to implement it into some of your higher intensity or longer workouts. You first want to get your mind used to your change of internal talk when your body is working at a comfortable effort level. Once you're solid in your talk, you can up the ante to race-simulated efforts. Most people will not fully simulate the physical rigors of a race in their training, but you need to be prepared with your self-talk in all aspects of your training so that on race day, when things start getting ugly, you can pull out your self-talk and plug it into your race experience naturally.

When the Going Gets Tough, The Tough Get...Rational

In sports psychology, there is a lot of talk about positive self-talk when teaching athletes to train and manage their internal chat. It concentrates on being optimistic, and if it's not, athletes may stress to pull their thoughts back to being optimistic. Optimism should always be your aspiration, but in the world of endurance sports, positive isn't always possible for the long haul.

When I first started learning about and using positive self-talk in my training and racing, I started at the beginning—noticing my general dialogue in various aspects of my athletic life. I then implemented positive self-talk words and phrases to replace the negative. I noticed over time that in events or training sessions of a few hours or shorter, I could remain positive for the most part. But carrying this process into Ironman events, 100-mile ultra running races, or continuous or staged multiday races, remaining positive was virtually impossible unless I flat out lied to myself.

Saying "I am light and strong" just doesn't sit right when you are at mile 85 of a 100-mile running race on one of the toughest stretches of trail in the country in the middle of the night, and you just clipped your blistered big toe on a rock and endo-ed into the creek because your hip flexors are too shot to lift your feet any higher than a shuffle. In situations like this, somehow even "patience" seems like a bunch of baloney.

You don't need 85 miles of running behind you to get to this particular head space; you can thwart your positive thoughts on a long training ride or in an international-distance triathlon if it's just not your day. In any case, if you can't seem to get positive, what do you do? You get rational.

Rational basically means lucid, balanced, coherent, or sane. If "positive" is eluding you, isn't sanity a pretty good second choice? Here's what your rational voice might look like.

Thought: "I'm so tired, I'm not sure I can keep going."

Thought stopping cue: "STOP!"

Replace negative thought with rational thought: "Walk and eat a gel packet," or, "Walk to the next telephone pole, then start running."

Rational self-talk speaks to the essential aspects of how you can stay in the game: eating, drinking, proper pacing, and just generally continuing to move forward. It prevents your mind from going to the negative. Rational self-talk gives your body instructions when it wants to quit. A friend who frequently uses rational talk commented, "I pick a spot on the road and I tell myself I will return to full mental and physical peak at that point. This helps me a lot more than trying to turn an emotion on a dime, which can become a bit of a punching bag for me sometimes."

In longer events or in events of any distance that challenge your fitness level, the body wants to quit when the going gets really tough. The mind must step in to prod the body forward. The body waits for a weakness to allow it to slow, but the mind doesn't allow it. Your mind propels. If you can't reach for positive to squelch the negative demons, reach for rational—your body will thank you and you'll keep the negative thoughts at bay.

Here are some more rational self-talk words and phrases that are helpful:

"Slow your pace."

"Pump your arms on this hill."

"Pick up your feet."

"Take an electrolyte tablet in 3 minutes."

"Start running at the next tree."

"Focus."

"Stay with me."

I have used rational self-talk in all of my Ironman races and have carried that process into many ultra running events and adventure races. I have never taken for granted that it will be there, I have trained it to be there—just like my positive self-talk. Rational self-talk, just like positive self-talk, can offer you satisfying event experiences. It can keep you present to your race strategy. Used in conjunction with your positive self-talk, it is a powerful tool for your mental toolbox.

AFFIRMATIONS

Affirmations are potent statements about something that is already true or something that has the possibility of coming true. They are a form of self-talk, but they deserve some attention because they can be applied slightly differently in practice.

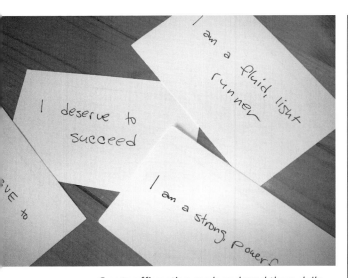

Create affirmation cards and read them daily.

I encourage athletes to use affirmations to reinforce current and desired views of self. To start, you can create a phrase or phrases that represent something you currently believe about yourself, such as, "I am a strong, powerful runner," or, "I deserve to finish."

In addition, choose a phrase or phrases that currently challenge your belief in self but are realistic for you to attain, such as, "I am a fluid, light runner," or, "I deserve to succeed."

To initiate the use of affirmations, choose four of these phrases: one referencing your general belief in self and one each referencing yourself as a swimmer, biker, and runner. Write each of them down on their own card, place these cards by your bed, and read them before you fall asleep at night and before you get out of bed in the morning. Every day. If you have a particular phrase you are challenged with such as, "I am a smooth swimmer," put the card within eyeshot of your desk or on your refrigerator.

Here are some examples of affirmations I have used recently:

"Pain is your ally."

"I am tenacious and experienced."

"I am a relaxed, methodical runner."

"I am boundless."

In creating your personal affirmations, it is important to be concise while being positive. Avoid negative statements like, "I will not be nervous." Instead say, "I will be calm and relaxed." You also want to keep your phrases in the present, such as, "I will..." and, "I am...." And most important, you need to engage with them regularly.

It is helpful to create a set of cards a few months prior to a big race. Create the cards specific to how you want to feel about yourself leading into that particular event, and then read your cards daily before that event. This works! You may choose to incorporate these phrases into your training and races, or keep them separate from your activity time. Either way, they are a powerful means of applying affirming self-talk into your day-to-day life.

MENTAL IMAGERY

Mental imagery is using your full spectrum of senses—sight, sound, touch, smell, emotions, and actions—to reproduce an athletic experience in your mind as vividly as if you were actually performing. Mental imagery is not meant to be spontaneous. The significance lies in its use as a structured, scripted mental practice.

With mental imagery, you can reduce event stress, generate positive emotions, manage pain, learn a new skill, reinforce good habits, and more. Use imagery to motivate your training, train your mind to stay focused and present, conjure intensity, and tap into your deep sense of confidence.

I've already shared imagery in motion through my experience in training for Hawaii Ironman '92: Each time I thought "flow," I would concentrate on my breath—seeing it as a white light moving through my body. When I said "flow," the breath initiated the feeling of relaxing for more speed. Focusing on my breathing and the white light, I would sink deeper into my body to generate a feeling of speed with less effort.

The manner in which you see yourself while you move is your imagery perspective. When I thought "flow," I could picture myself running—usually by looking out at the race course through my eyes or sometimes by looking at myself running on the course from an outsider's perspective. In practice, either perspective is effective, so it's important to use whichever one works for you.

Your objective in training this process and all mental imagery processes is to generate a very vivid experience—to truly view, hear, feel yourself moving as desired. Prior to my Ironman, I trained my imagery repeatedly and I could control it in the manner that allowed me to best produce my desired experience. When I first started practicing my imagery process, it was common for my mind to stray to other tasks. It was also common for me to imagine the opposite of what I was striving for—struggle. Many times I would shoot for flow and instead see and feel struggle. Gaining confidence over time with this process and with my training in general allowed me to train for control of my imagery process.

Just as I slowly taught myself to run with my personal version of flow, you can train for a more efficient swim stroke or develop a relationship with your discomfort in a race. For me, developing flow was not just about wanting to run with flow in the latter stages of an Ironman event, it was also about helping me manage my discomfort during events. The flowing breath became my means to negotiate pain, to breathe through the pain, to move with the pain, to tap into what the pain was communicating. Imagery can teach you that pain is a partner with valuable information to offer in an event. It helps you keep pace, listen to your body's needs, and address issues needing attention. Flow aided me not only in relaxing for speed, but it was a prompt to check in with my pain.

Refine and personalize your imagery. Spend time with it until it becomes a true reflection of who you are and who you aspire to be. Over time your imagery will become your greatest training partner. See, hear, and feel your way through your next race, and satisfaction will definitely be yours.

CREATING YOUR PRE-RACE ZONE

Bringing all of the contents of your mental toolbox together, it's time to address one particular area of your racing that warrants attention—pre-race. If you ever have spent days or even weeks prior to a race severely doubting your athletic abilities, you're in good company.

Prior to toeing the line, many triathletes experience fear, anxiety, or doubt and physical sensations such as nausea, weakness, or dizziness. Unfortunately, this is all quite common!

The first step in creating your pre-race plan is to gain an understanding of your arousal level before a race. Like me, you may tend to be on the overaroused end of the spectrum and need some solo quiet time rehearsing your race, stretching, or listening to calming music. Or you may be underaroused, feeling lazy, unmotivated, or uninterested in the event on race morning. In this case, try to draw on others' energy by chatting with your friends and talking up your race, or listen to music that pumps you up, stay in the transition area until right before you get in the water in order to

draw excitement from the other athletes.

Once you have determined where you lie on the arousal continuum, you can create a plan that will help you attain balance in your optimal performance zone. Here are some questions to consider in this process:

■ Do you want to create your own time schedule before a race, or are you willing to adjust your schedule to match with someone else's? Your time schedule can include everything from meal times, restaurant choices, and scheduled training times to what time you want to arrive at the event on race morning. The answers will determine whether you should travel to a race with a friend or family member or by yourself. Remember, you aren't required to adhere to anyone else's pre-race plan. Do what is best for your race.

■ Do you feed positively off of other people or do they distract your pre-race preparation? Even if you are okay being around others, you may need to decide what kind of energy you can tolerate. Hanging out with your excited, positive training partner is quite a different experience than hanging out with the training partner who is a stress freak who tries to draw everyone around her into her stressful space.

■ If you choose to listen to music, do you want music that calms you, lifts you, or somewhere in between? This can vary from race to race depending on your mood prior to an event. Be prepared with various options.

■ How much warm-up have you planned prior to your race? Give yourself plenty of time to execute your warm-up, organize your gear, hit the bathroom—again and again—as well as execute all of the other preparations needed before the gun goes off.

■ Do you want pre-race hugs or greetings from loved ones? If so, determine a specific place to meet away from the mayhem of the transition area and race start.

If you notice random pain or physical problems a couple weeks or a few days before a race, address them as best you can and then let them go. They may or may not be "real." If you are feeling doubt about your abilities, look back to when you started your training process for this race. Notice how far you have come in your physical and mental training. Allow yourself to feel confidence from this review.

After you have addressed the above issues, you can create a plan that will help guide you into your zone of optimal functioning. For overarousal, create a pre-race image that will relax you. You may choose to see and feel yourself on a beach, listening to the waves crashing on the sand. You may be able to gain the same sensation through listening to music. If you are underaroused, create an image that will heighten your senses and pull your energy up.

Add some time to your pre-race routine to rehearse your imagery and self-talk. Review your goals. Walk through your race in your mind one more time. Bring to mind the word cues you have prepared to use during the race. Say your affirmations once more.

Then, go and have some fun!

WAY OF THE CHAMPION BY DR. JERRY LYNCH

From my experience working over the last thirty years with hundreds of national and world-class champions, I can assure you that being a champion is *not* as far-fetched as you might imagine. It starts now by acting as a champion, committing yourself to practicing the habits and ways of a champion, choosing to engage in a lifestyle that demonstrates such qualities and characteristics on a consistent, daily basis. This "way of being" is, in the words of

scholar Joseph Campbell, "a hero's journey, an up-and-down, gain-and-loss odyssey of self-discovery as you become dedicated to exploring the unlimited boundaries of your full human potential in athletics and life. Along this journey the true champion must ask: does this journey have heart, passion, and love? If not, misery and failure will result. If so, success will be the by-product."

Although in athletics certain physical strengths are needed to excel, there are additional "ways" and qualities that separate the champions from the near champions, a host of internal, intangible characteristics that I refer to as the "stuff of champions." One such person who exemplifies these traits is distance runner Keith Foreman, who was told by a prominent, world-renowned college coach that he didn't have the "right stuff" to compete at that level, that he essentially didn't measure up. With champion-like qualities of courage, fortitude, determination, tenacity, and perseverance, Keith went on to become an all-American and only the fifth U.S. runner to break the four-minute-mile barrier. In my mind, Keith possessed the way of the champion...his heart and soul were into it. Keith truly was the quintessential warrior.

The way of champions in athletics and other arenas of life demands high self-esteem, self-awareness, integrity, and the ability to take the risks to improve while using failure as a teacher on the road to self-discovery. Where the average athlete and achiever are aware of everything when they think they should be, the champion is aware of all things at all times. Champions focus on consistent preparation and performance and know that all outcomes and results are natural by-products of strong commitments to a thorough, intense work ethic. In the words of Aristotle, "We are what we consistently commit to doing." Champions believe in themselves and display a strong desire to do whatever it takes to get it done. They fail, yet unlike the non-champion, tolerate such setbacks as natural, inevitable results of entering the competitive arena in sports and all walks of life. They are tenacious, fearless, audacious, proud, and confident in their ability to be this way, win or lose. Of course, they want to win on the scoreboard or get that contract in business and will do all that is necessary to gain that victory. Yet they know that such a win or outcome is never certain, and if it comes, it is usually the result of their inner victories.

Champions distinguish themselves from all others in that they are willing to sacrifice, suffer, and do all those things that the non-champions will not do.

Dr. Jerry Lynch is an author, public speaker, and sports psychology consultant.
He is the founder and director of Way of Champions (www.wayofchampions.com),
a performance consulting group geared toward helping others master
the inner game for peak performance in athletics and life.

BUILDING A MENTAL TRAINING PLAN

Building your mental training plan can start with expanding each type of goal category as well as evaluating your self-talk and pre-race arousal state. Keep in mind the goal guidelines while writing out your goals. Write down all of this information in your training log or in a personal journal—a place you have access to regularly.

For instance, write out the answers to all of the questions in "Self-Talk in Practice" as well as "Creating Your Pre-Race Zone." Then take each "Type of Goal" and spend some time addressing your goals in each category. Once you have walked through this process you can use the information as a guide to help you create specific Mental Training Programs for each area. Here are some examples of how that might work:

SAMPLE MENTAL TRAINING PROGRAMS

Training Goals	Strategy	Implementation
Improve freestyle	Take swim lessons	1x/week in Jan. & Feb.
Use positive self-talk	Create 3 word cues	Use in training 3x/week
Build confidence	Use positive self-talk	Use in training 3x/week
Get training partners	Join triathlon club	Jan. 1

Event Goals	Strategy	Implementation
Finish first triathlon	Be consistent in training	2x/bike 2x/run 2x/swim per week
Improve run split	Fuel properly	Define fuel plan and execute
Remain confident	Use cue words	Review them daily in training and pre-race

CHAPTER 10

Designing the Next Level

"In Patagonia a storm clears and the alpine monoliths stand like teeth set in a dragon's jaw. The last shreds of cloud fade into the firmament. The message broadcast from the peaks is as jarring as the scream of a train whistle. "Show yourself," they say. Few moments bristle with as much opportunity. And before such uncaring majesty, I wrestle my twin demons of fear and desire. Do I want this? Who am I? Is it good enough? I wonder every time.

"Those who don't seek out such moments of beauty, passion, and intensity don't know themselves as well as they should. People may say that alpinism is a fools' game full of meaningless risk, and they may be right, but I climb because I thirst to throw back the margins of my world. There remains so much that I do not know."

Greg Crouch, Enduring Patagonia

After basking in your post-season confidence and doing a bit of playing in the off-season, what the heck are you supposed to do next? There are myriad ways to organize your off-season time through recovery, playtime, and building your next season. In looking ahead, you may decide to refine your skill and speed to master shorter distance races or take your triathlon racing off-road. You can up the ante in distance to an international, half-Ironman, or Ironman-distance event, or create a combination of the above.

In this chapter, you'll learn how to ease into and make the best use of your off-season, ways to design the next level in your triathlon life by going longer or off-road and outline ideas on how to gain support for the next level of your racing through a rarely discussed topic—gaining sponsorship in triathlon.

OFF-SEASON OPTIONS

In the Northern Hemisphere, the triathlon season generally runs from March through October, with a few early- or late-season races sprinkled in. Most athletes in these areas will train for an early-spring start to their season and add races or events throughout the summer. Their most important, or A race, may lie near the middle or end of the season. But whichever way you slice your season, there will generally be challenging, focused periods when you are hitting your build-recovery cycles of training spot-on. These will be the most stressful times of your season and can be considered your midseason regardless of where these weeks actually fall in the year.

RECHARGE YOUR BATTERIES

After your final race in the fall, it is essential to take a break—physically and psychologically—from the rigors of prolonged, focused training. A consistent high-level workload is positive stress on your system. It gives you a training effect that can aid in top-level performances. But carrying this high level of stress year-round is a mistake and can hurt you in various ways.

Many athletes who train hard throughout the year end up injured, burned out, flat, or unmotivated for their first races of the season. Often they're unwilling to let go of their end-of-season fitness because they are concerned they will not be able to return to the same level of fitness in the future. But in addition to giving your muscles, tendons, joints, and physiology a much-needed break from the rigors of scheduled training, you also need to take a mental break from following a routine.

Taking some downtime from training is healthy in all regards and is also a lesson in trust. If you can trust that your body needs a break, you can trust that you will soon be fired up again and ready to get back into your routine. By the end of the season, you've worn your batteries down a bit. You need to recharge your mental and physical capacity for work. Trust in the time needed to recharge, and you'll come back even

stronger than you were at end of the previous season.

So forget all the worry surrounding your off-season recovery time and go out and play! Allow yourself to let go of definitive structure in your training, and the result will be a fresh, hungry, and rested mind and body.

The length of play or recovery time needed is dependent on the races in which you participated during your season and the training time devoted to those races. The longer the events and your season, the more recovery time might be needed. In general, after a full season of racing multiple events, settle into two to four weeks of playtime. If you really desire to train during this time, do. Go for a short jog or easy spin on the bike. But if the thought of a long ride or jumping in the pool makes you cringe, then don't.

PLAY, PLAY, PLAY

During off-season recovery time, allow yourself to play in activities that are not a part of your regular training regime. Take the rock climbing class you've been looking at. Get back in your kayak a couple of times a week, or dust off your mountain bike and hit the trails. Pull out the snowshoes or take a cross-country ski lesson. Try your first cyclocross race or yoga class.

Cyclocross in the off-season?

This is also an excellent time to do some "spring cleaning" in your life—catch up on personal projects, clean out your closet or filing cabinet, read a book, or engage in other hobbies you can't squeeze in while in full training mode.

Sleep in! Or enjoy those extra few minutes of being awake when you climb into bed to catch up on some reading or time with your spouse, as well as the blissful moments between the sheets each morning to rest your body and mind.

During the second or third week of your recovery, look for the spark to ignite. It's the first sign to rekindle the fire. You may notice that your energy is coming back or that you have lost energy due to lack of training. You may notice that you are starting to think about racing again next year, or that you have lost interest because you are feeling fat and lazy. These are all signs to get the process flowing again and start looking forward to moving and organizing the events in which you wish to participate.

To get the fire brewing again, you may need a kick start to stir things up again. Sign up for a 10K run, 100K fun ride, swim lessons, or that next season Ironman race. If recovery doesn't do it—the act of laying down some cash toward a goal will definitely ignite you.

JUMP-STARTING TRAINING

To jump into off-season base building, keep the focus on being kind to your body with easy, relaxed training sessions. Take your time getting back up to speed by using the following rules as a guide:

- Refrain from starting training where you left off. Start with a third of the training time you were doing midseason.
- For the first couple of weeks, train three to five days per week.
- Build your program by 10–15 percent of the total time training per week in each sport.
- Every fourth week, do an easy week and cut your mileage by 30 percent.
- On the fifth week, jump back to where you were at the end of week three, and continue your methodical build.
- Off-season is a perfect time to refine your skill base. Examine your freestyle stroke, work on spinning full circles on your bike, or have someone videotape you running, and then incorporate drills for improved form.
- Assess your gear to see where you can improve on speed and efficiency. Take advantage of end-of-season or post-holiday sales and get that new bike or wetsuit you've been coveting. Or use the extra darkness of winter to motivate you to get a new bike trainer for indoor cycling.
- If you are starting back in November or December, do minimal anaerobic work for a couple months, unless it's playful, infrequent, and impromptu.
- Use this time to build your aerobic base and gain a structural base of strength in your body. Slowly accrue miles and training time to get your body and mind ready for the rigors of a full training program.

■ Emphasize strength and core strength training with weights, plyometrics, or other types of strength work. Build up to doing your strength training program three times a week in the off-season.

Allow yourself to get creative with your training. Keep it light, easy, and fun for a few months while you are building your aerobic base. Ride in a different area. Check out a new masters swimming program or coach. Explore some new trails while running. Change it up—work on being adaptable.

Unless you live in an area where training outside may be unsafe due to snow, ice, or extreme weather, there is no reason to not get outside. A bit chilly? Wear the proper clothing to accommodate for cold or wind chill. Raining? You get wet anyway when you are swimming, so what's the issue? The plethora of high-tech clothing and shoes leaves you with no excuse to stay indoors on winter weekends, and chances are, you may have the roads or trails to yourself!

If you are consistent, steady, and disciplined, you will have a long, strong base come February and be in position to add speed to your program. Remember, after some downtime, it will take a while for you to get back into your usual routine and you may slip up and miss workouts more than you do during the season. Take the pressure off, enjoy your easy time on the roads, and you'll be back up to speed in no time.

If your training is intelligently structured, you will hit your first spring event ready to race with a solid core of strength. The more engaged you are with your play-time and your off-season training, the more enjoyable that first season race will be.

TAKING IT OFF-ROAD

In the mid 1990s, grassroots off-road triathlons starting popping up around the country. This deviation from the standard road triathlon came boldly to the public's eye through the 1996 Aquaterra on Maui, Hawaii. This event consisted of an ocean swim, mountain bike ride over dirt and lava rock, and a trail run. This exciting event attracted triathletes—some fresh off racing in Kona—as well as a strong mountain biking contingent. The fun, casual atmosphere of a mountain bike event combined with the hard-core, competitive savvy of road triathlon molded the essence of the Aquaterra event, as well as today's version of off-road triathlon racing.

With some exceptions, an off-road triathlon consists of an 800- to 1500-meter open-water swim, an 8- to 20-mile mountain bike ride, and a 2- to 7-mile trail run. There are many race promoters hosting off-road triathlons as part of their full season menus, but the highest profile off-road events are the XTERRA series put on by Team Unlimited.

You can find fifty XTERRA events around the United States as well as more than ten international race locations. XTERRA quickly branded itself as the name in off-road triathlon. USA Triathlon hosts a national off-road championship each year, and the International Triathlon Union (ITU) offered the first ITU World Off-Road

Championship in 2008. Off-road events provide an exciting, adventurous way to get into multi-sport racing for mountain bikers, trail runners, or for those who are interested in getting a little dirty.

GET TECHNICAL

Off-road triathlons are different from standard road triathlons in that the terrain for the cycling and running legs is generally on challenging, rough, steep, and hilly

Ned tearing it up on the mountain bike

terrain. The mountain biking in an off-road triathlon requires a much broader skill base than that of road cycling and should be taken quite seriously. On a road bike, you are trying to keep the rubber side down while cornering, descending, climbing, and riding straight. On a mountain bike, you are required to execute all of those movement variables while on dirt, sand, mud, rocks, gravel, roots, and just about anything that nature throws at your tires.

From a technical perspective, riding

MOUNTAIN BIKE CHAMP NED OVEREND: DOING TRIATHLON

I first started racing XTERRA triathlons in 1996, the first year they had the event on Maui. I took advantage of my mountain biking experience and finished third that year. I figured it would be no problem to polish my running and swimming skills and come back to win. The transition into becoming a real triathlete was more difficult than I expected.

I think an important character trait for a successful triathlete is humility, especially if you are coming from a strong background in one sport. Just because you have developed a strong aerobic engine in cycling, it does not mean you will be able to transfer it over to running, and especially swimming, without some focused work.

In the pool, I assumed since I had success coaching myself for cycling, I could figure out how to become a swimmer. I devoted a considerable amount of time and energy, but my time for 1500 meters barely improved and was never consistent. I was a pretty strong thrasher, I literally punished the water. After I swam for an hour, the maintenance people at the pool had to change the water in my lane because I had worn it out. I bought videos and books to try and learn the technique but what I really needed was a coach to prevent me from practicing bad technique.

In the running, my problem was an overuse issue. I had the stamina for long runs but not the biomechanics. I eventually learned that my ideal time spent training for the run was two sessions of 45 minutes to an hour and one run for 75 minutes; any more and I couldn't recover or I would develop overuse injuries. Keep in mind I was training for a two-and-a-half-hour event so I needed to be focusing on high intensity.

On the bike, I cut my hours back from 10–12 a week down to 6–8 (remember these are half on the mountain bike—mountain bike hours require more energy than road hours). The cutback in cycling was necessary to have enough recovery for high intensity run and swim training.

Ultimately I was competitive at XTERRAs, but it took some experimentation.

Ned Overend is a world champion mountain biker, six-time NORBA champion, two-time XTERRA champion, finisher of the 1980 Hawaii Ironman and has been inducted into the Mountain Bike Hall of Fame. He is still winning strong in his early fifties.

a road bike on pavement and riding a mountain bike on technical single track is comparing apples to oranges. The only thing that the fast road cyclist truly has in common with the fast mountain biker is fitness. And one thing that will set two equally skilled mountain bikers apart is their ability to manage fear and execute well under the stresses of technical riding.

You can look at the myriad of trail-specific running shoes to gain an understanding of the vast difference between road and trail running and the skill needed to run trails well. A road shoe offers support while being lightweight and cushy—all with the motive of making your movement through a predominantly linear plane of motion on pavement as comfortable as possible. Your foot tends to sit lower to the ground in a trail shoe and the shoe has an aggressive outsole to allow your foot to feel and claw its way through roots, rocks, and dirt. Trail shoes tend to be a bit heavier and stiffer for support of the foot and ankle on the torquing, abusive nature of rough terrain while offering some fore-shoe armor to protect the toes. You don't just run on trails, you run, jump, hop, and step up in all planes of motion while negotiating nature. Taking it off-road on the run in a triathlon warrants some serious trail time to hone the mind and leg muscles to the abuses specific to the trail.

Gaining comfort in off-road biking or running takes repetition and skill. The more you practice on bike and foot, the better you'll be at negotiating your fear on rough terrain.

Improve your off-road bike skills by getting some coaching from an experienced local mountain biker, watching a video, or reading up on skill execution off-road. Run trails as much as possible as well as enter a couple of trail run races prior to your off-road triathlon. The movements you make on dirt on bike and foot are not intuitive until you learn and practice them repeatedly.

Throwing in an off-road triathlon or two to your year is a fun, exciting way to spice up your season. The skill you'll obtain

while training off-road on the bike and run will also help you increase your prowess as a road triathlete. Mountain biking and trail running require a broad strength base, and this considerable power can be transferred to your road efforts.

GOING LONGER

A sprint-distance triathlon is a wonderfully concise distance to race. Why go longer? International-distance events are plenty long enough to earn you that post-race stack of pancakes—why up the ante to half-Ironman or Ironman? There are countless happy triathletes who focus their time and money on shorter distance races, and if you are new to the sport of triathlon, staying short to gain some experience or refine your speed makes sense. As a long-time client and short-course specialist, Sherri points out, "In a shorter triathlon, you can zip through, have fun without all the excessive wear and tear on life and limb, and still have a great sense of accomplishment." If going short excites you, then there is no point in upping the ante, especially if you are doing it because everyone else is doing it—not a good enough reason. The key to choosing any race distance is to focus on the length that beckons you in an intelligent and methodical manner.

But if the desire to go longer does pull at you, you may be sensing that there just might be more than you can imagine waiting at that finish line. Just as Greg Crouch recognized when faced with climbing in one of the harshest environments on earth, "There remains so much that I do not know," an ultra-distance triathlete may ponder the same when toeing the line of an Ironman event. If part of what you seek as a triathlete is a knowing of self, then longer distance events may be the perfect medium to nurture that desire for depth.

IF WE BUILD IT, THEY WILL COME

After the Hawaii Ironman became an intrigue in the sporting world, and then ownership of the race and the Ironman name were acquired by World Triathlon Corporation (WTC), the quantity of these ultra distance triathlons slowly expanded and events started popping up around the world. Soon there were a handful. Then seven or so events. Over the years WTC has methodically expanded the Ironman Series to a vast strip-mall of more than twenty top-quality events, in addition to the half-Ironman (70.3 miles) races they support and endorse.

Brand-name Ironman events are guaranteed to sell out. Top-quality half-Ironman races will also close their registration well before race day. Events are often full for

Huge spectator turnout for an Ironman start

the following year the day after the event takes place. What once was the elusive Holy Grail in triathlon is now readily available to those poised at their computer with credit card in hand. I have a client who whipped out her laptop at a dinner party, and with wine glass in hand, signed up for an Iron-man race. If you don't make the registration cutoff, there are various other ways to buy yourself a spot in a race.

WTC is working off the premise "If We Build It, They Will Come," and these owners of the powerful Ironman moniker appear to be on the mark. Why? What is the allure of devoting a half a year or more of one's life to train for 70.3 or 140.6 miles of pain and suffering?

EMBRACING THE UNKNOWN

Many people do endurance sport, and triathlon in particular, because it tests their resolve. They get value from those tests—information about strengths and clarity on weaknesses. Taking on an event that is longer than anything you've done before places you on the stage of the unknown. This can be a scary place, but if you are methodical and intelligent, you can manage that fear and move into your test with some sense of belief you can achieve. You may ponder, "Am I good enough?" When going long, the answers are loud and clear.

The people who choose to step onto that unknown stage and perform know the value in taking risks. Each long day of training or racing sets a new stage, a new opportunity, a new view of self, a higher value. There is significant value to going

longer than you've gone before, and those who have know this. Those who seek going longer, sense it, and may build their own opportunities to go longer.

"GOING LONGER" IN PERSPECTIVE

When considering taking your race distance up a notch, you need to embrace this change with eyes wide open. Going longer will not only place demands on your time, it will require you to change up your perspective on the sport in various ways. Here are a few perspectives to consider when looking at going longer:

Adapt or fail. In considering going longer, adapting—to training, lifestyle changes, cold water, and more—isn't just a perk that can help you get faster and be on top of your mental game, it's a requirement. In going longer, you either adapt or you fail.

If you've done a triathlon, you know that it's common to have difficult issues pop up—crashing on your bike, getting kicked in the face during the swim, forgetting where your bike is in the transition area, and so on. The longer the event, the longer the list can become.

The longer you race or train, the longer you are asking your body and mind to engage in some really tough forward move-ment. An Ironman isn't twice as hard as a half-Ironman, it is exponentially tougher. If you're racing a 7-hour half-Ironman event, you don't just need a bit more food and water than you do for an international-distance race, you need a lot more, and you need to refine your calorie intake to meet the demands of the distance.

To go longer, you need to learn to shrug off emotional responses to environmental discomfort and deal with it rationally, because 14, 15, or 17 hours are too long to be pissed off at the heat and wind. You are required to adapt to significant structural discomfort and mental struggle. These become part of your everyday existence in training, and you adapt to move with them and not fight them.

Revere the distance. When going longer, do not fear the distance, admire it. Respect yourself for taking on that distance. Celebrate your choice to step up to the line of a difficult event. You are selecting an endeavor most people would never entertain. Congratulations, you're opting to move out of your comfort zone and learn a great deal.

Any triathlete who has chosen to go longer can attest to their getting seriously humbled. If I ever find that I'm a bit too full of my grand fitness or strength, I quietly remind myself of the remaining distance in my race. My first Wasatch 100 trail running race, I felt fresh and strong on the 4000-foot, several-mile climb off the starting line. When noticing my aggressive pace, I immediately reprimanded myself, "Terri, you have 98 miles to go—slow down!" Now that is a quality reality check when going long.

Revel in the distance you are covering, and be humbled by the distance you are covering. These reminders will keep that distance in perfect balance with your race plan.

Embrace the mental game. The longer you go, the more critical your need to embrace your mental game. Having your goals laid out and your self-talk dialed in will not just help you have a faster time, they may make or break your ability to finish a race of serious distance.

When you train or race for several hours or more, you have no choice but to keep yourself company in your mind. You can be the negative, energy-sucking training partner, or you can be the helpful, rational training partner. The time you spend, or not, refining your mental game will decide who shows up in your head on race day. Just about anyone can get through a sprint- or international-distance race with a negative training partner chatting in their head, but it takes a mentally trained athlete to dial that self-talk to positive or rational for 5, 7, or 15 hours. Dial in your mental game, and you'll be assured of an effective mental companion come race day.

One of my clients, Jill, decided to run her first 50K trail race in her off-season. She summarized her experience with the following observations: "The mental capacity needed to complete this type of endurance event is monumental. The conversations you have with yourself are fascinating, from all perspectives: 'This is great.' 'Now it isn't.' 'That hurts.' 'Now it doesn't.' 'Can I finish?' 'I can do this!' 'Look at that, how beautiful.' 'Did I really sign up for this?' 'Paid for this, no less.' 'I'm so lucky to be out here.' 'I could be sitting in an office staring at a computer.'

"It's very easy to think 'I could be done right about now.' The funny thing is... there's no where to go but forward. So...you go. And go, and go some more. In the end, the reward is beyond measure. Sure the medal and t-shirt are cool, but the sense of accomplishment is quite unexpected. You relive each segment of the race and begin to remember the smallest details about the foliage, the terrain, the people, the snacks, the weather, the sounds, and the feeling. You then realize what you just did and smile."

Embracing your mental game will offer you the possibility of walking away from all events with a strong sense of personal satisfaction. Ignore your mental game, and a bad day on the roads can turn into what my adventure racing teammate so aptly observes, "A whole lotta pain and suffering."

Revel in the experience. A client who recently did his first Ironman in Hawaii had a very poignant goal for the race: "I'm so excited to go to this race, I really just want to race smart and take in the whole experience." His main objective was to finish the race. It being his first Ironman, he didn't know how that would play out. So he came up with a plan for pace and fuel, adapted it as needed along the way, and then metaphorically sat back and enjoyed every minute of the race. The result: a life-changing experience and a desire to go back and do it all over again.

Going longer is a journey in which you've never participated. If you allow yourself to put aside all the worry and hype and revel in the extended experience of your training and the race itself, you may come away with a refreshing view of life and yourself.

Success is relative. My personal suc-cesses in the distances that I have raced or trained are not about you. The way that I define success for me is based on my own experiences and interpretations of their value in my life, and yours need be based on similar criteria—for you.

Your distance-based successes and accomplishments are relative to your own experiences. There is no point in comparing your success to others—they do not live your life, nor you theirs. Each of us will have a definition of success that is relative to our own life. Period.

Refine your fuel plan. The human body can, amazingly, move forward for a few hours with little to no fuel. But if you go longer than a few hours without adequate calories, electrolytes, and water, you'll be forced to walk, or stop. I've seen athletes complete international-distance events on a couple hundred calories or less. I've seen people complete half-Ironmans on a bit more than that, but in both of these cases, they didn't have their best race, and there is a high probability they felt very poor post-race, and perhaps even for a few days after.

The longer you go, the more you are required to fine-tune your fuel plan. Consider adding some protein to your fuel plan, and be hyper-diligent about taking in that fuel on a consistent basis. Toward the end of an Ironman, your body is moving almost solely on what you are consuming. If you miss a food stop or are late in taking in calories or water, you can push yourself over an edge that will be quite challenging to recover from.

Create a fuel plan that is steady throughout your event—without missing a beat. Missing a feeding in a shorter race may mean that you have a poor performance and a post-race headache. Missing some much-needed calories over the long haul may mean that you miss out on your well-deserved finish line experience.

Patience is a virtue. Runners do not hit the wall in a marathon because of the distance; they hit the wall at mile 18, 20, or 22 because they either had an inadequate fuel plan, their training was insufficient for the distance, or they were not patient in their pacing of the distance.

Just as going longer requires your fuel plan to be dialed in, it also obliges you to be prudent in your early race pace. "My pace felt too easy the first 10 miles, so I went a bit faster than I had planned" is a common comment from wall-hitting marathoners.

Of course it's going to feel easy at the beginning! The best pace for you to run is the pace you can evenly sustain—for the entire 26.2 miles. To hold this pace at the beginning of the event feels effortless, so

CONVERSATION WITH MIKE REILLY: THE VOICE OF IRONMAN

Terri: How did you get started announcing for triathlon and for Ironman events in particular?

Mike: I actually got started announcing at a running event in San Diego in the late '70s. One of the first tri's I worked was the Bud Light USTS race in San Diego in 1980 with Scott Tinley, Mark Allen, Mike Pigg, and Dave Scott competing, not a bad start! The first Ironman I worked was with Mike Plant at the 1989 Hawaii Ironman. After witnessing Mark Allen and Dave Scott in an epic battle, then Rick and Dick Hoyt finishing their first Ironman, I was hooked. After nineteen years in Hawaii and over seventy Ironmans total worldwide, I never want it to end.

Terri: Athletes go to an event with personal goals. What are your goals when you pick up the mic at an event to become The Voice of Ironman?

Mike: My goal at each Ironman event is simple. Take care of the athletes, make sure they are recognized during the day and at the finish, entertained at the ceremonies, and given their just due for becoming a part of a very unique family. I am a strong believer it is not about being on the microphone trying to become a "personality." It is only about the athletes and the event. When they are taken care of and given the accolades they deserve, all else falls in place.

Terri: What impact does it have on you to know that thousands of athletes have a lifetime-defining moment in those four words you say, "You are an Ironman!"

it is critical that you are incredibly patient with this early effort. If you are not patient and not hitting your correct pace, you will not only slow down toward the end of the race, you may slow down significantly—1, 2, or more minutes per mile.

The place in triathlon where many forget to heed the virtue of patience is on the bike. Again I hear, "I felt so good on the bike, but my run didn't go so well." Triathlon is a swim, bike, and run event. So if you have a blazing swim and bike and blow up on the run, it won't matter if your bike was the fastest of the day for your age group—

your finish line result will be disappointing.

The longer you race in triathlon, the more patience is required. An inappropriately paced bike leg in an Ironman can leave a 3:30 marathon runner doing the Ironman shuffle on the run course. Because I have done so many long events, "patience" is one of the words I use in training to bring myself to a place of global reflection of my race. In Ironman events, patience often meant I put my blinders on during the bike leg. Being super fit and tapered for an Ironman equates to feeling like you are on fire on the bike. This is an exquisitely

Mike: It has a tremendous impact on me. The pure nature of what it means to so many athletes to hear those words can be very intimidating and yet gratifying. I have the honor to bestow on the finisher that incredible exclamation point to cap off maybe one of the best days of that person's life! That's why when people come up to me and say "you have the best job in the world," I say it isn't a job—it's a passion and honor I never take for granted.

Terri: Are there any particular moments you've had at the finish line that would epitomize what triathlon means to you?

Mike: Every finisher has their own individual story of what they went through to train and get to the finish. When I hear or talk about a particular person's hurdles they had to jump to succeed in this sport, it confirms the strength of what we do. That's why I look at each finisher and give them the accolades they deserve as if they're the very first one I've ever announced. That is the least they deserve from me.

Terri: What advice would you give a first-time Ironman participant?

Mike: Two words: *prepare* and *fun*. If you do the proper preparation, you will succeed. If you have fun along the way and during the event, you will be giving yourself the gift of a lifetime.

> *Mike Reilly is best known as The Voice of Ironman triathlons worldwide. As a race announcer, he has welcomed over 100,000 athletes across Ironman finish lines with the world famous phrase "You are an Ironman!" since 1989, and he's still going strong. Mike is vice president of major events at The Active Network, the world's largest sports online registration company.*

fun sensation but one that needs to be kept in perspective if you wish to have a strong total race experience.

When I said "patience" to myself, it would be my cue to look straight ahead and not at the people passing me. I would check in with my pace, given the distance left and the marathon looming, and I would relax into my own race plan.

In considering the possibility of going longer and having gained perspective on that process, there are a few areas to assess concerning your training and lifestyle for going longer.

INTELLIGENT PROGRESSION

The time frame in which you can intelligently progress to longer distances in your training and racing depends on several key factors.

The first area to assess is your general skill level. Acquiring enough skill on the bike and run to get yourself to the finish of a triathlon requires a marginal amount of focus, but being proficient enough in the water might take more effort. You need efficient enough technique to get yourself to the finish of a 1- to 2-mile (or longer) open-water swim without leaving yourself exhausted. For those new to the sport of swimming, that may take some coaching and time in the water.

As you progress in distance in training for each sport, take some time every couple months to do a longer sustained swim, bike, or run effort, then note your time, and how you feel afterward. For example, if you have been slowly increasing your swim distances in the pool, every once in a while do a straight 1- or 2-mile swim and note how comfortable it felt on a scale of 1 to 10 with 10 being really tough. Take note of your stroke count (per length) to see if it has dropped. Then a couple weeks later do the same length swim in open water. Note how you feel when you get out of the water.

You don't need to set any speed records in the water to get through the swim portion of a triathlon, but you do want to feel fairly fresh and ready to take on the other portions of your race.

TAKE INVENTORY

Have you had any injuries that are affecting your current training program? If so, are you addressing them with proper rest, rehab, and maintenance? When going longer, there is a good chance your body may rebel and exacerbate a preexisting injury. This doesn't mean you shouldn't go longer with a compromised body part, it just means you need to be especially vigilant about addressing its needs daily.

Another area to review is your overall experience with swim, bike, and run training, including the longest distances that you have trained and raced. If a first-year triathlete comes to me wanting to do an Ironman, and his life prior was that of a couch potato, I may suggest that he increase his experience through longer distance training in his swim, bike, or run before attempting the Ironman. He may decide to build up to a century bike ride or marathon to see how his body will cope with these stand-alone distances before he lays his money down for the big race.

It is important to evaluate not only your triathlon experience but your overall athletic experience when deciding to go longer. A former bike racer or ultra runner turned triathlete may take to training for a longer triathlon much easier than someone coming from a minimal to zero endurance background. That doesn't mean that if you have minimal experience you shouldn't sign up for that longer triathlon event next season. It just means that you will need to be smart and methodical in putting more distance on your inexperienced body.

MUSCLE MEMORY

Muscle memory is the idea that by continuously performing movement of a similar exercise, you will stimulate the body's adaptation process, and down the road, even if you stop doing this activity, your body will "remember" the gains and skill developed from the process. It may be the reason your body still retains the skill to ride a bike or swim after many years of not. And it could be one of the reasons an experienced distance runner can go out and do a 10- or 20-mile run after taking

a considerable amount of time away from running. Over time as a body adapts to training longer or faster, these subsequent changes can be retained as muscle memory from weeks, months, or years prior. In some ways, what you gain, your body never fully forgets.

I was one of those naive, overly excitable people who did an Ironman as my third or fourth triathlon. But even though I was brand new to the sport, I came from an extensive running background. In my early twenties, I knew how to swim pretty well, had already run a couple of marathons, and had spent my young years through college using a bicycle as my main form of transportation. I also had youth on my side. So when I trained for and raced in my first Ironman, the muscle memory I had developed at that point in my life carried me quite far in my preparation, and in the event itself. Your body's memory for past activity can aid your cause to go long. If you are without this memory, it may mean you have to be a bit more conscientious about your training build.

DESIRE

Have you felt excited and motivated to train for your shorter triathlon events, or have you struggled with getting in the adequate time? Do you look forward to your events, or are you constantly reaching for the desire to train and race?

If you don't have the desire to go after your sprint- or international-distance triathlon goals, there is a strong chance you'll fall short when preparing for a half or full Ironman. You need more than excitement about the prospect of training for a longer event; you need to have a deep core of desire to pull it off. As the weeks and months of training roll by, that desire will be strongly tested. If it was faulty to begin with, there is a good chance it will falter during peak training weeks. In checking in on your desire to go longer, you'll not only assess your ability to emotionally hang when the going gets tough, you'll also bring that desire to your conscious mind to draw upon for motivation at a later time.

CAN YOU LITERALLY MAKE THIS HAPPEN?

In intelligently progressing toward going longer, you finally need to do a general lifestyle assessment. What are your time constraints, commitments to work and family, or other entities that pull time from your week? Is your spouse supportive of your triathlon endeavors, and if not, is that important for you to address or not?

CONVERSATIONS WITH DAVE SCOTT: MOTIVATION

Terri: When you were in the thick of your career and you went through periods when you felt unmotivated or you didn't seem to care about your training and racing, what would you do to snap out of it?

Dave: I had a lot of this. My biggest hurdle was developing that psychological momentum. I was my worst judge and I set the bar too high. After winning a few of these things, I was a marked guy and I had to always be on and ready.

There were periods when I felt despondent, and I couldn't pull myself out of the funk. I'd think I need to do this, this, this, and there was no compromising. If I needed to workout 5 or 6 hours, I couldn't go out and just do a 40-minute run and an hour and a half bike. That didn't cut it. It was all or nothing, and that all or nothing really crippled me. I tried for a lot of years to try and get out of it.

I'd have periods when I'd go for ten days, nothing, zero, didn't do a thing and it was very self-destructive. It wasn't rest time, it was mental torture for me because I didn't know how to rest my mind.

So to try and overcome it, I had to set the absolute smallest goal and go back to the simplest common denominator that I use now, which is "I just need to be healthy for myself." Forget racing, forget the media, forget Mark Allen, Scott Tinley, anyone else. You're really unhealthy right now mentally and emotionally. I know I'm going to feel crappy the first time I go out, but if I got through these first three days I knew I could turn myself around.

In assessing your lifestyle, look at capacity for support from others as well as time constraints that may take you away from training efforts.

TRAINING BENCHMARKS

Once you've gained perspective on going longer and assessed that you are ready to take that next step: you need to take a look at specific benchmarks for your training time and distances in each sport and fit those into your training plan. From your current starting point in training, you can create guidelines for advancing your fitness, while hitting benchmarks along the way. These benchmarks will help you evaluate where you are in your process relative to your event date.

Generally, a safe progression during the build weeks of your training is a 10–15 percent increase of the total weekly time for swimming, biking, and running. For instance, if you are currently swimming 2 hours per week, your progression for the following week might be 2 hours and 15 minutes. Increase swim time over three weeks to 2 hours and 45 minutes a week. Take a recovery week, and then start your fifth week of training at 3 hours swimming and continue to build from there (for more information on this process see chapter 1).

Within this build and recovery process, you are hitting weekly time benchmarks within each week of training. Within your weekly program, you will build to the longest workouts you do in swim, bike, and run prior to your event. These could be the masters swimming workout in which you focus on distance sets or your long bike and long run sessions for the week.

Use the 10–15 percent rule to slowly build to meet these key long workouts. Ideally you'd like to hit these workouts several times or more during different build weeks prior to your event date.

See the table below for some benchmark guidelines for the swim, bike, and run within each race distance. They represent the distances or times, within swim, bike and run, which you should feel relatively comfortable completing in training before your selected race.

DISTANCE COMFORTABLY COMPLETED IN TRAINING SEVERAL TIMES OR MORE:

	swim	bike	run or walk/run
Sprint	500–800 yds	:45–1:00	:30–:45
International	1200–1500 yds	1:00–1:15	:45–1:00
Half-Ironman	2000–3000 yds	3:00–4:00	1:30–2:00
Ironman	3500–4200 yds	5:00–6:00+	2:30–3:30+

I'M OK WITH COBWEBS BY KAREN BURGESS

Virtually everyone who considers "moving up" to Ironman-distance triathlons has intentions of getting things in order prior to taking on the crux of training. We all know the training is tough and time-consuming. The daunting anticipation of long weekend training rides and runs tends to make you consider that the time to do more mundane tasks, such as laundry, will be compromised. You would be right. These preparations include cleaning the garage, clearing out closets, dusting, sorting the mail, and so on. Even though these are things I dislike doing, there is something about that distance that brings out the organization in us. I can tell you with certainty—don't bother. After a few months of build training, it won't matter.

You will begin to think it is normal to step over your bike gear and maybe even your bike at the front doorstep, fish gels and bars out from between the car seat because you forgot your energy food for a training session, or stare from the couch at the cobwebs on the ceiling and wonder how long they have been there. In fact, your living standards will regress to such a degree that you will think it is normal to notice bike grease on your leg, under your panty hose, during a business meeting. And the bike ride was two days ago. Trust me, I speak from experience.

Some people lose their mind while training for an endurance race of this caliber, and that does not mean they are not functional human beings, it simply means they are focused athletes—athletes who are training for one of the most respected and prestigious events in the world. Ironman. It takes a bit of lunacy to commit to something like this. No couch potatoes in this group. No late night parties, no sleeping in late on weekends—during training. In fact, "no" is a well-used word in an Ironman athlete's vocabulary. "No, I have to

THE POSSIBILITY OF SPONSORSHIP

Ever thought about devoting some time to gaining support for your racing? Has the thought remained a thought because you think, "I'm not good enough"? Think again. Sponsorship in sport is a mutually beneficial relationship between an athlete or athletes and a company or entity.

THINK LIKE THE COMPANY

Triathlon is a gear-intensive sport with a following of healthy, fit, high energy people who use that gear. In short, a breeding ground for promotion of products within the endurance market or those companies outside the industry wishing to grab a piece of triathlon's sexy persona. Talent in sport is one thing, and it might be the only thing a company wants, but most of the time they are looking beyond talent. They are looking for wholesome well-roundedness in ambassadors for their company.

In deciphering what a company's objectives are within sport and within triathlon, you need to do a bit of research. Ask some train," is the full phrase. Practice it, or make a sign. You have to be focused and committed to yourself and your race to accomplish the tasks at hand. Cobwebs be damned!

While training for my first Ironman race, I not only wore two different colored shoes to work and had the aforementioned bike grease incident, but I actually bought a new bathing suit rather than miss a swim workout when I discovered I had forgotten mine. Conventional wisdom and well-respected coaches will tell you that you need the support of your family and friends to help you through the massive amounts of training and discipline required, but what they fail to mention is that the support you need is reassurance that you are not, in fact, losing your mind. Because you will surely think you have.

Training for an endurance race is no small undertaking, and the emotions that go along with it can manifest themselves in the strangest ways. We come up with creative outlets to express ourselves within the confines of training and recovery, and our "lunacy" manifests itself in bizarre habits. While I could not seem to match my shoes or would forget a vital piece of training equipment, other athletes became obsessed with eating chocolate cake, or drinking vodka and sports drink in a bubble bath. (It is a male friend of mine and I am absolutely serious.) I am not a particularly sensitive person but found myself in tears at the drop of a hat while training for my first Ironman. The good news, I finished. The even better news, the next one gets "easier." At least in terms of shoe selection. May your training consist more of bubble baths and chocolate cake, and less tears! What is that they say? "Anything is possible."

Karen Burgess is a three-time Ironman. She currently employs a house-cleaning service to address the cobweb issue.

questions that will help you to try to narrow their marketing intent. Every company has a bottom line of wanting to promote and sell products, and it has been shown that people buy products that are used by successful athletes—"If I use that wetsuit, I will swim fast too." There is also a perception by the consumer that if a successful athlete is promoting a specific product, then it must be good.

The importance of all the research and supposition is to learn to look through a company's eyes in order to figure out what it would gain by developing a relationship with you. Not what you would gain, but what it would gain. It may have nothing to do with your athletic ability but lie in your personality, beliefs, profession, or the work you do with The Boys and Girls Club. Once you define what they would gain, then sell them that.

STEP OUTSIDE THE PROVERBIAL BOX

You can negotiate not only to be in media advertising, but also to help them come up with ideas as to how they can best use your image and talents. If you enjoy working with children, you can offer to come to their summer company meeting and put on a triathlon for the children of their employees. Offer to attend trade shows and talk to retailers about the company's product. There is no better endorsement to a retailer than someone who has product tested in the trenches of sport and come out satisfied.

Wearing a company logo is one small part of your sponsorship relationship. The sky's the limit as to what you can give them. Look at your talents and offer what you feel good about. Then make sure you can deliver.

YOU ARE YOUR PROPOSAL, YOUR PROPOSAL IS YOU

There are a couple of things to consider when creating the look and voice of the proposal you will present to a company. Take into account what the company that you are approaching may want to see, and, most important, personalize the information to represent you. Are you fun, intellectual, professional, passionate, organized? Then let those qualities shine in the way you present yourself on paper. While showing off your best stuff, be creative without being gaudy or flashy. Represent yourself strongly on the first pages and in your cover letter or email. Spend some extra time on that first section—it could make or break your getting a follow-up conversation. Have a qualified friend or training partner review your first draft.

The proposal should cover:

- What is triathlon?
- Who are you?
- What are your goals?
- What will you give the company?
- What do you want from the company in return?

Your proposal should include the following information, in this order:

Cover Sheet. With company logo, a photo relevant to the contents of the proposal, a title such as "Sponsorship Opportunities," and the event title or sport name for which you are pitching the proposal.

Table of Contents. Shows organization for a longer proposal in a business-like manner and allows them to review the contents upfront.

Overview. With subtitles; "Background and Mission," "Uniqueness" (yours, or the event which you are doing, or both), "Racing Schedule," or "Adventure Timeline." All of these may or may not be relevant to your proposal, but at minimum you should add the "Background and Mission" section, which defines your sport, why you do your sport, and why you are seeking help for these efforts. Get passionate. Get creative. Think globally. Dig for why you do what you do.

Your Bio. A one-page summary of your background with a couple of pictures, including a smiling head shot and an action shot. Include not only information about your triathlon experience and accomplishments, but also, relevant academic background, awards, parental status, the fact that you coach your daughter's softball team, or anything else interesting about you.

Opportunities. This is the part where you ask for what you want. I present this not as a "gimme," but as an "opportunity" for them to engage with. Start with a brief section called, "Sponsorship Benefits," a short summary of what they will get for working with you. Be creative and be expansive (give them options) while keeping it concise.

Evaluate the company's leverage then decide on your package options for that company.

Marketing Opportunities. In addition to listing what you will offer the company, include an additional page with "Online and National Marketing and Promotions," and "PR and Advertising Efforts." If you don't have a website, you can still offer promotions at events, in your work or personal life, or through a PR or marketing agent you may employ.

Why Do I Race? This is a piece about challenge, exploration, and attaining goals, and how those entities have defined your life. It lets the person reading take a peek inside you—the passionate athlete—if they choose. But more, it has the potential to inspire, and that is why you should include it.

Contacts and Terms. Though your contact info should be in an unobtrusive footer on each page, add it here again inclusive of all phone numbers and website. Terms are some legal talk defining the agreement.

BIKE SCHWEIZER **MAGAZIN**

Parlament: **velofeindlich** Stahlvelo: die Wiedergeburt
Frauen-Power: Jaquie Phelan

Internationaler Terminkalender

Triathlon: Körperstress

4. Ausgabe September/Oktober 1991 • Preis: sFr. 7.50 / DM 7.50 / ÖS 58

FOLLOW UP, FOLLOW UP, FOLLOW UP

When you are seeking support, it is common to have to send out many proposals in order to get one affirmative deal. Doing some upfront research or having direct inside contacts with a company can lower these numbers significantly, but if you are cold-calling your sponsorship efforts, you have to be willing to take a lot of rejection. Don't take it personally—these people don't even know you.

If you are meeting in person, bring a copy of your proposal and follow up with a digital copy. Once you've sent the cover email or letter, or had that first meeting, give them a bit of time to digest the information. Then follow up with a phone call. If they don't call you back right away, or ever, you are in good company. Call again.

It's easy to get discouraged in this process, but keep at it methodically until you get some kind of answer. Always be professional even if the deal is not going your direction.

If they show some sort of interest, set up a conference call or meeting to take it to the next discussion level. Keep notes on your communications with each company.

Be organized by taking notes on your phone conversations or meetings. Have an agenda, show leadership, be affirmative.

In addition to diligent follow-up on the front end, you will need to continue this process once you land the deal. Go beyond what you promised to deliver. Check in regularly with your company sponsors to let them know how your racing is progressing. Be personal, yet professional. Send them signed pictures from your events. Have integrity with your follow-through, just as you would with a friend, or someone you respect. Respect their efforts in supporting you, and show that respect often.

Getting sponsorship takes time. Gaining sponsorship for your triathlon life is like running a small business. I recommend that you either run that business with intensity and generate excellent proposals and follow-up, or don't bother. As a triathlete I was privileged to race all over the world on some incredible courses, while developing relationships with various athletes and race directors, with many of whom my friendships still stand. I could not have had those experiences on prize winnings alone. My efforts in gaining these opportunities were large, but the rewards are still priceless.

Appendix A:
Running Pace Chart

Mile Pace	MPH	5 Km	5 Miles	10 Km	15 Km	10 Miles	13.1 Miles	26.2 Miles
05:00	12.00	15:32	25:00	31:04	46:36	50:00	1:05:30	2:11:00
05:10	11.61	16:03	25:50	32:06	48:09	51:40	1:07:41	2:15:22
05:20	11.25	16:34	26:40	33:08	49:43	53:20	1:09:52	2:19:44
05:30	10.91	17:05	27:30	34:11	51:16	55:00	1:12:03	2:24:06
05:40	10.59	17:36	28:20	35:13	52:49	56:40	1:14:14	2:28:28
05:50	10.29	18:07	29:10	36:15	54:22	58:20	1:16:25	2:32:50
06:00	10.00	18:38	30:00	37:17	55:55	1:00:00	1:18:36	2:37:12
06:10	9.73	19:10	30:50	38:19	57:29	1:01:40	1:20:47	2:41:34
06:20	9.47	19:41	31:40	39:21	59:02	1:03:20	1:22:58	2:45:56
06:30	9.23	20:12	32:30	40:23	1:00:35	1:05:00	1:25:09	2:50:18
06:40	9.00	20:43	33:20	41:25	1:02:08	1:06:40	1:27:20	2:54:40
06:50	8.78	21:14	34:10	42:28	1:03:41	1:08:20	1:29:31	2:59:02
07:00	8.57	21:45	35:00	43:30	1:05:15	1:10:00	1:31:42	3:03:24
07:10	8.37	22:16	35:50	44:32	1:06:48	1:11:40	1:33:53	3:07:46
07:20	8.18	22:47	36:40	45:34	1:08:21	1:13:20	1:36:04	3:12:08
07:30	8.00	23:18	37:30	46:36	1:09:54	1:15:00	1:38:15	3:16:30
07:40	7.83	23:49	38:20	47:38	1:11:27	1:16:40	1:40:26	3:20:52
07:50	7.66	24:20	39:10	48:40	1:13:01	1:18:20	1:42:37	3:25:14
08:00	7.50	24:51	40:00	49:43	1:14:34	1:20:00	1:44:48	3:29:36
08:10	7.35	25:22	40:50	50:45	1:16:07	1:21:40	1:46:59	3:33:58
08:20	7.20	25:53	41:40	51:47	1:17:40	1:23:20	1:49:10	3:38:20
08:30	7.06	26:24	42:30	52:49	1:19:13	1:25:00	1:51:21	3:42:42
08:40	6.92	26:56	43:20	53:51	1:20:47	1:26:40	1:53:32	3:47:04
08:50	6.79	27:27	44:10	54:53	1:22:20	1:28:20	1:55:43	3:51:26

Mile Pace	MPH	5 Km	5 Miles	10 Km	15 Km	10 Miles	13.1 Miles	26.2 Miles
09:00	6.67	27:58	45:00	55:55	1:23:53	1:30:00	1:57:54	3:55:48
09:10	6.55	28:29	45:50	56:58	1:25:26	1:31:40	2:00:05	4:00:10
09:20	6.43	29:00	46:40	58:00	1:27:00	1:33:20	2:02:16	4:04:32
09:30	6.32	29:31	47:30	59:02	1:28:33	1:35:00	2:04:27	4:08:54
09:40	6.21	30:02	48:20	1:00:04	1:30:06	1:36:40	2:06:38	4:13:16
09:50	6.10	30:33	49:10	1:01:06	1:31:39	1:38:20	2:08:49	4:17:38
10:00	6.00	31:04	50:00	1:02:08	1:33:12	1:40:00	2:11:00	4:22:00
10:10	5.90	31:35	50:50	1:03:10	1:34:46	1:41:40	2:13:11	4:26:22
10:20	5.81	32:06	51:40	1:04:13	1:36:19	1:43:20	2:15:22	4:30:44
10:30	5.71	32:37	52:30	1:05:15	1:37:52	1:45:00	2:17:33	4:35:06
10:40	5.63	33:08	53:20	1:06:17	1:39:25	1:46:40	2:19:44	4:39:28
10:50	5.54	33:39	54:10	1:07:19	1:40:58	1:48:20	2:21:55	4:43:50
11:00	5.45	34:11	55:00	1:08:21	1:42:32	1:50:00	2:24:06	4:48:12
11:10	5.37	34:42	55:50	1:09:23	1:44:05	1:51:40	2:26:17	4:52:34
11:20	5.29	35:13	56:40	1:10:25	1:45:38	1:53:20	2:28:28	4:56:56
11:30	5.22	35:44	57:30	1:11:27	1:47:11	1:55:00	2:30:39	5:01:18
11:40	5.14	36:15	58:20	1:12:30	1:48:44	1:56:40	2:32:50	5:05:40
11:50	5.07	36:46	59:10	1:13:32	1:50:18	1:58:20	2:35:01	5:10:02
12:00	5.00	37:17	1:00:00	1:14:34	1:51:51	2:00:00	2:37:12	5:14:24
12:10	4.93	37:48	1:00:50	1:15:36	1:53:24	2:01:40	2:39:23	5:18:46
12:20	4.86	38:19	1:01:40	1:16:38	1:54:57	2:03:20	2:41:34	5:23:08
12:30	4.80	38:50	1:02:30	1:17:40	1:56:30	2:05:00	2:43:45	5:27:30
12:40	4.74	39:21	1:03:20	1:18:42	1:58:04	2:06:40	2:45:56	5:31:52
12:50	4.68	39:52	1:04:10	1:19:45	1:59:37	2:08:20	2:48:07	5:36:14
13:00	4.62	40:23	1:05:00	1:20:47	2:01:10	2:10:00	2:50:18	5:40:36
13:10	4.56	40:54	1:05:50	1:21:49	2:02:43	2:11:40	2:52:29	5:44:58
13:20	4.50	41:25	1:06:40	1:22:51	2:04:16	2:13:20	2:54:40	5:49:20
13:30	4.44	41:57	1:07:30	1:23:53	2:05:50	2:15:00	2:56:51	5:53:42
13:40	4.39	42:28	1:08:20	1:24:55	2:07:23	2:16:40	2:59:02	5:58:04
13:50	4.34	42:59	1:09:10	1:25:57	2:08:56	2:18:20	3:01:13	6:02:26

Mile Pace	MPH	5 Km	5 Miles	10 Km	15 Km	10 Miles	13.1 Miles	26.2 Miles
14:00	4.29	43:30	1:10:00	1:27:00	2:10:29	2:20:00	3:03:24	6:06:48
14:10	4.24	44:01	1:10:50	1:28:02	2:12:02	2:21:40	3:05:35	6:11:10
14:20	4.19	44:32	1:11:40	1:29:04	2:13:36	2:23:20	3:07:46	6:15:32
14:30	4.14	45:03	1:12:30	1:30:06	2:15:09	2:25:00	3:09:57	6:19:54
14:40	4.09	45:34	1:13:20	1:31:08	2:16:42	2:26:40	3:12:08	6:24:16
14:50	4.04	46:05	1:14:10	1:32:10	2:18:15	2:28:20	3:14:19	6:28:38
15:00	4.00	46:36	1:15:00	1:33:12	2:19:49	2:30:00	3:16:30	6:33:00
15:10	3.96	47:07	1:15:50	1:34:14	2:21:22	2:31:40	3:18:41	6:37:22
15:20	3.91	47:38	1:16:40	1:35:17	2:22:55	2:33:20	3:20:52	6:41:44
15:30	3.87	48:09	1:17:30	1:36:19	2:24:28	2:35:00	3:23:03	6:46:06
15:40	3.83	48:40	1:18:20	1:37:21	2:26:01	2:36:40	3:25:14	6:50:28
15:50	3.79	49:12	1:19:10	1:38:23	2:27:35	2:38:20	3:27:25	6:54:50
16:00	3.75	49:43	1:20:00	1:39:25	2:29:08	2:40:00	3:29:36	6:59:12

Appendix B: Sample Schedules

These sample training and tapering schedules are a reference to help you fine-tune your own program. Each week of training takes into account the important variables of consistency, variety, and rest and recovery—all are important ingredients to racing your best.

Each program offers a guideline to use heart rate training and perceived exertion to determine your intensity levels for training as well as some motivational tips or goals for each week of training. The four-week programs highlighted are not the recommended amount of time needed to prepare for an event in full. These sample schedules are just that, samples. Remember, you are unique and your training program should be suited to your abilities and time constraints.

SAMPLE TRAINING SCHEDULES

Use the following guidelines when reviewing these schedules:

TRAINING LEVELS

Level 1: Recovery
  Used for: Recovery, warming up, cooling down, baseline endurance
  Perceived Exertion: 9–10, you can talk easily, effort is extremely easy
  HR Range: 65–75% of max

Level 2: Aerobic
  Used for: Improving aerobic capacity, warming up, cooling down, longer races until fitness increases
  Perceived Exertion: 11–13, conversations are comfortable, effort is easy
  HR Range: 75–80% of max

Level 3: High-End Aerobic to Low Anaerobic
  Used for: Improving lactate system, intervals, hill repeats, tempo training, long to moderate distance races depending on fitness
  Perceived Exertion: 14–15, short conversations are possible, effort is moderate to challenging
  HR Range: 80–85% of max

Level 4: Lactate or Anaerobic Threshold
  Used for: Improving ability to mobilize lactate for longer periods, intervals, hill repeats, effort is challenging to difficult, moderate to short races depending on your fitness
  Perceived Exertion: 16–18, difficult to speak
  HR Range: 85–90% of max

Level 5: Sub-maximum to Maximum Effort
  Used for: Training fast twitch to develop speed, intervals, hill repeats, sprint events
  Perceived Exertion: 19–20, breathing is labored, effort is very difficult
  HR Range: 90–100% of max

BEGINNER–SPRINT-DISTANCE TRIATHLON

Four-week schedule for a beginner training for a sprint-distance triathlon

WEEK 1

	Monday	Tuesday	Wednesday	Thursday	Friday	Saturday	Sunday
Stretch	15 min	15 min	15 min	15 min	15 min	15 min	15 min
Bike		30 min (L2–L3)				45 min (L2–L4)	
Run or walk/run			20 min (L1–L2)				30 min (L1–L2)
Swim		400 yds		400 yds			
Walking lunges		2 x 10			2 x 10		
Push-ups		2 x 10			2 x 10		
Abs		20			20		

Notes: **Bike** on a flatter stretch of road. Spin easy and focus on releasing the downward pressure on your pedals during the recovery phase of your pedal stroke. **Run** the entire workout at the levels indicated if you have been a consistent runner coming into this program. Or walk 2 minutes, run 2 minutes, alternate this for the duration. Unless you are swimming masters, **swim** 100 yards any stroke or drill (L2); kick 100 yards (with a kickboard) (L2); 2 x 50 yards freestyle with 15-second rest between each (L3); 100 yards any stroke (L2).

WEEK 2

	Monday	Tuesday	Wednesday	Thursday	Friday	Saturday	Sunday
Stretch	15 min	15 min	15 min	15 min	15 min	15 min	15 min
Bike		40 min (L1–L2)		40 min (L2–L3)		50 min (L2–L4)	
Run or walk/run			25 min (L1–L2)				35 min (L1–L2)
Swim		600 yds		600 yds			
Walking lunges		2 x 10		2 x 10			
Push-ups		2 x 10		2 x 10			
Abs		30		30			

Notes: **Swim** 100 yards any stroke or drill (L2); kick 100 yards (with a kickboard) (L2); 4 x 50 yards freestyle with 15-second rest between each (L4); pull 100 (L3); 100 yards any stroke or drill (L2). Do same swim workout on Thursday, but replace 4 x 50 with 2 x 100 with 15-second rest between each (L4). On Saturday, **bike** at least two 1-minute climbs during the ride; push each climb to L4. **Run** the entire workout at the levels indicated if you have been a consistent runner coming into this program. Or walk 2 minutes, run 2 minutes, alternate this for the duration.

WEEK 3

	Monday	Tuesday	Wednesday	Thursday	Friday	Saturday	Sunday
Stretch	15 min	15 min	15 min	15 min	15 min	15 min	15 min
Bike		35 min (L2–L3)				60 min (L2–L4)	
Run		10 min (L1–L2)	30 min (L1–L3)				40 min (L1–L2)
Swim		900 yds		900 yds			15 min (L2)
Walking lunges		2 x 15		2 x 15			
Side-shuffle lunges		2 x 10		2 x 15			
Push-ups		2 x 15		2 x 15			
Abs		40		40			

Notes: **Run** the workouts at levels indicated, or, on Wednesday and Sunday, alternate between walking 2 minutes and running 4 minutes for the first 15 minutes. Then do four 2-minute hill efforts at L3 (fast hiking) with a 2-minute jog at L1 between each. Alternate walking and running for the remainder of workout. **Swim** 200 yards of any stroke or drill (L2); kick 100 (with kickboard) (L2); 4 x 50 yards freestyle, with 15-second rest between each (L4); pull 200 (L3); 200 yards of any stroke or drill (L2). On Thursday workout, increase kick to 2 x 100 with 15-second rest between each (L4); pull 100 (L2). On Saturday, **bike** at least three 1-minute climbs during the ride; push each climb to L4. On Sunday, **swim** is open water; practice diving through waves and swimming past the surf line.

WEEK 4 (RECOVERY WEEK)

	Monday	Tuesday	Wednesday	Thursday	Friday	Saturday	Sunday
Stretch	15 min	15 min	15 min	15 min	15 min	15 min	15 min
Bike		30 min (L2–L3)		40 min (L1–L2)			40 min (L1–L2)
Run			20 min (L1–L2)				
Swim		800 yds		800 yds			15 min
Walking lunges		2 x 10		2 x 10			
Side-shuffle lunges		2 x 10		2 x 10			
Push-ups		2 x 10		2 x 10			
Abs		40		40			

Notes: **Swim** 100 yards of any stroke or drill (L2); kick 100 (with a kickboard) (L2); 2 x 200 yards freestyle, with 40-second rest between each (L4); sprint 4 x 25 yards freestyle (L4); 100 yards of any stroke or drill (L2). On Thursday workout, swim 100 yards of any stroke or drill (L2); kick 2 x 100 yards with 10-second rest between each (L2); 200 yards freestyle (L4); 200 yards pull (L2); 100 yards any stroke or drill (L2). Sunday swim is open water. **Run** for the duration or alternate between walking 2 minutes and running 5 minutes. Make the Sunday **bike** a leisurely ride through a new neighborhood.

BEGINNER–INTERNATIONAL-DISTANCE TRIATHLON

Four-week schedule for a beginner training for an international-distance triathlon

WEEK 1

	Monday	Tuesday	Wednesday	Thursday	Friday	Saturday	Sunday
Stretch	15 min	15 min	15 min	15 min	15 min	15 min	15 min
Bike		45 min (L2–L3)		35 min (L1–L2)		60 min (L2–L4)	
Run			30 min (L1–L2)				40 min (L1–L2)
Swim		700 yds		700 yds			
Walking lunges		2 x 10		2 x 10			
Push-ups		2 x 10		2 x 10			
Abs		20		20			

Notes: **Bike** on a flatter stretch of road. Spin easy and focus on releasing the downward pressure on your pedals during the recovery phase of your pedal stroke. For the 60-minute ride, include two 1-minute climbs, push each climb to L4. **Run** entire workout at the levels indicated if you have been a consistent runner coming into this program. Or walk 2 minutes, run 2 minutes, alternate for the duration. Unless you are swimming masters, **swim** 200 yards any stroke or drill (L2); kick (with a kickboard) 100 yards (L2); 6 x 50 yards freestyle with a 15-second rest between each (L3); 100 yards any stroke or drill (L2).

WEEK 2

	Monday	Tuesday	Wednesday	Thursday	Friday	Saturday	Sunday
Stretch	15 min	15 min	15 min	15 min	15 min	15 min	15 min
Bike		50 min (L2–L3)		45 min (L1–L2)		75 min (L2–L4)	
Run		25 min (L1–L2)	35 min (L1–L2)				50 min (L1–L2)
Swim		1000 yds		900 yds			
Walking lunges			2 x 10		2 x 10		
Push-ups			2 x 10		2 x 10		
Abs			20		20		

Notes: **Bike** for the 75-minute ride, include at least four 1-minute climbs, push each climb to L4. **Swim** 200 yards any stroke or drill (L2); kick (with a kickboard) 100 yards (L2); 6 x 50 yards freestyle with a 15-second rest between each (L4); pull 200 yards (L3); 200 yards any stroke or drill (L2). On Thursday workout, increase kick (with a kickboard) to 2 x 100 yards with a 10-second rest between each (L2); 3 x 100 yards freestyle with a 15-second rest between each (L4); pull 100 yards (L2); 100 yards any stroke or drill (L2). **Run** at the levels indicated, or on Wednesday and Sunday, alternate between walking 2 minutes and running 3 minutes for the duration of the workout.

WEEK 3

	Monday	Tuesday	Wednesday	Thursday	Friday	Saturday	Sunday
Stretch	15 min	15 min	15 min	15 min	15 min	15 min	15 min
Bike		45 min (L2–L3)		55 min (L1–L2)		85 min (L2–L4)	
Run		20 min (L1–L2)	40 min (L1–L3)		20 min (L1–L2)		60 min (L1–L2)
Swim		1200 yds		1200 yds			15 min (L2)
Walking lunges			2 x 15		2 x 15		
Side-shuffle lunges			2 x 10		2 x 15		
Push-ups			2 x 15		2 x 15		
Abs			40		40		

Notes: **Run** workouts at the levels indicated, or on Wednesday, alternate between walking 2 minutes, running 4 minutes for the first 15 minutes, then do four 2-minute hill efforts at L3 (fast hiking), jogging 2 minutes at L1 between each. Focus on using your upper body and arm swing for power on each hill. Alternate walking and running for the rest of the workout. On Friday, alternate between walking 2 minutes and running 5 minutes, and on Sunday alternate between walking 1 minute and running 3 minutes. On Saturday, **bike** at least four 1-minute climbs, pushing each climb to L4 on each climb. **Swim** 200 yards any stroke or drill (L2); kick 100 yards (L2); 10 x 50 yards freestyle with a 15-second rest between each (L4); pull 200 yards (L3); 200 yards any stroke or drill (L2). On Thursday workout, increase kick to 2 x 100 yards with a 10-second rest between each (L2); 2 x 100 freestyle with 15-second rest between (L4). On Sunday, **swim** is open water; practice diving through waves and swimming past the surf line.

WEEK 4 (RECOVERY WEEK)

	Monday	Tuesday	Wednesday	Thursday	Friday	Saturday	Sunday
Stretch	15 min	15 min	15 min	15 min	15 min	15 min	15 min
Bike		45 min (L2–L3)		45 min (L1–L2)		60 min (L1–L2)	
Run			30 min (L1–L2)				40 min (L1–L2)
Swim		1500 yds		1500 yds			15 min (L2)
Walking lunges			2 x 10		2 x 10		
Side-shuffle lunges			2 x 10		2 x 10		
Push-ups			2 x 10		2 x 10		
Abs			40		40		

Notes: **Swim** 300 yards any stroke or drill (L2); kick 100 yards (L2); 4 x 200 yards freestyle with a 40-second rest between each (L4); 4 x 25-yard sprints (L4); 200 yards any stroke or drill (L2). On Thursday workout, 200 yards any stroke or drill (L2); kick 2 x 100 yard with 10-second rest between each (L2); 500 yards freestyle (L4); pull 2 x 200 yards (L2); 100 yards any stroke or drill (L2). Sunday swim is open water; practice diving through waves and swimming past the surf line. **Run** at the levels indicated, or alternate between walking 2 minutes and running 5 minutes for the duration of workout. Easy neighborhood **bike** ride on Saturday!

SAMPLE TAPERING SCHEDULES

TWO-WEEK TAPER FOR A BEGINNING TRIATHLETE TRAINING FOR A SPRINT-DISTANCE TRIATHLON

WEEK 1

	Monday	Tuesday	Wednesday	Thursday	Friday	Saturday	Sunday
Stretch	15 min	15 min	15 min	15 min	15 min	15 min	15 min
Bike		40 min (L2–L2)		40 min (L2–L4)		50 min (L2–L4)	
Run		15 min (L1–L2)	40 min (L2–L4)				35 min (L1–L2)
Swim		1200 yds		1200 yds			20 min
Walking lunges			3 x 15		3 x 15		
Side-shuffle lunges			3 x 15		3 x 15		
Push-ups			3 x 15		3 x 15		
Abs			40		40		

Notes: On Wednesday **run** entire workout at levels indicated, or alternate between walking 1 minute and running 5 minutes for the first 15 minutes. Do five 2-minute hill repeats at L4, walk 1 minute between each. Alternate between walking 1 minute and running 5 minutes for the duration of the workout. On Sunday, walk 1 minute, run 4 minutes, alternate for the duration, or run the entire workout at the levels indicated. On Thursday **ride**, easy spin for 20 minutes at L2, then three 90 second hill repeats at L4 with a 1-minute recovery between each. Finish ride at L2. On Saturday ride, first 20 minutes at L2, then two 3-minute intervals at race pace with 3 minutes of easy spinning at L2 between each. Finish ride at L2. **Swim** 200 yards any stroke or drill (L2); kick 4 x 50, no board for 25, stroke (not freestyle) for 25, mix it up (L2); 2 x 200 freestyle with 50-second rest between each (L4); pull 3 x 100 with 20-second rest between each; 100 any stroke or drill (L2). On Thursday, 100 any stroke or drill (L2); pull 100 with 15-second rest between each (L3); kick 4 x 50, no board for 25, stroke (not freestyle) for 25, mix it up (L2); drill 3 x 100 kick on stomach, right arm, left arm, swim, each 25 (L2); 4 x 75 yards freestyle with 10-second rest between each (L4); 2 x 50 sprint with 10-second rest between each (L4); 100 yards any stroke or drill (L2). Sunday swim is open water.

WEEK 2

	Monday	Tuesday	Wednesday	Thursday	Friday	Saturday	Sunday
Stretch	15 min	15 min	15 min	15 min	15 min	15 min	15 min
Bike		35 min (L1–L2)		30 min (L1–L4)		10 min (L1–L2)	E
Run			20 min (L1–L4)				C
Swim		1000 yds		800 yds		10 min	A
Walking lunges		1 x 10					
Push-ups		1 x 10					R
Abs		20					

Notes: **Swim** 200 yards any stroke or drill (L2); kick 100 (with kickboard) (L2); 8 x 50 with 15-second rest between each (L4); pull 200 (L4); 100 yards any stroke or drill (L2). On Thursday, 200 yards any stroke or drill (L2); kick 2 x 100 with 10-second rest between each (L2); 4 x 100 with 15-second rest between each (L4); pull 2 x 100 with 30-second rest between each (L3); 100 yards any stroke or drill (L2). Saturday swim is open water. **Run** 10 minutes at L1–L2, run three 30-second intervals at L4 with 1-minute of walking between each. Finish the run at L1. On Thursday, **bike** 10 minutes at L1–L2, do five 30-second intervals at L4 with 1 minute of easy spinning between each. Finish ride at L1. **Race** on Sunday!

TWO-WEEK TAPER FOR A BEGINNING TRIATHLETE
TRAINING FOR AN INTERNATIONAL-DISTANCE TRIATHLON

WEEK 1

	Monday	Tuesday	Wednesday	Thursday	Friday	Saturday	Sunday
Stretch	15 min	15 min	15 min	15 min	15 min	15 min	15 min
Bike		50 min (L1–L2)		60 min (L2–L4)		75 min (L2–L4)	
Run		25 min (L1–L2)	50 min (L1–L2)		50 min (L1–L2)		45 min (L2–L3)
Swim		1600 yds		2200 yds	1500 yds		20 min
Walking lunges		3 x 15		3 x 15			
Side-shuffle lunges		3 x 15		3 x 15			
Push-ups		3 x 15		3 x 15			
Abs		40		40			

Notes: **Swim** 300 yards any stroke or drill (L2); kick 6 x 50, no board for 25, stroke (not freestyle) for 25, mix it up (L2); 3 x 200 with 50-second rest between each (L4); pull 2 x 100 with 20-second rest between each (L4); 100 yards any stroke or drill (L2). On Thursday, swim 300 yards any stroke or drill (L2); pull 2 x 200 with 15-second rest between each (L3); kick 4 x 50, no board for 25, stroke (not freestyle) for 25 (L2), mix it up; 3 x 100 kick on stomach, right arm, left arm, swim, 25 each (L2); 10 x 75 with 10-second rest between each (L4); 5 x 50 sprint with 10-second rest between each (L4); 200 yards any stroke or drill (L2). On Friday, swim 200 yards any stroke or drill (L1); kick 4 x 100 on stomach, right arm, left arm, swim, 25 each (L2); pull 200 (L3); swim 100, 200, 100 with 30-second rest between each (L4); pull 200 (L3); 100 any stroke or drill (L2). **Run** entire workout at levels indicated, or alternate between walking 1 minute and running 5 minutes for first 15 minutes. Do five 2-minute hill repeats at L4 (running) and walk 1 minute between each. Alternate between 1 minute of walking and 5 minutes of running for duration of workout. On Thursday, **bike** easy for 20 minutes at L2, then ride six 90-second hill repeats at L4 with a 1-minute recovery spin between each. Finish the ride at L2. On Saturday ride, easy spin for 20 minutes at L2, then three 5-minute intervals at race pace with a 3-minute easy spin between each (L2). Finish the ride at L2.

WEEK 2

	Monday	Tuesday	Wednesday	Thursday	Friday	Saturday	Sunday
Stretch	15 min	15 min	15 min	15 min	15 min	15 min	15 min
Bike		40 min (L1–L2)		40 min (L1–L4)		10 min (L1–L2)	
Run			30 min (L1–L4)				
Swim		1200 yds		1200 yds		10 min (L2)	
Walking lunges		1 x 10					
Push-ups		1 x 10					
Abs		20					

R A C E

Notes: **Swim** 200 yards any stroke or drill (L2); kick 100 (with kickboard) (L2); 8 x 50 with 15-second rest between each (L4); pull 2 x 200 with 20-second rest between each (L4); 100 yards any stroke or drill (L2). On Thursday, swim 200 any stroke or drill (L2); kick (with a kickboard) 2 x 100 with 10-second rest between each (L2); 4 x 100 with 15-second rest between each (L4); pull 3 x 100 with 30-second rest between each (L3); 100 yards any stroke or drill (L2). Open-water swim on Saturday. **Run** 10 minutes at L1–L2, do three 30-second intervals at L4 with 1 minute of walking between each. Finish run at L1. **Bike** 10 minutes at L1–L2, do five 30-second intervals at L4 with 1 minute of L2 easy spinning between each. Finish ride at L1. **Race** on Sunday!

Glossary

A race. The most important events of the season in reference to performance with the goal of a personal best or a peak performance. Usually an athlete will have two to three A races in a season; there may be only one. These are the ones you want to prime for. *See also* B race, C race.

active recovery. Can include the cool down at the end of a training bout, as well as methods that actively restore the body with fluids and vital nutrients that will aid recovery.

aero bars. Various styles of handlebars that position the rider in a more aerodynamic position than a standard drop handlebar. Often used for time trials.

aero tubing. Bike frame tubing that is wing or teardrop shaped.

aerobic. In the presence of oxygen.

anaerobic. Without oxygen.

anaerobic threshold. Onset of blood lactate accumulation during exercise or the exercise intensity at which lactic acid is produced faster than it can be metabolized. *See also* lactate threshold.

B race. Moderately important events but not important enough to generate a complete taper or plan the season around. B races are excellent events to use as benchmarks to test fitness, try a new fuel plan, new bike, or race pace.

ballistic stretching. Passive stretching done with a bouncing motion. Not recommended.

baseline endurance. A training level used to generate a foundation of aerobic fitness.

baseline flexibility. A person's genetic predisposition to flexibility. How far a person can stretch comfortably without training flexibility.

bilateral breathing. Alternating breathing on both sides of the body while swimming freestyle.

biomechanics. Mechanics of the body.

bonk. General fatigue resulting from muscle glycogen depletion. When glycogen stores are severely threatened, brain function is impaired.

Borg Scale. A 15-point scale used to determine a person's perceived exertion during exercise.

brick workout. A workout combining two or more disciplines executed one after another without a break in between. In triathlon this usually entails a bike/run workout.

build training. A training cycle methodically designed to produce positive training results over time.

build-recover cycle. A full periodization cycle. *See also* periodize.

burnout. An exhaustive, psychophysiological malfunction in response to repeated efforts to try to adapt to training.

C race. Events an athlete wants to do for fun and camaraderie and as a diversion to training but not necessarily for top performance.

cadence. Revolutions per minute of pedaling on a bicycle.

calorie. A unit of heat and a form of energy.

carbohydrates. Used in numerous roles in living things, such as the storage and transport of energy and structural components. They play a major role in the working process of the immune system, fertilization, pathogenesis, blood clotting, and development. Carbs are an important part of the human diet.

dead shoes. Running shoes that are broken down to the point at which they should no longer be used.

deep-water running. Simulating the act of running while suspended in deep water while wearing a foam belt for flotation.

drafting. To ride or swim closely behind another rider or swimmer to make maximum use of his slipstream.

draft-legal. A triathlon event that allows drafting on the bike portion of the race.

drag. The aerodynamic force exerted on an airfoil, airplane, or other aerodynamic body that tends to reduce its forward motion.

drivetrain. A group of components on a bicycle that generate power to propel the bike.

electrolyte. Any substance containing free ions that behaves as an electrically conductive medium. Found in sports drinks and available in the form of tablets. During endurance events, electrolytes help keep the blood sugar

and hydration scale in balance.

fast twitch. Pertaining to muscle fiber that contracts relatively rapidly, used particularly in actions requiring maximum effort for a short duration such as sprinting.

fat. A category of molecules important for many forms of life, serving both structural and metabolic functions. Fats are an important part of the human diet.

foot bed. A mass-produced foot support that is inserted into a shoe.

four-week periodization. Dividing training into four-week periods to work toward accomplishing specific goals. An athlete builds training over a three-week period and then takes an easier week during week four to allow the body to fully integrate the training. This is done to best plan build phases, peaks, and recovery phases within a training cycle.

glycogen. A polysaccharide of glucose (Glc) that functions as the primary short-term energy storage in cells.

heart rate. The number of times a heart beats in a minute. *See also* maximum heart rate, resting heart rate.

heart rate monitor. A device that records heart rate in real time.

heart rate range. Heart rate array presented in percentage of maximum heart rate, i.e. 80–85 percent of maximum heart rate.

high-end aerobic. The upper end of an athlete's aerobic training level.

hill repeats. Repetitions of high-intensity work followed by periods of rest or low activity. Done on an incline.

hyponatremia. Also known as "water intoxication." Dangerously low levels of sodium concentration in the blood.

ice bath. To sit or stand in very cold water or water laced with ice to aid recovery.

international distance. A triathlon that includes a 1.5K swim, a 40K bike ride, and a 10K run. *See also* Olympic distance.

intervals. Repetitions of high-speed and high-intensity work followed by periods of rest or low activity.

kickboard. A small, flat flotation board that a swimmer uses in order to focus forward movement on kicking only.

lactate system. Uses glucose (or glycogen) for energy in the absence of oxygen.

lactate threshold. See anaerobic threshold.

long-course event. Also known as a half-Ironman event, which includes a 1.2-mile swim, 56-mile bike, 13.1-mile run.

masters swim. An organized, coached swim workout for adults.

maximum heart rate. The maximum number of times a heart can beat in one minute's time.

negative split running. When the latter part of a run effort is faster than the initial or middle sections, or when a runner consistently and gradually increases their pace over the duration of the run.

Olympic distance. A triathlon that includes a 1.5K swim, a 40K bike ride, and a 10K run. *See also* international distance.

orthotic. A customized, molded foot support that is worn in a shoe.

overtraining. Too much training stress resulting in a malfunction in training adaptation.

overuse injury. An injury incurred by repetitive use.

pacing. Executing a particular speed for a given distance and event.

passive recovery. Methods such as massage, nutrition, and sleep used to aid in training recovery.

pedal stroke. A full revolution of the pedals on a bicycle.

peleton. The large, main group in a bicycle road race.

perceived exertion. A perceived measure of expenditure during activity.

periodize. Modulating volume and intensity of training over time to both stimulate gains and allow recovery.

plyometrics. Any exercise where the muscle is contracted eccentrically and then immediately concentrically. The muscle is stretched (i.e., loaded) before it is contracted. A good example is push-ups with a clap in-between each push-up.

positive recovery. Recovery that may offer training gains, such as sleep.

power meter. A device on a bicycle that measures the power output of the rider.

PR. Personal record for a particular distance or event.

pronate. The heel bone angles inward and the arch tends to collapse. This flattens the arch as the foot strikes the ground.

proprioceptive neuromuscular facilitation stretching. A type of flexibility exercise that combines muscle contraction and relaxation with passive and partner-assisted stretching. Also known as PNF stretching.

protein. Large organic compounds made of amino acids. Proteins are essential parts of organisms and participate in every process within cells. They are an important part of the human diet.

pull buoy. A flotation device that swimmers place between their legs to bring their legs to the surface of the water and eliminate the need to kick.

race wheels. Usually a lighter, more aerodynamic wheel than a training wheel, normally ridden only during races.

racing flats. Running shoes that are usually much lighter than training shoes. Normally used only during races or faster training sessions.

recovery heart rate. Heart rate one minute after an athlete stops exercising.

resting heart rate. The number of times the heart beats in one minute when an athlete is at complete rest.

rim tape. Specialized tape placed on the inside of a bicycle rim to cover the nipple holes and protect the tube from the rim.

seat tube angle. The geometric angle between the top tube and the seat tube of a bicycle frame triangle.

set. One group of repetitions of an exercise.

speed work. Intervals, hill repeats, tempo training, or other training that involves an increase in speed.

spinning. When a cyclist turns the pedals around lightly and quickly, while in a low (easy) gear.

sprint distance. A triathlon with a 0.5-mile swim, 13-mile bike, 3-mile run, plus or minus a bit of distance in each.

static stretching. Holding a body position while engaging a muscle group in a stretch. Stretching until a gentle elongation of the muscle is felt and holding that position.

streamline. The most hydrodynamic position a person can take while accelerating underwater. A swimmer must tuck the head into the collar bone, pointing both arms straight ahead in a tight line. The underside of both arms should be pressing on the back of the head.

stride length. The distance covered in one step of running.

strides. Multiple steps of running, or a build up of running speed over 100 yards followed by 100 yards of easy jogging.

super-sets. A set of strength training exercises that group two or three exercises together, alternating until all sets are complete for each exercise.

supinate. An outward rotation of the foot so the sole is upward and the outer edge of the sole bears the body's weight.

swim start position. An athlete's placement within the context of all of the other competitors at the start line of a race.

tempo training. Consists of a warm-up phase, a tempo pace phase, and a cool-down phase. Tempo pace is run at the athlete's anaerobic or lactate threshold, or a different predetermined intensity level.

time trial. A solo bike race against the clock.

time-trial design. A bicycle frame with a steeper road seat tube geometry of around 78 degrees.

time trial position. The aerodynamic position of the rider on a bicycle.

training effect. The cardiovascular and structural "advancement" that the body attains through training. In order to gain training effect, an athlete needs both training stress and recovery/rest. The effect that training has on an athlete's body, physiologically, structurally, and cardiovascularly.

training wheels. Wheels on a bicycle used primarily for training sessions.

transition area. The area at a triathlon venue provided for athletes to transition from one sport to the next. It houses racks to hold bicycles and a small section of ground space for the shoes, clothing, and gear of each athlete.

traumatic injury. Damage or harm to the structure or function of the body caused by an outside agent or force.

ultra running. Running longer than a traditional 26.2-mile marathon.

Resources

BOOKS

CYCLING

Armstrong, Lance. *It's Not About the Bike.* New York: Broadway. 2001.

___. *Every Second Counts.* New York: Broadway. 2003.

Armstrong, Lance, and Chris Carmichael. *Lance Armstrong Performance Program.* Emmaus, Pennsylvania: Rodale. 2000.

Bernhardt, Gail. *The Female Cyclist: Gearing Up a Level.* Boulder, Colorado: VeloPress. 1995.

___. *Training Plans for Multisport Athletes: Your Essential Guide to Triathlon, Duathlon, Xterra, Ironman, and Endurance Racing.* Boulder, Colorado: VeloPress. 2002.

Carmichael, Chris. *Training Tips for Cyclists and Triathletes.* Boulder, Colorado: VeloPress. 2001.

Edwards, Sally, and Sally Reed. *The Heart-Rate Monitor Book for Cyclists.* 2nd edition. Boulder, Colorado: VeloPress. 2002.

Harr, Eric. *Ride Fast: Get Up to Speed on Your Bike in 10 Weeks or Less.* New York: St. Martins Press. 1999.

Van Den Bosch, Paul. *Cycling for Triathletes.* Aachan, Germany: Meyer & Meyer Verlag. 2005.

Wallenfels, Linda. *Triathlete's Guide to Bike Training.* Boulder, Colorado: VeloPress. 2000.

Zinn, Lennard. *Zinn and the Art of Triathlon Bikes: Aerodynamics, Bike Fit, Speed Tuning and Maintenance.* Boulder, Colorado: VeloPress. 2003.

GENERAL

Aschwer, Hermann. *Tips for Success.* Aachan, Germany: Meyer & Meyer Verlag. 1997.

Babbitt, Bob. *25 Years of the Ironman Triathlon World Championship,* 2nd edition. Aachan, Germany: Meyer & Meyer Verlag. 2000.

Barfield, Mark. *Starting Triathlon.* North Pomfret, Vermont: Trafalgar Square. 2002.

Carty, Michelle. *Racing to the Finish.* Huntington Beach, California: Creative Teaching Press. 1997.

Cox, Lynne. *Swimming to Antarctica.* New York: Random House. 2004.

Dahlkoetter, Joanne. *Your Performing Edge.* Mechanicsburg, Pennsylvania: Stackpole Books. 1999.

Donnelly, Julie, and Zev Cohen. *The Pain-Free Triathlete.* Nanuet, New York: Makai Press. 2002.

Donnelly, Julie, and Zev Cohen, and Kevin McKinnon. *The Triathlon for Youth:*

Training a Healthy Introduction to Competition. Aachan, Germany: Meyer & Meyer Verlag. 2003.

Edwards, Sally. *Triathlon: A Triple Fitness Sport*. New York: McGraw-Hill. 1979.

___. *Triathlons for Kids*. Sacramento: Heart Zones Company. 1988.

___. *Triathlons for Fun*. New York: Winning International. 1988.

Edwards, Sally, Rebecca Brocard Yao, and Kaari Busick. *The Complete Book of Triathlon*. New York: Random House. 1997.

Evans, Marc. *Triathlete's Edge*. Champaign, Illinois: Human Kinetics. 2003.

Fitzgerald, Matt. *Complete Triathlon Book*. New York: Warner Books. 1999. Articles from *Triathlete* magazine.

Harr, Eric. *Pocket Personal Coach: 356 Tips to Energize Your Body, Mind, and Spirit*. Marin County, California: Citron Bay Press. 1995.

___. *The Everyday Athlete: Achieve Greater Fitness, Motivation, and Exercise Results in Just Three Steps*. New York: St. Martins Press. 2003.

___. *Triathlon Training in Four Hours a Week: From Beginner to Finish Line in Just Six Weeks*. Emmaus, Pennsylvania: Rodale. 1999.

Harr, Eric, and Dara Torres. *The Portable Personal Trainer: 100 Ways to Energize Your Workouts and Bring Out the Athlete in You*. New York: Bantam Dell Publishing Group. 2003.

Hobson, Wes, Clark Campbell, and Mike Vickers. *Swim, Bike, Run*. Champaign, Illinois: Human Kinetics. 1997.

Holland, Tom. *The 12-Week Triathlete: Train for a Triathlon in Just 3 Months*. Beverly, Massachusetts: Quayside Publishing Group. 2001.

Jonas, Steven M.D. *Triathloning for Ordinary Mortals*. New York: W.W. Norton and Co. Inc. 2002.

Kearns, Brad. *Breakthrough Triathlon Training: How to Balance Your Busy Life, Avoid Burnout, and Achieve Triathlon Peak Performance*. New York: McGraw-Hill. 2001.

Luchtenberg, Dietmar. *Supplementary Training for Endurance Sports: Optimize Performance—Avoid Overloading*. Aachan, Germany: Meyer & Meyer Verlag. 2003.

Maffetone, Phil. *The Maffetone Method: The Holistic, Low-stress, No-pain Way to Exceptional Fitness*. Camden, Maine: Ragged Mountain Press. 2000.

___. *In Fitness and In Health*. Stamford, New York: D. Barmore Productions. 1997.

McKinnon, Kevin. *A Healthy Guide to Sport: How to Make Your Kids Healthy, Happy, and Ready To Go*. Aachan, Germany: Meyer & Meyer Verlag. 2000.

Mica, Roman, Heather Ramsey, and Randy Gredner. *My Training Starts Tomorrow: The Everyman's Guide to Ironfit Swimming, Cycling, and Running*. LaVergne, Tennessee: Lightning Source. 2002.

Mora, John. *Triathlon 101: Essentials for Multisport*. Champaign, Illinois: Human Kinetics. 1995.

Schindler, John. *Triathlons*. Milwaukee, Wisconsin: Gareth Stevens Publishers. 2000.

Town, Glenn P. *Science of Triathlon Training and Competition.* Champaign, Illinois: Human Kinetics. 1985.

Trew, Steve. *Triathlon.* North Pomfret, Vermont: Trafalgar Square. 1997.

Warren, Barbara, Mark Allen, and Warren Ash. *Lifelong Training.* Aachan, Germany: Meyer & Meyer Verlag. 1999.

IRONMAN

Crutcher, Chris. *Ironman.* New York: Harper Collins Childrens Books. 1999.

Donnelly, Julie, Zev Cohen, and Paul Van Den Bosch. *The Ironman Made Easy: A Maximum of Achievement in a Minimum of Time.* Aachan, Germany: Meyer & Meyer Verlag. 2003.

Fauteux, Ray. *Ironstruck: The Ironman Triathlon Journey.* Lulu.com. 2003.

Friel, Joel, and Gordon Byrn. *Going Long: Training for Ironman-Distance Triathlons.* Boulder, Colorado: VeloPress. 1999.

Huddle, Paul, Roch Frey, and T.J. Murphy. *Start to Finish: Ironman Training, 24 Weeks to an Endurance Triathlon.* Aachan, Germany: Meyer & Meyer Verlag. 1999.

O'Shaughnessy, Michael. *Blue-Collar Ironman: An Introduction to Lifelong Triathlon Training.* Philadelphia: Xlibris Corp. 2002.

Petschnig, Stefan. *10 Years of Ironman Triathlon Austria.* Aachan, Germany: Meyer & Meyer Verlag. 2003.

Rodgers, Tom. *The Perfect Distance: Training for Long Course Triathlon.* Boulder, Colorado: VeloPress, 2002.

Scheppler, Bill. *The Ironman Triathlon.* New York: Rosen Publishing Group. 1997.

LOGBOOK/DIARY

Friel, Joel. *The Triathlete's Training Diary.* Boulder, Colorado: VeloPress. 2007.

Mora, John. *Triathlete Workout Planner.* Champaign, Illinois: Human Kinetics. 2001.

MEDICAL/NUTRITION

Baker, Joe, and Whitney Sedgwick. *Sport Psychology Library: Triathlon.* Morgantown, West Virginia: Fitness Information Technology. 2001.

Bernardot, Dan. *Nutrition for Serious Athletes.* Champaign, Illinois: Human Kinetics. 2000.

Burke, Edmund. *Precision Heart Rate Training.* Champaign, Illinois: Human Kinetics. 1998.

Carmichael, Chris, and Jim Rutberg. *Chris Carmichael's Food for Fitness: Eat Right to Train Right.* New York: G.P. Putnam and Sons. 2004.

____. *Chris Carmichael's Fitness Cookbook.* New York: G.P. Putnam and Sons. 2005.

Dean, Sheila. *Nutrition and Endurance: Where Do I Begin.* Aachan, Germany: Meyer & Meyer Verlag. 2003.

Girard Eberle, Suzanne. *Endurance Sports Nutrition,* 2nd edition. Champaign, Illinois: Human Kinetics. 2003.

Maffetone, Phil. *Eating for Endurance.* Stamford, New York: D. Barmore Productions. 2000.

Miller, Saul, and Peggy Maass Hill. *Sport Psychology for Cyclists.* Boulder,

Colorado: VeloPress. 1999.

Murphy, T.J., and Chris Chorak. *The Unbreakable Athlete: Injury Prevention.* Aachan, Germany: Meyer & Meyer Verlag. 2003.

Ross, Michael J. *Maximum Performance: Sports Medicine for Endurance Athletes.* Boulder, Colorado: VeloPress. 2003.

Ryan, Monique. *Sports Nutrition for Endurance Athletes,* 2nd edition. Boulder, Colorado: VeloPress. 2002.

Seebohar, Bob. *Nutrition Periodization for Endurance Athletes.* Boulder, Colorado: Bull Publishing. 2004.

Taylor, Jim, and Terri Schneider. *The Triathlete's Guide to Mental Training.* Boulder, Colorado: VeloPress. 2001.

Ungerleider, Steven. *Mental Training for Peak Performance.* Emmaus, Pennsylvania: Rodale. 1996.

Vonhof, John. *Fixing Your Feet: Prevention and Treatments for Athletes,* 2nd edition. Court Manteca, California: Footwork Publications. 2001.

PERSONAL EXPERIENCE/HISTORY

Babbitt, Bob. *Ironman: Life Stories from the Ironman Triathlon.* New York: Simon & Schuster. 1999.

Booth, Jane. *Transformed by Triathlon: The Making of an Improbable Athlete.* San Mateo, California: Fast Foot Forward Press. 2003.

Cook, Jeff. *The Triathletes: A Season in the Lives of Four Women in the Toughest Sport of All.* New York: St. Martins Press. 1988.

Kearns, Brad. *Can You Make a Living Doing That? True Life Adventures of a Professional Triathlete.* Palo Alto: TriMarket. 1991.

Madson, Dan. *Swim, Bike, Run, Laugh!: A Lighthearted Look at the Serious Sport of Triathlon and the Ironman Experience.* LaVergne, Tennessee: Lightning Source. 2001.

Plant, Mike. *Iron Will: The Heart and Soul of the Triathlon's Ultimate Challenge.* Boulder, Colorado: VeloPress. 1995.

Schwartz, Bob. *I Run, Therefore I Am Nuts.* Champaign, Illinois: Human Kinetics. 2001.

Staples, Stuart. *Not Normal Behaviour: From Novice to Ultra-Distance Triathlete.* United Kingdom: Upso. 2001.

Thom, Kara Douglas. *Becoming an Ironman: 1st Encounters with the Ultimate Endurance Event.* Holcottsville, New York: Breakaway Books. 1997.

Tinley, Scott. *Racing the Sunset: An Athlete's Quest for Life After Sport.* Guildford, Connecticut: Lyons Press. 1999.

____. *Scott Tinley's Winning Triathlon.* New York: McGraw-Hill. 1992.

____. *Triathlon: A Personal History.* Boulder, Colorado: VeloPress. 1994.

Waaesche Kislevitz, Gail. *First Triathlons: Personal Stories of Becoming a Triathlete.* Halcottsville, New York: Breakaway Books. 2005.

____. *The Spirit of the Marathon.* Halcottsville, New York: Breakaway Books. 2003.

Williams, Jayne, and Tim Anderson. *Slow Fat Triathlete.* Cambridge, Massachusetts: Marlowe and Company. 2000.

RUNNING

Dreyer, Danny, and Katherine Dryer. *Chi Running*. New York: Fireside Press. 2004.

Fee, Earl. *The Complete Guide to Running.* Aachan, Germany: Meyer & Meyer Verlag. 2005.

Galloway, Jeff. *Marathon: You Can Do It.* Bolinas, California: Shelter Publications. 2001.

___. *Galloway's Book on Running.* Bolinas, California: Shelter Publications. 2002.

Karnazes, Dean. *UltraMarathon Man.* New York: Penguin Books. 2005.

Kowalchik, Claire. *The Complete Book of Running for Women.* New York: Pocket Books. 1999.

Lynch, Jerry, and Warren Scott. *Running Within.* Champaign, Illinois: Human Kinetics. 1999.

Mierke, Ken. *The Triathletes Guide to Run Training.* Boulder, Colorado: VeloPress. 2001.

Moore, Kenny. *Bowerman and the Men of Oregon.* Emmaus, Pennsylvania: Rodale. 2006.

Sandrock, Mike. *Running with Legends.* Champaign, Illinois: Human Kinetics. 1996.

SWIMMING

Bernhardt, Gail, and Nick Hansen. *Workouts in a Binder: Swim Workouts for Triathletes.* Boulder, Colorado: VeloPress. 1998.

Colwin, Cecile. *Breakthrough Swimming.* Champaign, Illinois: Human Kinetics. 2002.

Denes, Thomas, and Desiree Ficker. *The Waterproof Triathlete: Waterproof Workouts for Triathletes.* Kensington, Maryland: Ancient Mariner Aquatics. 2003.

Laughlin, Terry. *Triathlon Swimming Made Easy.* New Paltz, New York: Total Immersion Inc. 1999.

___. *Freestyle Made Easy.* New Paltz, New York: Total Immersion Inc. 2004.

Tarpinian, Steve. *Triathletes Guide to Swim Training.* Boulder, Colorado: VeloPress. 2001.

TRAINING

Allen, Mark, and Bob Babbitt. *Mark Allen's Total Triathlete.* New York: McGraw-Hill. 1994.

Anderson, Owen Ph.D, *Lactate Lift Off.* Lansing, Michigan: SSS Publishing. 1998.

Aschwer, Hermann. *The Complete Guide to Triathlon Training.* Aachan, Germany: Meyer & Meyer Verlag. 1999.

Ash, Henry, Scott Tinley, and Barbara Warren. *Lifelong Success, Triathlon: Training for Masters, Ironman Edition.* Aachan, Germany: Meyer & Meyer Verlag. 1999.

Bernhardt, Gail. *Triathlon Training Basics.* Boulder, Colorado: VeloPress. 2000.

___. *Training Plans for Multisport Athletes.* Boulder, Colorado: VeloPress. 1996.

Blahnik, Jay. *Full Body Flexibility.* Champaign, Illinois: Human Kinetics. 2004.

Buxton, Karen, and E.M. Buxton. *Triathlete's Guide to Off-Season Training.* Boulder, Colorado: VeloPress. 2000.

Finch, Michael. *Triathlon Training.* Champaign, Illinois: Human Kinetics. 2000.

Friel, Joel. *The Triathlete's Training Bible.*

2nd edition. Boulder, Colorado: Velo-Press. 2005.

Huddle, Paul, Bob Babbitt, and Roch Frey. *Starting Out Triathlon: Training for Your First Competition*. Aachan, Germany: Meyer & Meyer Verlag, 1999.

Katai, Steve, and Colin Barr. *The Complete Idiot's Guide to Triathlon Training*. New York: Penguin Books. 2007.

Maffetone, Phil. *Training for Endurance,* 2nd edition. Stamford, New York: D. Barmore Productions. 2000.

Price, Robert. *The Ultimate Guide to Weight Training for Triathlon*, 2nd edition. Cleveland: Price World Enterprises. 2001.

Slaemaker, Rob, and Ray Browning. *Serious Training for Endurance Athletes*. Champaign, Illinois: Human Kinetics. 1996.

St. John, Allen. *The Triathlete's Training Diary for Dummies*. Hoboken, New Jersey: John Wiley and Sons. 1997.

WOMEN

Doan, Karen, and Lisa Lynam. *Triathlon for Women: Triathlon–a Mind-Body-Spirit Approach for Female Athletes*. Aachan, Germany: Meyer & Meyer Verlag. 2002.

Edwards, Sally. *Triathlons for Women*. Boulder, Colorado: VeloPress. 1998.

___. *Triathlons for Women: Triathlon Training for All Levels—Beginner to Advanced*, 2nd edition. Sacramento: Heart Zones Company. 1996.

YOGA

Carillo, Anthony. *Iron Yoga*. Emmaus, Pennsylvania: Rodale. 2005.

Couch, Jean. *The Runner's Yoga Book*. Berkeley, California: Rodmell Press. 1979.

DVDS

Triathlon—Racing Faster. Endurance Films.

What It Takes. Endurance Films. Follows four elites through their training.

Campbell, Clark. *The Blueprint: Training Plans and Strategies for Triathletes,* Championship Productions. 2005.

Campbell, Clark and Clay Hedrick. *The Swim: Technique and Training for Triathletes,* Championship Productions. 2005.

___. *The Ultimate Training, Technique, and Strategy Series for Triathletes*. Championship Productions. 2005.

Carillo, Anthony. *Iron Yoga*. Companion to the book of same name.

Collins, Michael. *Triathlon Transitions*. Endurance Films.

Dreyer, Danny. *Chi Running: A Revolutionary Approach to Effortless, Injury-free Running*. chirunning.com. Companion to the book of same name.

Emich, Gary and Phil DeGirolamo. *Lane Lines to Shore Lines: Your Complete Guide to Open-Water Swimming*. Championship Productions. 2007.

Friel, Joel and Ken Mierke. *Evolution Running*. Endurance Films.

Friel, Joel and Wes Hobson. *The Science of Triathlon*. Endurance Films. Nine hours of lecture.

___. *Triathlon through the Eyes of the Elites.*
Endurance Films. Nine hours of lecture.
Hummel, Barbara. *Water Running for the Serious Athlete.* 2003.
Jacobsen, Troy. *Spinervals Fitness Series.*
Spinervals.com. Four titles.
___. *Spinervals Competition Series.*
Spinervals.com. Twenty-seven progressively harder workouts.
___. *IronGirl Series—Ride, Run, Strength.*
Spinervals.com. Three workouts: cycling, weights, running.
___. *Spinervals Strength and Conditioning Series.* Spinervals.com. Seven DVDs.
Laughlin, Terry. *Freestyle Made Easy—Total Immersion Technique.* Total Immersion.
Marsh, David. *Swimming Faster Freestyle.*
Championship Productions. 2005.
Pipes-Nelson, Karlyn. *Go Swim Freestyle.*
Go Swim Productions.
Schmitz, Eric. *Triathlon Core—DVD and eBook.* Binder and Workbook with DVD.
___. *Endurance Core.* Endurance Films.
Zohlman, Lee. *Performance Stretching.*
Endurance Films.

CLUBS AND ORGANIZATIONS

UNITED STATES
New York Road Runners
9 East 89th Street
New York, NY 10128
www.nyrr.org

US Cycling Federation
1 Olympic Plaza
Colorado Springs, CO 80909
719-866-4581
www.usacycling.org

US Masters Swimming
PO Box 185
Londonderry, NH 03053-0185
800-550-SWIM
www.usms.org

USA Track and Field
(National Office)
132 East Washington Street, Suite 800
Indianapolis, IN 46204
317-261-0500
www.usatf.org

USA Triathlon
1365 Garden of the Gods Road, Suite 250
Colorado Springs, CO 80907-3425
719-597-9090
www.usatriathlon.org

XTERRA (TEAM Unlimited)
720 Iwilei Road, Suite 290
Honolulu, HI 96817
801-521-4322
www.xterraplanet.com

INTERNATIONAL
British Triathlon Association
PO Box 25
Loughborough, Leics, LE11 3WX
UK
01509 226165
www.britishtriathlon.org

European Triathlon Union
998 Harbourside Drive, #221
North Vancouver, BC V7P 3T2
Canada
604-904-9248
www.etu-triathlon.org

International Triathlon Union
998 Harbourside Drive, #221
North Vancouver, BC V7P 3T2
Canada
604-904-9248
www.triathlon.org

Irish Triathlon Association
98 Charlesland Court
The Glen, Greystones, Co. Wicklow
Ireland
www.triathlonireland.com

Scottish Triathlon Association
Glenearn Cottage, Edinburgh Road
Port Seton, EH32 0HQ
Scotland
www.tri-scotland.org

Triathlon Australia
20 Rodborough Road
PO Box 6039
Frenchs Forest, DC NSW 2086
Australia
02 9972 7999
www.triathlon.org.au

Triathlon Canada
1185 Eglinton Avenue East, #704
Toronto, Ontario M3C 3C6
Canada
416-426-7180
www.triathloncanada.com

Triathlon New Zealand
67 Davis Crescent
Newmarket, Auckland
New Zealand
09-524-6959
www.triathlon.org.nz

ONLINE RESOURCES

www.trinewbies.com
　　Resources for starting out
www.pccoach.com
　　Resources for books, heartrate
　　monitors, videos, etc.
www.spinervals.com
　　DVDs for cycling and running
www.endurancefilms.com
　　DVDs for triathlon, cycling, running
www.slowtwitch.com
　　Forums, news and opinions
www.trisports.com
www.triathletemag.com
　　Triathlete magazine
www.insidetri.com
　　Inside Triathlon
www.competitor.com
　　Competitor magazine

Index

About the Author

Adventure racer, triathlete, ultrarunner, and neophyte mountaineer Terri Schneider, MA, has established herself as a premiere ultra-endurance athlete. Terri has completed twenty-two Ironman triathlons, finishing ten times among the top five women. She has participated in seven Eco-Challenge® Expedition Competitions; the Mild Seven Outdoor Quest in China; the ESPN X-Games Adventure Race; the Raid Gauloises in Tibet and Nepal; seven-day running stage races in Costa Rica, the Sahara Desert, and the Gobi Desert; and in several 100-mile endurance runs. More recently she has devoted her time to ultrarunning and mountain climbing.

Terri's masters degree is in Sports Psychology; her research focused on risk taking and team dynamics. Her BS is in Exercise Physiology and she has studied myofascial release therapy. She is a motivational speaker on topics including training, teamwork, motivation, sports psychology, endurance, and risk taking. Terri is co-author of *The Triathletes Guide to Mental Training* and a contributor to *Applying Sport Psychology: From Researcher and Consultant to Coach and Athlete*, and *The Thrill of Victory, the Agony of My Feet: Tales from the Wild and Wonderful World of Adventure Racing*. She has coached triathletes, adventure racers, runners, cyclists, and swimmers for twenty-five years. Terri lives in Santa Cruz with her dog, Gryphon. To learn more, visit www.terrischneider.net.

THE MOUNTAINEERS, founded in 1906, is a nonprofit outdoor activity and conservation club, whose mission is "to explore, study, preserve, and enjoy the natural beauty of the outdoors.... " Based in Seattle, Washington, the club is now the third-largest such organization in the United States, with seven branches throughout Washington State.

The Mountaineers sponsors both classes and year-round outdoor activities in the Pacific Northwest, which include hiking, mountain climbing, ski touring, snowshoeing, bicycling, camping, kayaking, nature study, sailing, and adventure travel. The club's conservation division supports environmental causes through educational activities, sponsoring legislation, and presenting informational programs.

All club activities are led by skilled, experienced instructors, who are dedicated to promoting safe and responsible enjoyment and preservation of the outdoors.

If you would like to participate in these organized outdoor activities or the club's programs, consider a membership in The Mountaineers. For information and an application, write or call The Mountaineers, Club Headquarters, 300 Third Avenue West, Seattle, WA 98119; 206-284-6310. You can also visit the club's website at www.mountaineers.org or contact The Mountaineers via email at clubmail@mountaineers.org.

The Mountaineers Books, an active, nonprofit publishing program of the club, produces guidebooks, instructional texts, historical works, natural history guides, and works on environmental conservation. All books produced by The Mountaineers Books fulfill the club's mission.

Send or call for our catalog of more than 500 outdoor titles:

The Mountaineers Books
1001 SW Klickitat Way, Suite 201
Seattle, WA 98134
800-553-4453
mbooks@mountaineersbooks.org
www.mountaineersbooks.org

OTHER TITLES YOU MIGHT ENJOY FROM THE MOUNTAINEERS BOOKS

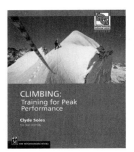

**Climbing: Training for Peak Performance,
2nd Edition**, *Clyde Soles*
"Whatever your talent, experience, and ambition,
if you climb you would do well to read
Clyde Soles' training manual." —Jon Krakauer

50 Trail Runs in Southern California
Stan Swartz, Jim Wolff, Samir Shahin
"A super resource—the trails are defined in
terms that both the novice and experienced
trail runner can appreciate." —Nancy Hobbs,
All-American Trail Running Association

50 Trail Runs in Washington,
Cheri Pompeo Gillis
Comprehensive regional guide to the most
beautiful and challenging places to trail
run throughout Washington State

**High Infatuation: A Climber's
Guide to Love and Gravity**
Steph Davis
"Davis's clean, fresh prose and honest and open
examination of herself make *High Infatuation* an
enjoyable, quick read...a nice addition to the annals
of mountaineering literature." —*Rock and Ice* magazine

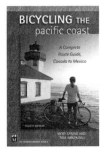

**Bicycling the Pacific Coast: A Complete Route
Guide, Canada to Mexico, 4th Edition**
Vicky Spring, Tom Kirkendall
"[A] no-holds-barred look at doing the mighty
Coast Highway on two wheels." —*The Oregonian*

Leadership the Outward Bound Way
Outward Bound USA
Dynamic and effective leadership skills from
the organization that has spent decades helping
people discover their own potential to lead.

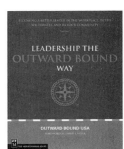

Available at fine bookstores and outdoor stores, by phone at
800-553-4453, or on the web at www.mountaineersbooks.org

THE MOUNTAINEERS BOOKS